SAGE was founded in 1965 by Sara Miller McCune to support the dissemination of usable knowledge by publishing innovative and high-quality research and teaching content. Today, we publish over 900 journals, including those of more than 400 learned societies, more than 800 new books per year, and a growing range of library products including archives, data, case studies, reports, and video. SAGE remains majority-owned by our founder, and after Sara's lifetime will become owned by a charitable trust that secures our continued independence.

Los Angeles | London | New Delhi | Singapore | Washington DC | Melbourne

Migration, Trafficking and Gender Construction

Migration, Trafficking and Gender Construction

Women in Transition

Edited by
Roli Misra

Foreword by
Paula Banerjee

$SAGE | Stree

Los Angeles | London | New Delhi
Singapore | Washington DC | Melbourne

First published in 2020 by

SAGE Publications India Pvt Ltd
B1/I-1 Mohan Cooperative Industrial Area
Mathura Road, New Delhi 110 044, India
www.sagepub.in

SAGE Publications Inc
2455 Teller Road
Thousand Oaks, California 91320, USA

SAGE Publications Ltd
1 Oliver's Yard, 55 City Road
London EC1Y 1SP, United Kingdom

SAGE Publications Asia-Pacific Pte Ltd
18 Cross Street #10-10/11/12
China Square Central
Singapore 048423

STREE
16 Southern Avenue
Kolkata 700 026
www.stree-samyabooks.com

Published by Vivek Mehra for SAGE Publications India Pvt Ltd. Typeset in 10.5/13 pt Caslon SSi by Fidus Design Pvt. Ltd, Chandigarh.

Library of Congress Cataloging-in-Publication Data Available

ISBN: 978-93-81345-47-4 (HB)

SAGE Stree Team: Aritra Paul, Amrita Dutta and Neena Ganjoo

To
My parents for teaching me humility and humanity

Thank you for choosing a SAGE product!
If you have any comment, observation or feedback,
I would like to personally hear from you.

Please write to me at **contactceo@sagepub.in**

Vivek Mehra, Managing Director and CEO, SAGE India.

Bulk Sales

SAGE India offers special discounts
for purchase of books in bulk.
We also make available special imprints
and excerpts from our books on demand.

For orders and enquiries, write to us at

Marketing Department
SAGE Publications India Pvt Ltd
B1/I-1, Mohan Cooperative Industrial Area
Mathura Road, Post Bag 7
New Delhi 110044, India

E-mail us at **marketing@sagepub.in**

Subscribe to our mailing list
Write to **marketing@sagepub.in**

This book is also available as an e-book.

Contents

Foreword by Paula Banerjee   ix
Acknowledgements   xv
Introduction by Roli Misra   xvii

PART I
Migration, Trafficking and Work

1. Labour Migration in Bangladesh: Experiences of
   the Chittagong Hill Tracts (CHT) Indigenous
   Women Workers   3
   Ena Tripura

2. Dynamics of Female Migration in India:
   Issues and Concerns   26
   Sandhya R. Mahapatro

3. Interface between Migration and Trafficking:
   A Case of Tribal Minor Girls from Jharkhand   47
   Gomati Bodra Hembrom

4. Places of Migrants' Hope: Bosnian Women in Migration   78
   Sanela Bašić

5. Violence, Forced Migration and Vulnerability of
   the Adivasi Women in Western Assam   99
   Nazimuddin Siddique

6. Towards Emancipation or Bondage? Rohingya
   Women's Narratives from Bangladesh Refugee
   Camps and Indian Jails   113
   Sucharita Sengupta

PART II
Migration and Assimilation

7. Female Migrants at the Doors of Fortress Europe:
   The Case of Slovenia   145
   Sanja Cukut Krilić

8. Care Relations of Resettled Refugees: Case Study,
   Finland   167
   Kati Turtiainen

9. Requestioning Identity: Female Descendants of
   Immigrants from Former Yugoslavia in Slovenia   189
   Mateja Sedmak

10. Precariousness of Migrant Women: Between
    Structural Constraints and Coping Strategies   209
    Mojca Pajnik and Veronika Bajt

About the Editor and Contributors   224

Foreword

MIGRATION CAN BE CONSIDERED as the most divisive problem of not just the last few decades but probably that of the last century. *Migration, Trafficking and Gender Construction* should therefore be recognized as a timely and a necessary contribution on an issue that has clearly been acknowledged as one of the important and critical issues of the recent past and of current times. It is a truism, however, that migrations have always taken place, but the Global North, where the discourse on migration first began, had for a long time perceived it to be a problematic of the Global South. Even though there were large-scale migrations during the colonial period, for example, many people from European countries such as Ireland entered the Americas. However, because it was largely a movement of the white people at the cost of the Native Americans it was not considered as a crisis. As for migration of the African-Americans or the racial 'other', they were considered as beasts of burden so their migration was never questioned as their presence was required for their labour.

In the last century the three great migratory movements did not affect the Global North to any serious extent. The partition in 1947, and the ensuing political violence and the havoc, continued to be seen as a problem of South Asia and not a problem of colonialism that was caused by the Global North. The foundation of Israel and the massive displacement of the Palestinians, which is still continuing in present times, was perceived as a problem of the Arab world and not of the Global North, and the Cultural Revolution of China (1966–1976) was seen as a problem of Communism and not of migration. The post-war movement of refugees was again perceived as a result of the onset of the Iron Curtain. Also when people left the Soviet Union and Eastern Europe it was not viewed as a problem, rather they were welcomed in the Anglo-American world as it re-enforced the perception of the moral superiority of the 'democratic' North.

The prevailing discourse in the West had been to view migrations from the Global South not as a result of colonialism but as an effect of endemic poverty and underdevelopment. The West progressively termed migration as a crisis when people who looked different tried to enter within their borders. From the Middle Ages it has been a policy of the Western world order to try to keep out the racial 'other', failing which to confine them within a ghetto. The Jewish ghetto in Venice (1516) was the oldest one in Europe. With the influx of non-white people to the West migration progressively began to be recognized as a Crisis. The non-white people had aspirations to move to the Global North because they correctly associated their marginality with colonial rule that made race the bedrock of acquisition of benefits such as citizenship, power-sharing and attainment of material benefits and resources. So countries in the Global North marked such movements as crisis that necessitated policies and laws that gave the authority to respective states as to who should be taken and who shunned. Because more people were stopped from entering the northern borders, policies and laws were formulated and the hordes that were moving were homogenized as a faceless, nameless mass and in no way were they humanized in the narratives because the moment they appeared as individuals their claims for rights and resources could not be legitimately ignored. At the centre of resource sharing was the question of citizenship and who belonged was a conscious decision made by the ruling elite. Those who were considered as unworthy of being recognized as a citizen were either to be tolerated as a precarious group who might provide cheap labour or be forced out, joining the ranks of the 'nowhere' people. The forced migrants or the refugees progressively became the precariat who were stopped if possible from entering and tolerated as service providers only when they could not be restricted to the borders. Their political presence was to remain peripheral. This state of affairs continued and progressively became entrenched in the Global North.

The breakup of the Soviet Union and Yugoslavia in the 1990s required a change in the discourse and of the refugee regime. Migrants from Ukraine moved to Europe and to Slovenia, to the more affluent states of Europe, but these were white people. However, these migrant situations brought to the fore another axis of vulnerability that resulted: migration as a result of marginalization on the basis of gender. Conflicts in the former Yugoslavia in the 1990s for the first time brought it within the cognizance of the Global North that rape can be an instrument of war and women's sexual marginalization often leads to migration. It is true that in many other conflicts such as that between the two Pakistans, rape has been used as an instrument of war but the recognition came after conflicts in the former Yugoslavia.

About a gendered analysis of forced migration, Eileen Pittaway and Linda Bartolomei say that for too long, the prevailing discourse about refugee women and girls has been about a vulnerable minority. This has been reinforced by media stories and fundraising advertisements which depict them as helpless and hopeless. It is true that these women are vulnerable but so are the men who become victims of forced migration. So why privilege women's experience is something that we are often asked. 'While sharing with men and boys the same basic needs for food, water, shelter, sanitation and security, they do have additional and significantly different needs. The most important difference is that of endemic and often systemic sexual and gender-based violence against women and girls. Men and boys are also victims of sexual and gender-based violence, which again generates the need for different and appropriate responses'.[1] If one negates the sexual abuses faced by the Rohingya women both in their state of origin or in their host countries then one misses the larger picture of why a gendered analysis is important.

Today, the North finds that its old discourse of forced migration that was presented in the 1951 Convention and the 1967 Protocol does not fit the contemporary situation of migrants from Syria, Iraq, Libya, Afghanistan and Bangladesh, almost all taking routes led by traffickers/smugglers, without due process, for seeking asylum. The reality of migration hitherto provided by the North and led by the diplomats in Geneva and New York that was touted as a global phenomena and the discourse that was built around it had specific impact largely over European and American understandings and not over global justice systems. While the borders of Europe changed as a consequence of the formation of the Schengen regime, the boundaries between the figure of the refugee and that of the migrant also shifted. The rise of the figure of the legitimate asylum seeker and the clear-cut distinction between asylum seekers and economic migrants, that plays an important role in current debates, was hardly ever and more so in current times, based on the reality. As the distinction between asylum seekers, refugees and economic migrants all shift and collide, the old legal framework becomes unworkable. The distinction between voluntary migrants and forced migrants shows itself as majorly flawed and emerges as a false distinction. Therefore, it is time now to begin a new and different discourse on forced migration that this volume initiates.

The South also constructed a migration narrative that was often skewed. The reality is that migration is a phenomenon that has been present throughout history, with people moving away from conflict and for economic reasons, to escape environmental disasters, to be with kith and kin. In the South, the awareness of difference was not on the basis of race, but on caste and religious lines. People did not live in ghettos, but often were accommodated near the rich and privileged who needed their services but marginalization existed. The literature on refugees followed a different terrain from that in the Global North but even then it was full of clichés that set a pattern and that might be interesting to explore. I will endeavour to explain through broad sketches how the narratives evolved. To begin with we were given the literature of victimhood in which the refugees were portrayed only as victims. It cannot be denied that in large parts these refugees were victims but by fixing their identities as victims these authors lost much of the richness of refugee experience because as victims the refugee identity was never fixed as those of refugees. Even in the worst of times refugees constantly tried to negotiate with the powers that be and challenged their given identities. They proved their agencies through such challenges.

By fixing their identities as victims and not problematizing that victimhood, the refugees were for a long time displaced from the centre stage of their own narratives. With the ascendance of cultural studies in West Bengal the refugee experience was reduced to the memory of partition that seemed to have traumatized refugees to such an extent that all other experiences paled in comparison. Historians and social scientists belonging to the genre of cultural studies, largely depending on oral narratives, settled on the notion that the violence and trauma associated with losing one's home was the definitive aspect of the refugee psyche. Authors such as Sandip Bandyopadhyay, Dipesh Chakrabarty and Manas Ray discussed the imaginative mappings of the refugee lives through memories. The understanding was that a refugee lived in his/her memories whether of pre-partition belongings or of post-partition localities. For Dipesh Chakrabarty what was definitive for the refugee was the memory of their *chere asha gram*, which literally translates as the village that they left behind. This village symbolized their yearnings for their *desh* or home country.[2]

These writings did not contradict the victimhood narrative but added a new dimension to it. Such narratives were usually anecdotal and reductive, challenging the understanding of refugee experience not through multiplicity but through singularity. Often it was the author's own experience that was privileged over group experiences and it is through such discourses that the author reclaimed agency.

Besides the memory lane there appeared a number of writings from the 1990s that discussed institutional responses to the arrival of forced migrants from both the West and the East. These writings by authors such as Samir Das and Monica Mandal discussed how the newly born governments operating within the imperatives of the state and nation building exercise came to terms with the influx of such huge population groups. Older scholars such as Prafulla Chakrabarti had argued that the government's work in the field of relief and rehabilitation was one of non-performance.[3] The measures that were taken by these governments could be categorized under relief and rehabilitation and according to Das, Mandal and others the government did the best that it could. Samir Das is of the opinion the government had to respond positively to the influx of refugees because after 1954 the government figured that the refugees were unlikely to go back and 'hence, had to be accepted as an inalienable part of the Indian nation'.[4]

What is interesting in much of these narratives, both in the North and the South is that the discourse always had an institutional response. The Global North reduced the refugees to a law and order problem and so the unwanted refugees were to be kept away through law. As a result of this, refugee discourses thrived in departments of law. In the South, however, the narrative was focussed on how rehabilitation was to be addressed, which was reduced to how many blankets were to be distributed and how much food was to be allocated. From there it was but once step to deducing that refugees were merely a drain and so unwanted. Although the paths taken by the Global North and the South were different, the discourses arrived at were similar because both considered refugees as unwanted. The similar treatment of refugees from Africa to Europe and Myanmar to South and Southeast Asia is a case in point. This volume challenges such a debilitating discourse.

It also highlights another reality culled from experiences from the Balkans and from South Asia or the fact that there seems to be a feminization of migration, where women move on their own for economic reasons (Chapters 1, 2, 6, 8, 9). Ultimately the propelling factors are poverty, resource crunch, or post-conflict stagnation of resources, and so on. To concentrate only on the vulnerability of refugee women, either through the axis of race, religion or because of gender can be a disservice to these women. As many feminist scholars have shown us the service that these women give to their host countries as well as to their families is a testimony to their strengths. This volume bears witness to that reality of migration and forced migration. It has to be read to address such lacunae.

Paula Banerjee
Professor, Department of South and
Southeast Asian Studies,
University of Calcutta

Acknowledgements

THIS VOLUME IS A collective venture that has depended on the contributions of several authors. I am deeply indebted to the contributors for their patience and hard work, and for co-operating so generously in this venture. Without their time and efforts this book would not have materialized. The authors have patiently redone their chapters on time in response to the requirements of the book. I would like to put on record our thanks to Shipra Srivastava, my former research assistant, and Vishnu Kumar, working as research staff in my project, in the Department of Economics, University of Lucknow, for helping in the process of editing this book. My special thanks to Urec Mojca, University of Ljubljana, Slovenia, Subhangi Herath, University of Colombo, and Parvin Sultana from Dhubri, Assam, for connecting me to the contributors in Slovenia, Finland and Bangladesh, respectively. I would also like to thank Stree for their support in enabling this book to take form.

This work would not have been possible without the sustained encouragement of my family and friends who always believed in me and stood by me during the completion of this book. Lastly this book owes a lot to the lives of women whose identity took newer shapes through migration and whose role and stories fill the pages of this book.

Introduction

THIS BOOK BRINGS together essays from India, Bangladesh, Finland, with references to Ukraine and Russia and the Balkans after the breakup of Yugoslavia that caused many women to migrate, providing insights on women's migration in general. These address how migration at times is voluntary, at times enforced, and how women cope. Individuals have to respond to the larger forces operating on them. Migration may have a constraining effect on those who move, not only in structural terms by limiting available options or in cultural terms because of translocating lives, but also as it may entail exploitation, emotional and psychological abuse. Apart from forced displacement caused by conflict or natural disasters, migration is often undertaken with the hope of a better life. There is thus a need to understand and study these nuances and complexities; merely looking at migration as a result of push and pull factors is not enough; this often overlooks the agency of the migrating population. While 'push' tends to reduce the movement to an individual's rational decision without taking into account the other impacting factors, 'pull' tends to delve in economic determinism. There is hence a need to understand the phenomenon with a more holistic approach.

Any theory of migration must account for it in terms of race, religion, nationality, sense of belonging and nostalgia. The differential experience of women in a gendered world cannot be overlooked. This book is an attempt to bring forth such experiences. This is important because despite the rising number of female migrants, women are not given equal importance as compared to men in matters of migration as they are still not considered as equal actors. Migration is still seen as a man's decision. Women migrants are often seen as dependants. Their economic contribution might be overlooked. However women do not always migrate with families. They might migrate alone, maybe because of harsh economic conditions or to escape a patriarchal society or an abusive marriage. Just like varied reasons behind migration, the experience of migrant women is also diverse. And whatever may be the reason behind migration, it has become a reality. No serious study of migration can escape this aspect.

The decisions of women are shaped by multiple factors, individual needs, aspirations along with availability of jobs, for instance. Once women migrate, on the one hand they may face certain restrictions in terms of social and cultural rights/liberties; on the other hand the very act of movement may have enabling and empowering capacities. These various factors need to be looked into to understand the phenomenon. This book within its many limitations has tried to look at these issues through the collection of ten essays.

Migration has been identified as a survival strategy for all those who have been victims of social, economic and political conditions in their place of residence. Over a period of time many theories have explained the causes of migration and the main causes are confined to the push and the pull factors, mentioned earlier. Lee (1966) reformulated Ravenstein's theory (1885), emphasizing more on the internal (or push) factors, outlining the impact that intervening obstacles have on the migration process.

Gender aspects of international migration have not found place in theories of international migration partly because of the assumption that most migrant workers were men and women are their dependents. Even though this problem has been alleviated over the past two decades, not very many scholars have made sufficient attempts to theorize international female migration in a comprehensive manner. This is partly because these theories did not focus on the experiences of the female migrants but were confined to looking into the causes of migration (Boyd and Grieco 2003). Massey (1998) coined the term 'the age of migration' to describe the increase in mobility and mentioned the feminization of migration as a new migration pattern. This theory focussed mainly on the quantitative increase in women's mobility worldwide.

Migration also opens up new avenues in the theoretical spectrum. While liberal feminists often pointed out to the public-private divide as the core of feminist theory, such binaries and dichotomies are destabilized during conflicts. Women are exposed to the public sphere predominantly held by men; socializing patriarchal values, home has a different meaning for migrant women. The relationship with home of women in the diasporas, women who migrate for work, women who are forcefully displaced reveal that home is intricately linked to the sense of belonging not only to a place but also to a community and a culture.

The gendered aspect of migration has been discussed in Navnita Chadha Behera's edited volume (2006). It emphasizes the need to differentiate the reasons underlying why men and women migrate. While conflict-induced migration rarely has a scope of choice or agency and is often forced, the essays in our book try to explore the possibility of economic empowerment of these women presented by migration. The writers suggest that while the structural implications of migration should be looked into, individual experiences of migration also bring forth fresher aspects for study.

Susan Kneebone and Felicity Rawlings-Sanaei (2007) address some of the major trends that have affected forced migration. Asylum is often perceived as a disguise for economic migration. Hence there is a focus on finding 'real' asylum seekers. Human rights organizations have rightly questioned this framework which fails to safeguard the interest of the asylum seekers, rather amounts to a restrictive externalization which limits asylum seekers to already poorer regions that are unfairly asked to host refugees.

Paula Banerjee (2005, 2013) analyses the issue of internal displacement, specifically of women, and how far laws regulating internally displaced persons have been fruitful. Unlike other books that point out the limitations of legalistic framework in safeguarding the rights of the internally displaced, this book time and again goes back to the applicability of the UN Guiding Principles to internally displaced people in South Asia. Paula Banerjee and Anasua Basu Ray Chaudhury (2011) talk about ethnographic compilation based on the complex interrelationship between gender and political borders in South Asia, in the context of West Bengal, Jammu and Kashmir and Northeast India. The authors have discussed how the power and control of one state ends and the other begins, converting borders into zones, intertwining the struggles of women and their differences within a state.

Meenakshi Thapan (2006) looks at migration as a process which changes, modifies or redefines identities. Immigrant women have to construct identities which draw both from the past and the present, arguing that cultural identities are not territorially rooted; are both enduring and extraordinarily flexible. Partha S. Ghosh (2016) argues that collective violence is the prime factor behind migration in South Asia. Since boundaries were redrawn, a large number of people have moved across borders. There is no legal regime based on which migration laws are to be made. As such refugees, migrants, illegal settlers and stateless persons are often bundled together.

Samita Sen (2016) talks about marriage migration as a one way journey where women are disconnected from their natal roots and women circulate between their natal and conjugal families. She also talks about bride trafficking. Ravinder Kaur (2010) gives a detailed study of the migration of brides of Bengal to far-flung states, thereby focussing on their sexual, reproductive labours besides economic labour in which the women are trapped.

Conflict is one of the prominent reasons that often lead to forced displacement and movement of people (Banerjee 2013). In our book conflict-induced migration and its impact on women have been presented. Conflict is understood in the broader sense and includes inter-state conflicts, internal conflicts, ethnically driven insurgencies and secessionist movements. Conflicts often force not only individuals, families but at times entire communities to migrate to a new place due to a perceived fear (see Chapters 1, 5 and 6).

There is a need to compare the reasons and consequences of migration taking place in different countries at different points so that commonalities and differences in the multicultural movement of people can be looked into. In this context this volume attempts to give readers an insight about the migration which affected India, Bangladesh and Europe too, which had been witnessing unending influx of people from the former USSR and Yugoslavia after their disintegration. These countries have their own history of migration altering the geography, demography and economy of the nations post-partition. As Samaddar suggests (2016), it is also important to master the art of writing event-centric history to bring out the depths of the phenomenon of forced migration, which is the focus of this book. For centuries the major causes of population movements have been invasions and wars.

In the second half of the 1980s, migration from the Balkans took place in two sets of countries. The first set was of the sending countries comprising Yugoslavia and Turkey and the second set comprising Albania, Bulgaria and Romania, which were the receiving countries. Balkan countries also faced problems of asylum seekers until they restricted them from entering their territories. After the crisis of the 1990s, the region since 2012 again witnessed another strong wave of migration when the civil wars of Iraq and Syria, led to a heavy influx of people in Eastern Europe. Turkey and Hungary closed their doors to these migrants. Displaced persons from Syria, Iraq and Afghanistan fled war or political persecution and sought asylum (Salamon 2016).

When a nation-state is created and borders are re-drawn, it divides people, victimizes them, affecting both men and women. The disaggregated experiences need to be studied separately. Conceptually, taking the gendered aspect into consideration one may understand the features of power relations within gender which otherwise might be overlooked. And empirically such an initiative has to some extent led to the exploration of newer areas of enquiry—transnational identity, health and human rights of migrants and so on. While looking at migration through the lens of gender, there is a need to ensure that the experiences of Third World women are not essentialized and seen through the eyes of the West. Women in Third World countries find themselves at a greater distance from the state and its various manifestations, as compared to their western counterparts. Lack of education, poor infrastructure, economic vulnerability and lack of information often leave these women more dependent on their own meagre resources than on state support. Many studies on migration to a great extent have been gender-blind.

All these aspects raise newer concerns in the study of women and migration. Are they always the passive players in this process or do they have their voices too in decision-making? It is with this question in mind that chapters were invited from the contributors who have been working on either migration studies or gender studies. The ten chapters, which have been written exclusively for this book, give various insights about the gendered aspect of migration through narratives, case studies and secondary data across different regions and countries. Despite the differential gender relations prevailing in different parts of the world, absence of the mother and the housewife poses similar problems in the countries studied even though the intensity and the nature of the problem could be different. Women's experience of displacement needs to be acknowledged as women are important stakeholders in rehabilitation. Policies must address their problems. Migration impacts women differently. Displacement leaves women with a sense of uprootedness. Traditionally the home has been the domain of women, the loss of which leaves them with a sense of longing.

Part I, 'Migration, Trafficking and Work' discusses economic migration. With changing times women make up a large component of this migrant population. Earlier they migrated as family members of male migrants. But now they often migrate as active agents. As a result, they not only contribute remittances to the home country but also contribute to the economy of the host country. Their new found economic role has in turn shaped their own identity as well as compelled the host country to take cognizance of their contribution. This has resulted in the host country devising different policies to accommodate these women as well as help them in different ways.

In Chapter 1, 'Labour Migration in Bangladesh: Experiences of the Chittagong Hill Tracts (CHT) Indigenous Women Workers', Ena Tripura talks about the discrimination faced by the indigenous communities of Bangladesh who are distinct from one another as well as from the mainstream, in terms of religion, language, traditions and culture. After the foundation of Bangladesh in 1971, the indigenous people of the CHT lost their land to outsiders, leading to severe displacement. In the hope of a better life, many young indigenous men and women migrated into the cities to work in factories of the export industry where they faced new problems. Exploitation, discrimination, sexual harassment are endemic, and make their experiences to be of a particular nature.

In Chapter 2, 'Dynamics of Female Migration in India: Issues and Concerns', Sandhya Mahapatro refers to Census data which show that the trend of female migration is increasing over the years and constitutes over two times more migrants than men. However, in the majority of migration research in India women are treated as associational migrants, who have either migrated due to marriage or moved with family because of their position and nature of relationship with men. Nevertheless, globalization and the associated socio-economic transformation have slowly been effecting structural changes in the economy in terms of the creation of gender-specific employment opportunities. An attempt is made to explore the economic motivation for migration by addressing two issues: First, to study the socio-economic and spatial characteristics and the changes in the pattern of women's migration. Second, to understand the determinants, specifically the economic ones, that relate to female migration behaviour.

In Chapter 3, 'Interface between Migration and Trafficking: A Case of Tribal Minor Girls from Jharkhand', Gomati Bodra Hembrom discusses intersectionality between gender and migration. In sum, gender is a central, constitutive element in explaining the migration process. In the last few decades, there has been mass migration of single tribal women and girls aged between 12 to 26 years who migrate to Delhi to work as domestic workers. Many of them are unmarried minors. An overview of the gender hierarchy, prevalent in the tribal communities of the eastern India in states like, Jharkhand, Odisha and Chhattisgarh determine migration behaviour. The Rohingya refugee also fall into a pattern of trafficking (Chapter 6). The dynamics of migration decision-making are very much related to the sex-specific tribal gender roles and societal expectations. In this region a very strong nexus of migration and trafficking of the minor tribal girls has emerged. In this way an attempt has been made to provide a link between migration, trafficking and the gendered labour market.

In Chapter 4, 'Places of Migrant's Hope: Bosnian Women in Migration', Sanela Bašić gives an insight about the migrant population and the various motivations behind the movement of people. It explores more specifically the life narratives of migrant women in an attempt to understand and shed light on how the migrant process and status affect the economic and social position of women. According to statistics, 37 percent of Bosnians lived abroad in 2014. The greatest outflow of migrants occurred in the early 1990s. This massive

displacement was triggered initially by the political conflict surrounding Bosnia's move for independence from the former Republic
of Yugoslavia. In 1992, two million people out of a total of 4,377
million were forcibly moved; 1.2 million were internally displaced;
while one million sought refuge in western European countries. In
the post-war period, the time following the Dayton Peace Agreement
in 1995, approximately 800,000 former refugees returned to Bosnia.
Today, emigration is primarily motivated by poverty and a lack of
economic opportunity. Beyond the examination of those important variables, however, migration as a phenomenon has drawn little
research attention from Bosnian social scientists.

In Chapter 5, 'Violence, Forced Migration and Vulnerability
of the Adivasi Women in Western Assam', Nazimuddin Siddique
deals with the issue of forced migration consequent to the perennial
conflicts in the northeastern state. Siddique discusses the continuous violence that has severely affected post-independence Assam,
which is increasingly getting mired in deeper turmoil than ever
before. This is unfolding fundamentally because of the escalating rifts
between various communities in the heterogeneous state. Ceaseless
'othering' of a number of marginal communities by the ruling political elites of the state too have significantly contributed in these series
of longstanding violence.

An enquiry through the gendered prism, explores the vulnerability
of the women as group—as victims and as survivors—and also
discusses the Bodo movement, where the major victims in the
conflict were, by and large, Adivasis and Muslims. In this chapter
the focus has been on the Adivasis. The latter are a heterogeneous
community of social groups such as the Oraon, Munda, Khariya,
Santhals, Gonds, Kisangs, Nagesias, brought from the Chota Nagpur
region to the Assam tea plantations as coolie labour. Interestingly,
though tribals, the Bodos are not termed as Adivasis. Nor do they
see themselves as Adivasis. Adivasi women have been the worst
sufferers in the violence. In Chapter 6, 'Towards Emancipation
or Bondage? Rohingya Women's Narratives from Bangladesh
Refugee Camps and Indian Jails', Sucharita Sengupta describes the
complexities and dilemmas facing the refugee women who also try
to exercise agency in this milieu.

'Part II', 'Migration and Assimilation' delves into what happens once migration has taken place. No country can deny the truth of migration. Irrespective of causes, most countries have now become home to a diverse multicultural population. Most countries have devised various techniques to cope with the inflow of migrants. These steps aim at assimilating the migrants in some way or the other to ensure that there is no social upheaval in the countries. How do women from the diasporic community handle this fragmented identity? They are caught in between the traditions of their homelands and the modernity of their new homes. In Chapter 7, 'Female Migrants at the Doors of Fortress Europe: The Case of Slovenia', Sanja Cukut Krilić traces the effects of an increasingly restrictive EU migration policy towards third-country nationals on female migrants from the former Soviet Union who reside in Slovenia who have been given a sexualized image that affect their integration. It argues that such an approach to migration management has contributed to increasing insecurity and vulnerability of third-country nationals residing in the EU, privileging marriage as an institution and conceptualizing the rights of marriage migrants in Slovenia mainly in relation to their partners. Krilić reveals the heterogeneity and diversity of their experiences and reclaims their agency in challenging such stereotypical notions.

In Chapter 8, 'Care Relations of Resettled Refugees: Case Study, Finland', Kati Turtiainen has thrown light on the resettlement of the refugees to Europe and especially to Finland. The data consist of the interviews of experiences of resettled refugees. Refugees are often selected on the grounds of vulnerabilities, such as chronic illnesses, woman at risk or age. Here, the premise is that refugees must form functional care relations in the early stages after arrival to a new country: to whom do the informants form the primary care relations in early stages of arrival to Finland? No major gender differences are seen in the data. The only difference is that single mothers and male victims of torture are benefiting from the strong presence of public settlement and integration services. In Chapter 9, 'Requestioning Identity: Female Descendants of Immigrants from Former Yugoslavia in Slovenia', Mateja Sedmark focuses on an aspect of the migration experience that critically marks the whole person: this will be identity or a subjective answer to the question 'Who am I?' in relation to requisitioning one's ethnic, cultural, and state affiliation. Based on the case of female descendants of immigrants who had left the territories of the former Socialist Federal Yugoslavia and moved to Slovenia (as one of the constituent republics of the once common state), an attempt is made to reject assumptions of the existence of singular and exclusive identities, and to present the complex, plural, hybrid and trans-cultural nature of ethnic and state affiliations.

In Chapter 10, 'Precariousness of Migrant Women: Between Structural Constraints and Coping Strategies', Mojca Pajnik and Veronika Bajt discuss the precarious position of migrant women in the labour market of Slovenia, and reflect how the welfare policies, or the lack thereof, affect the migrants' lives, interviewing women who have migrated to Slovenia from different countries in the last 15 years. Drawing on the concept of intersectionality, the chapter debates the various relations between the structural constraints and migrant women's individual experiences.

One common factor underlying all the chapters is that the impact of male labour migration on the institution of family or society significantly differs from female labour migration across countries. The aim of this edited volume is an attempt to bridge the research gap in available literature to some extent and also to provide reading material to the researchers, academicians and readers as a ready reckoner.

Roli Misra
Associate Professor
Department of Economics
University of Lucknow

NOTES

1   Eileen Pittaway and Linda Bartolomei, 'From Rhetoric to Reality: Achieving Gender Equality for Refugee Women and Girls,' *World Refugee Council* Research Paper no. 3, August 2018: 3; https://www.cigionline.org/sites/default/files/documents/WRC%20Research%20Paper%20no.3_0.pdf, accessed on 23 October 2018.

2   Dipesh Chakrabarty. 'Remembered Villages,' *Economic & Political Weekly* (10 August 1996): 2143.

3 Prafulla K. Chakrabarti, *The Marginal Men: The Refugees and the Left Political Syndrome in West Bengal* (Kalyani: Lumiere Books, 1990): xxiv.

4 Samir Kumar Das, 'Refugee Crisis: Response of the Government of West Bengal', in *Refugees in West Bengal*, edited by Pradeep Kumar Bose (Kolkata: Mahanirban Calcutta Research Group, 2000):11.

REFERENCES

Banerjee, Paula, ed., 2013. *Unstable Populations, Anxious States: Mixed and Massive Population Flows in South Asia.* Kolkata: Samya.

———. 2010. *Borders, Histories, Existences: Gender and Beyond.* New Delhi: SAGE Publications.

Banerjee, Paula, and Anasua Basu Ray Chaudhury. 2011. *Women in Indian Borderlands.* New Delhi: SAGE Publications.

Banerjee, Paula, Sabyasachi Basu Ray Chaudhury, and Samir Kumar Das. 2005. *Internal Displacement in South Asia: The Relevance of the UN's Guiding Principles.* New Delhi: SAGE Publications.

Behera, Navnita Chadha, ed. 2006. *Gender, Conflict and Migration.* New Delhi: SAGE Publications.

Boyd, M., and Grieco, E. 2003. 'Women and Migration: Incorporating Gender into International Migration Theory'. Retrieved from http://www.migrationinformation.org/Feature/print.cfm?ID=106, accessed on 13 August 2017.

Ghosh, Partha S. 2016. *Migrants, Refugees and the Stateless in South Asia.* New Delhi: SAGE Publications.

Kaur, Ravinder, 2010. 'Bengali Bridal Diaspora, Marriage as a Livelihood Strategy', *Economic & Political Weekly* (henceforth *EPW*) 5, 5 (30 January).

Kneebone, Susan, and Felicity Rawlings-Sanaei, 2007. *New Regionalism and Asylum Seekers: Challenges Ahead.* New York: Berghahn Books.

Lee, Everett S. 1966. 'A Theory of Migration', *Demography* 3, 1: 47–57.

Massey, D. 1998. *Worlds in Motion: Understanding International Migration at the End of the Millennium.* London: Oxford University Press.

Ravenstein, E. G. 1885. 'The Laws of Migration', *Journal of the Statistical Society of London* 48, 2: 167–235.

Salamon, Neza Kognovsek. 2016. 'Asylum Systems in the Western Balkan Countries: Current Issues', *International Migration* 54, 6. Retrieved from https://onlinelibrary.wiley.com/doi/abs/10.1111/imig.12273, accessed on 16 March 2019.

Samaddar, R. 2016. 'Forced Migration Situations as Exceptions in History?' *International J. Migration and Border Studies* 2, 2: 99–118.

Sen, Samita, 2016. 'Marriage, Migration and Trafficking in Bengal: Impossible Mobility', *EPW* 51, 44–45 (5 November).

Thapan, Meenakshi, 2006. *Transnational Migration and the Politics of Identity.* New Delhi: SAGE Publications.

PART I

MIGRATION, TRAFFICKING AND WORK

1

Labour Migration in Bangladesh: Experiences of the Chittagong Hill Tracts (CHT) Indigenous Women Workers

ENA TRIPURA

LABOUR MIGRATION INVOLVES the movement of people from one place to another for economic betterment. A migrant labourer or worker is one who migrates to a different place, either nationally or internationally, in pursuit of work. While vast numbers of people still migrate from rural to urban areas within their own country, the number of international migrant workers reached as high as around 244 million world-wide (United Nations 2015: 5), women have remained invisible in the studies of migration for a very long time; their socio-economic contribution and unique experiences have not been taken into account by migration experts. In the 1960s and 1970s migration theories often assumed that most migrant workers were men, and women were merely dependents. However by the 1980s, due to the feminization of poverty and changes in world economic policies, which created a demand for women's cheap labour, women's participation both within and outside labour markets significantly increased as they became family breadwinners (Paiewonsky 2009).

Women, both single and married, have started moving on their own, independently from their families, in search of job in cities or other countries rather than travelling as companions to their husbands, father, or other male family members. It is very clearly visible among

3

the Bangladeshi women in general, and among the indigenous women of the Chittagong Hill Tracts (CHT) in particular. In recent decades, the indigenous people from the CHT, with medium to higher level education (8 years of study to Bachelor Degree Certificate), have been migrating to the big metropolitan cities of Bangladesh to work in factories which manufacture goods for export. According to the information provided by the Kapeeng Foundation and the Parbatya Chattagram Jana Shanghati Samiti (PCJSS), two indigenous organizations, there are more than 70,000 indigenous workers in different factories of the export industry in Bangladesh (Kapeeng Foundation 2013; PCJSS cited in Asia Indigenous Peoples Pact 2011). Accurate gender disaggregated data on indigenous migrant workers is not available, however, according to Chakma, half of these labourers are women. The majority of them have junior school certificates (8 years of study) and few have higher studies such as bachelor degrees (Chakma 2010). Based on the estimates and also personal observation, looking at the Chittagong bus stops early in the morning, it is reasonable to assume that there are substantial numbers of CHT indigenous women working in different factories located in different cities of Bangladesh.

Bangladesh is a predominantly Muslim country where women's mobility is restricted by religious orthodoxy, and women are expected to stay at home cooking, cleaning, and caring for family members while men earn money for their families and deal with the outside world. Bangladesh became independent from Pakistan in 1971 through the 9 months long liberation war which left the country devastated with multidimensional aspects of poverty. The export industries were established in 1978 in different cities of Bangladesh to create employment opportunities for the war-stricken nation. Since then, a large numbers of rural women have been migrating to the cities of Bangladesh and to other countries such as Malaysia, Singapore, Taiwan, Hong Kong and the Middle East for work (Dannecker 2005, Ullah 2007). Much of the literature focuses on the experience of these Bangladeshi female migrant workers and more specifically on the garment workers. However, less attention has been given to the experience of the CHT indigenous women in Bangladesh who have migrated to different metropolitan cities within the country looking for work in the absence of overseas migration opportunities for them. This chapter critically examines the experience of these indigenous women workers, and the benefits they receive from the employment opportunities in factories located in the cities of Bangladesh, whether it has brought any changes in their cultural practices and gender relationships within their families and communities back in the CHT.

ETHNOGRAPHY OF THE INDIGENOUS COMMUNITIES OF CHT

The CHT is situated in the southeastern part of Bangladesh and comprise 10 percent of the total land. It shares a border with Myanmar in the south and the southeast and with India in the north and the northeast. The CHT is the only hilly area in Bangladesh with multiple river valleys, which make it a very unique and distinct region from rest of the country in terms of geographical features, socio-economic and political culture. At present the CHT has three hill districts: Bandarban, Rangamati and Khagrachari. Historically the region has been a home to eleven indigenous communities: Chakma, Marma, Tripura, Tanchangya, Bwam, Mro, Chak, Khumi, Khyang, Lushai and Pankho. The CHT indigenous people are distinct from the mainstream population of Bangladesh in terms of race, religion, language, culture, economy and political history. They are closer to the people of neighbouring Northeast India and Myanmar in terms of physical appearance and culture. In addition, there are differences as each community has a separate language, dress and belief system. All the major religions such as Christianity, Buddhism and Hinduism are represented among the CHT people. The Marma, Tanchangya and Chakma are Buddhist. The Tripura are mainly Hindu except for a few who have converted into Christianity. The Mro community people still follow their Animist religion called Krama. The other minor indigenous communities such as Lushai, Pankho and Bwam are of the Christian faith. However, all communities have their own traditional cult and include traditional elements in formal religious practice (C. K. Roy 2000).

Traditionally, the majority of the CHT indigenous communities use the Tibeto-Burman family of languages in both their spoken and written form, although some of the scripts used are on the decline. Among the indigenous communities, the Chakma and Tanchangya languages have close connections with Assamese and the local Chittagonian Bengali dialect but over the centuries they have got their own distinctive identity (ibid.). The Marma people speak in Arakanese dialect while Tripura speak Kokborok, which is closely related to Bodo and Dimasa languages of Assam state of India. The other minor indigenous communities also have their own languages, which are closely connected to the Kuki-Chin language of Nagaland (Mohsin 2003). However, for inter-community interaction Bengali, Marma and Chakma communities' languages are widely used. All the communities have their own hand-woven dresses with distinctive patterns and vibrant colour combinations. They craft their clothes with the figures and colours of flowers, birds and other objects found in their surrounding natural environment. Traditional dresses are still worn every day, especially during special occasions such as weddings and festivals and feasts (Dewan 2002).

Irrespective of the differences indigenous people have always lived in social harmony with one another. Just like the differences they also have similarities in many aspects. For instance, they are all dependent on nature and natural resources for living. Their main economy is agriculture, which includes jhum cultivation (dry land rice planted on hill sides), wet land cultivation, fruit orchards and horticulture. The majority depend on jhum for subsistence as CHT has only around 3 percent (3.2%) of its total land suitable for intensive plough cultivation (hence wet land cultivation) while the rest is hilly terrain, suitable only for jhum (C. K. Roy 2000), burning vegetation and then planting crops.

HISTORICAL BACKGROUND OF THE CHT

The British coined the name 'Chittagong Hill Tracts' during their occupation, and annexed it as a part of British India in the 1860s. Earlier, the chief judiciary of the indigenous people was community-based, with one chief from every community. In 1881, the British divided the CHT into three administrative circles, the Mong, Chakma and Bohmang circles, and appointed a chief for each (Aminuzzaman and Kabir 2005). Irrespective of ethnic differences, all the inhabitants of a circle were brought under the judicial administration of the circle chief. In 1900, the British divided the CHT area into three districts, Khagrachari, Rangamati, and Bandarban, to represent the state laws. They established a dual administrative system with a deputy commissioner appointed to oversee the chiefs in the three districts (ibid.). The chiefs 'retained power over customary matters' (Mohsin 2003) and also worked as advisors for the deputy commissioner. Since then, the CHT has always had a dual administration system representing both customary and state laws. However, under the 1900 CHT Regulation Act, the CHT was identified by the British as a 'totally excluded area'; outsiders were not allowed to settle in the CHT for the sake of protecting indigenous communities and their cultural distinctiveness (Raja D. Roy 2004).

In 1947, Pakistan and India emerged as two separate states. Pakistan comprised two provinces: East and West Pakistan. During partition, the CHT indigenous chiefs wanted to retain the CHT as a native state, but the Boundary Commission of Great Britain 'rewarded' East Pakistan with the CHT in 1947, being influenced by the Pakistani political leaders (Aminuzzaman and Kabir 2005). The Pakistani government amended the CHT Regulation Act of 1900 many times. The excluded area status of the CHT was changed to a 'tribal area' in 1964 against the will of the native people (Raja D. Roy 2004) and the government encouraged migration of Bengali Muslims from the plains to CHT. In the 1960s, the Pakistani government built a dam over the Kaptai River that runs into the CHT, to generate hydro-electric power. The project benefited the people of the plains, but submerged 40 percent of the arable land in the CHT under water. Thousands of indigenous people became homeless and migrated to India or became internally displaced. The indigenous people have not received proper compensation for their loss (ILO 2000).

After the independence of Bangladesh from Pakistan in 1971, the Bangladesh government refused to give autonomy and recognition to the indigenous people in its first constitution enacted in 1972. The constitution of 1972 declared all citizens of Bangladesh to be Bengali. Article 3, of part 1 of the constitution defined Bengali nationalism as:

The unity and solidarity of the Bengali nation, which deriving its identity from its language and culture, attained sovereign and independent

Bangladesh through a united and determined struggle in the war of independence, shall be the basis of Bengali nationalism. (Thompson 2007)

By making the Bengali language the centre of nation-building, other cultural communities within Bangladesh were excluded. The indigenous people called upon the then prime minister, Sheikh Mujibur Rahman, demanding the autonomy and retention of the CHT Regulation Act of 1900; but these demands were rejected and he advised indigenous people to assimilate into the new Bengali nation or be threatened with marginalization through further migration of Bengalis into CHT (Aminuzzaman and Kabir 2005). After Sheikh Mujibur Rahman was assassinated in 1975, military rulers seized power. In the light of the change in the political dynamics of the country the indigenous leaders started their insurgency movement. Consequently, the government deployed a large number of military personnel into the region. Simultaneously, 450,000 Muslim Bengalis from outside were settled in the region in 1979–1984 to outnumber the indigenous peoples, causing further displacement and dispossession of indigenous people from their ancestral land and natural resources (Raja D. Roy 2004). Political unrest and guerrilla warfare continued for more than two decades between the government military and the Shanti Bahini (the armed forces of the indigenous people). Being ousted from their heartland and homes, thousands fled into the deep forest of the CHT and 70,000 indigenous people took shelter in India as refugees (Hossain 2013). The 1951 UN Convention on Refugees, which was later extended by the 1967 protocol, defines a refugee to be any person who

owing to well-founded fear of being persecuted for reasons of race, religion, nationality, membership of a particular social group or political opinion, is outside the country of his nationality and is unable or, owing to such fear, is unwilling to avail himself of the protection of that country; or who, not having a nationality and being outside the country of his former habitual residence as a result of such events, is unable or, owing to such fear, is unwilling to return to it. (1951 UN Convention on Refugees cited in Kumar 2009)

Under this definition, the 70,000 indigenous people who fled to India are refugees; hence they are different from the young labourers of the CHT who work in cities in factories of the export industry who have been identified as migrant labourers in this chapter. Migrants are persons who make their own decision to move from one place to another for economic betterment, comfort or fulfilling a desire that could not be met in their present location. Though a migrant makes an overtly voluntary decision to move, in many cases a migrant does not always have much choice but moves to another place to avoid extinction, or physical torture and extreme poverty; these types of migrants can be called forced migrants. A migrant can be temporary or permanent while a person's refugee status is being decided and is usually temporary and ceases once the refugee avail protection of his/her country of origin voluntarily (ibid.).

THE CHT PEACE ACCORD

The armed conflict officially ended in 1997 through the signing of the CHT Peace Accord, and most refugees have been repatriated to Bangladesh. However, the Peace Accord is not yet fully implemented, and the refugees have not received proper rehabilitation. The communal clashes in the forms of kidnapping, rape, murder and arson attacks continue between the indigenous people and the Bengali Muslim settlers. At present, the Bengali settlers have become the majority ethnic group in the CHT and the privatization of land has drastically increased. Most of the land is currently owned by settlers, a few rich indigenous elites, corporate agencies and the forestry department of Bangladesh. Indigenous people who are completely dependent on natural resources for their living have been highly affected (Schendel, Mey and Dewan 2000). After the Peace Accord a commercial economy has slowly spread into the region. The indigenous people face multiple barriers in contributing and benefiting from the economic growth in the region because of lack of skill, capital investment and ethnic discrimination in accessing services (Asia Indigenous Peoples' Pact 2007). Many indigenous youths found themselves in difficult socio-economic situations without better livelihood options. Indigenous women have become more vulnerable socially and economically. After the increased privatization of land, men have become the owner of most of the lands, which is passed on to sons; with the exception of Marma, women do not get inheritance rights, fearing that women may take away community land by marrying Bengali men (Raja D. Roy 2004).

DEVELOPMENT OF EXPORT INDUSTRY IN BANGLADESH

When the CHT was going through socio-economic and political crisis, the export industry started flourishing in the big cities of Bangladesh, offering wider employment opportunities in the early 1980s. It has led to a large numbers of poor and landless people migrating to the cities to work. Quite quickly, the number of women in the metropolitan cities of Bangladesh increased; they are mostly young women in their twenties and too poor to be concerned about religious taboos and social stigma (Nana 2002). Prior to the development of the export industries the people of Bangladesh did not see such a large number of women outside of their homes (Hossain 2012). According to Kibria, both push and pull factors form the basis of women's migration to work in the factories of the export industries including in the Export Processing Zones (EPZs). Push factors include poverty, family crises, and frustration, while the pull factors include the desire for socio-economic standing (Kibria cited in Khosla 2009). By migrating to cities they earned their living from factory work.

In CHT this news was given to the indigenous people by the settlers, which then became a lucrative opportunity for many indigenous youths to escape frustration, economic difficulties and hardship. It has also opened an opportunity for many indigenous youths to escape the political. Many young people have migrated to cities as factory labourers since 1990 (ILO 2000). The majority of the migrant workers, both Bengali and indigenous, work in the garment industry as it is the most dominant export industry in Bangladesh. At present, the garment industry earns 81 percent of Bangladesh's export income and employs 4 million workers of which 70 percent are female, mostly young women with no or very limited education, who migrated from rural to urban areas (Hossain 2012).

POSITIVE IMPACTS OF EXPORT INDUSTRY ON WOMEN WORKERS

Many scholars and public figures have identified the development of export industries in Bangladesh as a milestone towards women's empowerment (Siddiqi 2009). Mahmud says that female migration and participation in the workforce in the export industry empowers women by way of giving them greater mobility, income contributions for their families, political awareness, and labour supply (Mahmud cited in Ahmed and Khatun 2008). The then foreign minister of Bangladesh, Morshed Khan, identified industrialization and women's participation as a golden opportunity. He said that

> It is a silent revolution that has taken place in our country. For the first time in a Muslim country, hundreds of thousands of women in their late teens and early 20s are wearing cosmetics, carrying handbags and walking to work every day. There is no way in Bangladesh that this government or any other government can send them back to the kitchen. (Morshed Khan cited in Bradsher 2004)

Acker and others observe that earning money by means of factory work is definitely better than not having any wage at all. It increases income, self-confidence, assertiveness, and helps women to escape familial control (Acker 2004 cited in Richards and Gelleny 2007). As a result of working in industry, women's financial contribution to their families has increased. Women who work in export industries contribute, on average, 46 percent of their total family's income. This improves their status within the family to the extent that they have an influence on family decision-making, can avoid forced marriage, choose their husbands by themselves, and send their children to school. They can afford higher quality food, medical care, and better clothing than other poor women who do not work (Paul-Majumder and Begum 2000).

GENDER DISCRIMINATION AND STEREOTYPES IN THE WORKPLACE

Despite their hard work and overtime work, women still receive lower wages than men. Paul-Majumder and Begum state that a female worker's income is equivalent to only about half that of a male worker's income. The gender gap, in terms of income, has increased over time. Female workers continue to be employed, in large numbers, in low skilled jobs. Conversely, males dominate in jobs which require technological skills and are awarded better wages. Women's lower payment is often justified on the grounds that female workers are said to be less efficient, uneducated, and less experienced (ibid.). The gender difference in terms of promotion is acknowledged in many articles. The promotion rate of female workers in export-based industries is very low. A female worker who works as a helper may get promoted to an operator, but hardly any female operators are promoted to positions with a higher payment, such as manager, supervisor or quality controller. Being in the lower positions, women are often forced to work 6 to 7 days per week and two shifts a day, but often their overtime is not recorded and they do not get paid based on the time spent working (Khosla 2009). Long hours and repetitive work combined with few breaks and poor working conditions cause hazardous health problems for women. Factories of export industries, including EPZs, produce goods for the international market, but do not always abide by the international standards regarding work environments. The factory rooms are usually overcrowded and have very little ventilation. The fibres and dust from the raw materials used in the production, as well as vapours from the dyes used to colour fabrics, contain toxic chemical substances which are frequently suspended in the air throughout the work room (Paul-Majumder and Begum 2000). In this situation, more women than men suffer from weight loss, headache, hearing problems, eye problems and fatigue as they hold low skilled jobs where occupational hazards are greater (Khosla 2009).

The lack of efficient amenities for workers, such as proper canteens, pure drinking water and toilets are also mentioned by a number of researchers. Paul-Majumder and Begum argue that on average there is one toilet for every 61 female workers compared with one toilet for every 31 male workers (2000). Furthermore, most of the factories do not conform to appropriate building standards with fire prevention and safety measures installed. Many hundreds of garment workers are killed or injured in factory fires and building collapses, where most of the casualties are women. The most recent example of this occurred on 24 April 2013 when Rana Plaza at Savar in Dhaka collapsed, and more than 1000 workers were killed and 2500 workers were seriously injured (Alam and Biplob 2013; North 2013).

Female workers are also subject to sexual violence as identified across the literature. In Dhaka, during the 1990s, female garment workers constituted only 2 to 3 percent of the total workforces. However, 11 percent of all rape cases filed with the Dhaka metropolitan police was from garment workers (Paul-Majumder and Begum 2000). Siddiqi expands on this, arguing that verbal abuse by line managers and supervisors is very common. They often insult workers, hurling insults at their parents, saying things like 'Daughter of a whore, so you've come with lipstick on. Go home and show your *bhatar* (family head/breadwinner), don't show off here!' (Siddiqi 2004 cited in Siddiqi 2009).

ISSUES OF INDIGENOUS WOMEN WORKERS

According to Chapola, and also my own experience of interacting with the CHT indigenous women workers, the indigenous women travel to cities in small groups, following their personal network with other indigenous workers. On their arrival in cities they first face cultural shock by seeing people of diverse backgrounds who come to the cities with different objectives. They experience a completely different lifestyle in terms of 'housing, transportation, social interactions, and majority Bengali cultures and practices' (Chapola 2009). The life experience and problems of these women are different from indigenous men and their Bengali counterparts which always remain beyond the attention of any authority.

EMPLOYEES' ATTITUDES TOWARDS INDIGENOUS WOMEN WORKERS

The CHT indigenous women are generally preferred by factory managers and supervisors for their honesty, hardwork and dedication to work. A manager of the Chittagong EPZ said that they prefer Khyang indigenous women over Bengali women because 'Khyang indigenous women are well known for their hard work, honesty, sincerity, weaving skills, obedience and loyalty' (ibid.). As a result of their personal characteristics, indigenous women are central to the maximization of profit for their employers. However, indigenous women do not receive any extra benefits; rather, they are often victimized by their Bengali co-workers who are jealous of them. Many Bengali co-workers complain that indigenous people are given priority by the employers, which they think is unfair. In their interviews with Wazed, many Chakma indigenous women said that Bengalis do not feel comfortable working with indigenous women who they believe to be taking their jobs. Their Bengali co-workers often treat indigenous women badly (Wazed 2012), and some of the supervisors also think similarly and behave in a discriminatory way towards indigenous workers by imposing excessive workloads, and accusing them of mistakes done by other Bengali workers (ILO 2011). Hardly anybody notices the discrimination, harassment and exploitation that indigenous women face in workplaces and outside. Nobody thinks it is unfair to pay them lower wages. According to Mitra (2005), women generally receive lower pay than men in any kind of waged work irrespective of ethnicity. Similarly, in Bangladesh in all sectors of informal employment, indigenous men are offered less payment than the Bengali men if the employer is Bengali. Indigenous women are even paid less than the indigenous men as compared to their Bengali counterparts doing the same kind and amount of work (Wazed 2012). This means indigenous women workers earn even less than 3,000–4,000 taka per month which in Bangladesh is not sufficient for a person to live in a city. This is why garment industry workers, mostly Bengali, who earn more than the indigenous workers, are demanding that the minimum wage to be increased to 8,000 taka (BBC 2013).

As a result of being non-Muslim, indigenous women are left to work very hard to make up for the worker shortage, as export factories always try to accommodate the demands of foreign buyers on time (Rock 2007). Also, it is because of their being of different religious faiths, the employers prefer to hire them to fill the gap of worker shortage during the Muslim religious festivals. It would have been fair and just if they also enjoy paid leave during their religious events and other traditional festivals such as Boisabi. There are no national holidays for indigenous people to celebrate their biggest traditional event.

REPRESENTATION IN TRADE UNION AND OTHER NETWORKS

Indigenous women are more vulnerable to workplace harassment and injustice, and they do not have any representation in the trade unions. In the export industries, organizing trade unions may not be illegal, but is very difficult to organize, especially in the factories located within the EPZs (Hale and Wills 2007). The factories located inside the EPZs are exempt from the protection of the country's labour legislation. 'These zones are geographical enclaves surrounded by high fences with armed security guards who control access and often also discipline workers and prevent their action' (ICFTU 1996 cited in Hale and Wills 2007). In factories where there is a trade union, it is predominantly controlled by male workers with a few Bengali women workers who are not very interested in addressing issues related to women such as workplace harassment, maternity leave and childcare facilities, let alone the issues of indigenous women (Hossain 2012). There is no opportunity for indigenous women to be part of the trade union because of socio-cultural barriers.

Indigenous women workers are mainly limited to their small peer networks that help them migrate to cities or with whom they share accommodation. The members of such networks tend to be mostly women and are either neighbours, or relatives, or friends coming from the same locality. These types of networks help them in sending money home, sharing rent, food items and lending or borrowing money in necessary. Silvy and Rebecca (2003: 81) in their Social Capital discussion on the Indonesian crisis said that there are some close networks in combination of male and female migrant workers in the cities of Indonesia. In such networks women are expected to have restricted mobility, controlled behaviour, and shoulder all the reproductive household roles. A similar situation is visible among the CHT indigenous workers in the cities of Bangladesh. The CHT indigenous men working in cities think it is their responsibility to maintain their society and community's reputation by controlling women's behaviour and movement. Women are often not included in their discussions and networks. It limits women's opportunity to gain further knowledge, skills and negotiation power which might allow them to get promotion in their job. There are some indigenous male workers who work as supervisors and managers in the factory (Chapola 2009) but no single indigenous women working as supervisor or manager has been reported yet.

ACCOMMODATION PROBLEMS

Finding accommodation is one of the biggest challenges that all female migrant workers face. The challenge is bigger among indigenous women in general and biggest among the indigenous women from small communities. Compared to Bengali women, indigenous women are often required to pay higher rent just because of their different ethnicity (Research Initiatives and ILO 2011). In order to share the rent, indigenous women often need to live by gathering as many as thirty people in one large room. The types of accommodation they can afford are urban slum houses that have problems with gas, water, electricity and toilets. They often cook in the same room where they sleep (Afsar 2003). Living independently and alone in the city often carries with it negative connotations; so the landlords do not want to rent their houses to unmarried indigenous women who migrate to the cities alone, unaccompanied by their male family members. Based on the stereotypical understanding of the indigenous people, Bengali landlords often think that unmarried indigenous women in cities might get involved in illegal activities such as prostitution. Sonali, an indigenous Khyang woman who works in a factory, shared her experience of dealing with a landlord in Chittagong:

> I am an unmarried indigenous woman. The landlord told me directly that a single woman might be in danger; they can be spoilt anytime if they live without purushmanush (male person). Also, he gave a strange look at my indigenous appearance. He was curious how I came into the city from the deep jungle of the Hill Tracts. He was surprised as to why I am not going to other migrated indigenous people to live with them. Then I was surprised why he asked such a question, but I didn't argue with the landlord, why did I have to find other indigenous people to live with? I didn't try to convince them about my virtuousness as I felt city people and

city rules are very strange, especially for indigenous women. (Sonali cited in Chapola 2009)

Many people, including indigenous women who migrate to cities, often presume that living in the city, far away from family, will be less stressful and more relaxing and liberating, and that traditional responsibilities towards their family, children and husband no longer need to be fulfilled. They can cook and clean easily at their leisure (ibid.). It can be true for some educated and fortunate indigenous women who have a better job and can afford to live by themselves in better housing within a congenial neighbourhood or with friends. However, for less educated indigenous women who work as factory labourers and have no alternative options but to share accommodation with Bengali co-workers, they can never live how they like. They face problems because of their cultural and language differences.

CULTURAL DISCRIMINATION

In the media such as newspapers, magazines, television shows and academic literatures, indigenous people are always represented as primitive and uncivilized who live with animals and eat snakes, ants and cockroaches; even though that is not always true (Vinding and Kampbel 2012). As a result, their Bengali housemates and co-workers typically look at indigenous women's cooking with suspicious and curious eyes. Sonali, explained that one day when she was cooking 'hilly' food (crab and bamboo shoots) her Bengali room-mates surrounded her and asked many embarrassing questions about indigenous people's food (Chapola 2009). In the same way they get treated like an untouchable by their co-workers in the workplace. The Bengali workers do not like to share canteen facilities with them and often refrain from coming in contact with the cooking utensils used by indigenous people for fear that the dishes many have been used to cook 'haram' food (Wazed 2012). Fearing further social exclusion and ridicule, indigenous women always compromise in terms of cooking, cleaning, eating and sleeping. They try their best not to annoy their housemates and co-workers by eating indigenous food and by their different behaviour. Instead, they try to eat Bengali food, although their own cuisine is their favourite. They always tend to smile, irre-spective of what they feel in their hearts (Chapola 2009).

In order to show they are not different from Bengali women, indigenous women wear Bengali dress in the workplace as well as outside the workplace. Indigenous women's colourful traditional dresses are considered to be indecent according to Bengali values (Raja D. Roy 2004). By wearing Bengali dress, leaving their colourful traditional attire behind, indigenous women try to comply with Muslim Bengali sense of decency, so as to protect themselves from humiliating comments and treatments even though they don't really like the Bengali attire (Asian Indigenous Peoples Pact 2007). An indigenous women worker said, referring to Bengali women:

> 'They feel orna is their abru, ijjat [honour and purdah]. Sometimes, if my orna is displaced from my breast, I have seen that street boys give a strange attention on my breast which is much uncomfortable for me. I feel orna reminds other people that there are something special hidden things or body parts to cover it up. Bengali women are making their breasts attractive and giving special attention by covering with an extra-large piece of cloth on the top of a kameez!' (Sonali cited in Chapola 2009)

This statement clearly expresses that Sonali, the indigenous women worker, does not really feel comfortable wearing orna, a large piece of long cloth put on top of a kameez, to cover her breasts. She wears it to avoid the vulgar attention from Bengali men, and to maintain the Bengali standard of decency. In so doing, many indigenous women workers have adopted Bengali culture and have developed good Bengali language skills. However, despite their continuous hard efforts to assimilate and to fit into the Bengali culture, they are easily identifiable because of their different physical appearance which they cannot hide unless they wear veils. In Bangladesh, many women (Muslims) wear veils as they are socially and religiously expected to wear it as a symbol of modesty, and to maintain distance with others. The culture of wearing veils has increased in the recent years being influenced by Saudi Arabia as Bangladesh has many migrant workers in Saudi Arabia and other Muslim countries of the Middle East. Indigenous women wear salwar-kameez, the dress of the West Pakistani Punjabi, which is known as one of the Bengali dresses by the indigenous people as they see Bengali women wearing the dress. However, the CHT indigenous women do not wear veils amongst their own communities and in cities, except those who are married to Muslim men and are expected to wear veils by their husbands or mothers-in-law.

Indigenous people are more open and frank in interaction with people. They do not maintain a strict religious taboo on women's mobility and women are accustomed to eating, working and chatting with men in the jhum fields. Indigenous men regard human bodies as natural, not to be hidden away and not to be ashamed of. Many Bengali Muslim people see indigenous people's ways of living as a sign of loose morals; women are seen with negative stereotypical assumptions of being loose characters, easily obtainable for sexual services. Hence, these women workers receive indecent proposals from Bengali men who want to take sexual advantage or to convert them to the Muslim faith. One of the women, Mili, said that she was disturbed by one of her Bengali male co-workers who wished to establish an inter-personal relationship. Her refusal did not stop him from continuously bothering her. Mili could not complain about this to the authority fearing that she would be fired from her job (Mili cited in Research Initiatives and ILO 2011).

SEXUAL VIOLENCE AND ITS FAR REACHING IMPACTS

Sexual violence is one of the more gender-specific forms of violence that women face. Indigenous women are at a higher risk of sexual violence than Bengali women workers. The police do not want to look into a case of physical and sexual abuse against indigenous women. In many cases, indigenous victims are arrested by police and accused of having been seductive towards men, with references to their indecent dress, characteristics and cultural practices (Asian Indigenous Peoples' Pact 2007). This is because the majority of the Bengali people always presume indigenous women are promiscuous. Megna Guhathakurta said, such stereotypical thinking 'is one of the main reasons for the discriminatory and inhumane attitudes towards indigenous women that make them justify their actions' (Guhathakurta cited in Asian Indigenous Peoples Pact 2007). Consequently, the number of migrant indigenous women being raped, abducted and forcefully married has been on the increase. There have been cases where indigenous women who refuse to marry Bengali men and who refuse to convert to Islam have been murdered. Many Garo indigenous women of the plains who work in beauty parlours in Dhaka city are married to Muslim Bengali men. Typically, their marriage is not based on love but exists for the sake of their security in the city. The same can be applied to CHT indigenous women who work in the export industry and who become easy prey to Bengali men in the cities (Mohsin 2002).

As in their own societies, women of the CHT play a very important role as custodians of traditional culture and values. It is the indigenous women who have an intricate knowledge of forest food items, nutrition values, medicinal plants, and have knowledge of weaving and handicrafts as well as methods for preparing and preserving food in a traditional way. If women do not engage in these indigenous economic activities, then by living in cities, cultures may lose their source of knowledge. Hence, women are expected to strictly adhere and conform to the social norms. Any kind of deviation receives severe reprimands. In addition, it is the indigenous women who are the biological bearers of the indigenous nations. Staying away from home always creates suspicion as to their sexual purity (Raja D. Roy 2004). People often gossip that they get close to their male bosses for material gain and foreign buyers get the line managers to arrange for time with them. This gossip is so powerful that often many indigenous men, even the ones who work in the same factory, do not want to marry those women who work in factories in the cities. On one hand, because of this stigma and hard life in the city, many indigenous women want to quit their jobs and the city life, but no better options are available to them. Thus they get stuck in factory work and their numbers increase day by day. An indigenous woman, Maya, says: 'I wish I could leave the job at once! But what a fate … I have been continuing and it's more than a year now!' (Maya cited in Chapola 2009).

Initially, women are cautious regarding Bengali people inside and outside the workplace. First, they disapprove of Bengalis who like to flirt with women even if they have wives. Second, they are apprehensive of marrying Bengali men because their marriage would not be accepted by their indigenous community, and also because they think Bengali men are very dominating regarding women and do not allow them any freedom in terms of religion, dress and mobility. There are also some indigenous women workers who do not want to marry less smart and less educated indigenous men who live in the villages. Seeing no better option, many of them marry Bengali men for the sake of security in the city. Once they marry a Bengali man, they never return to their indigenous societies and are cut-off from all networks in the hilly areas. Consequently, they are alienated from their indigenous communities and traditions. The parents of these women do not have anyone to look after them in their old age. Even though property inheritance and bloodlines flow from father to son, it is mostly the daughters who are more attached and responsible for their elderly parents. In addition, parents of these women who marry Bengali men are sometimes socially ostracized, or taunted by their neighbours, relative, and other community people. If they have a younger sister, it often works as a barrier to getting married to an eligible indigenous man with a good family background.

CONCLUSION

The CHT indigenous societies are also negatively affected by the work-motivated migration of indigenous women into the cities. Indigenous communities are losing a large segment of young and educated women who work and live in the cities, isolated from their families and communities. It is a kind of 'brain drain' for the communities as these educated young women have much more potential to contribute to the society, compared to the uneducated and elderly women who remain home. The benefit indigenous women get by working as labourers in the city is very minimal compared to the sufferings and challenges faced after migration. They have been affected by state-sponsored migration of outsiders to the CHT, by the increased privatization of land, and the wealth created by the competitive market-based economy in the region.

Due to lack of capital and required skills they face barriers in benefiting from this new economic growth in the region. In such a situation, the available employment in factories in cities definitely sounds very lucrative for them. These pull and push factors lead to their migration to the cities. However the prevalence of gender- and ethnic-based discrimination in the labour market means that they cannot get jobs that offer better remuneration and working conditions. So these young women mainly take on the lower- strata factory jobs in the industrial zones with lower payment. The experiences of migrant indigenous women workers can never be comparable with those of other factory workers of Bangladesh. By paying them less and imposing extra workload to these honest and hardworking indigenous women workers, it is their employers who are making maximum profits from their migration.

REFERENCES

Afsar, R. 2003. 'Internal Migration and the Development Nexus: The Case of Bangladesh', Bangladesh Institute of Development Studies, Dhaka, Bangladesh: 1–16, Retrieved from http://www.eldis.org/vfile/upload/1/document/0903/Dhaka_CP_6.pdf, accessed on 19 June 2012.

Ahmed, S., and M. Khatun. 2008. 'Gender Relations in Postmodern Societies: Impact of Globalization on Women's Position', *Journal of Knowledge Globalization* 1, 2: 109–25.

Alam, H., and B. H. Biplob. 2013. 'Hope Regained: Rescuers Suspend Using Heavy Equipment after Miraculous Rescue of Reshma', *The Daily Star*, 11 May 2013: 1.

Aminuzzaman, S. M., and A. H. M. Kabir. 2005. 'Bangladesh: A Critical Review of the Chittagong Hill Tract (CHT) Peace Accord', Working Paper No 2, United Nations Development Programme. Retrieved from http://regionalcentrebangkok.undp.or.th/practices/governance/documents/Bangladesh000.pdf, accessed on 12 September 2013.

Asian Indigenous Peoples Pact. 2007. 'A Brief Account of Human Rights Situation of the Indigenous Peoples in Bangladesh'. Retrieved from http://www.iphrdefenders.net/docs/Bangladesh%20%20CN%20edited%20_clean%20copy_%5B1%5D.pdf, accessed on 20 June 2012.

——. 2011. 'Bangladesh: Conference of Pahari Shramik Kalyan Forum held in Chittagong to Strengthen Movement of Labourers' Rights of Indigenous Labourers'. Retrieved from http://www.aippnet.org/index.php/daily-sharing/574-bangladesh-conference-of-pahari-shramik-kalyan-forum-held-in-chittagong-to-strengthen-movement-for-labourers-rights-of-Indigenous-labour, accessed on 24 September 2013.

BBC, 2013. 'Bangladesh Seeks 77% Rise in Wage For Garment Workers'. Retrieved from http://www.bbc.com/news/business-24800279, accessed on 2 August 2017.

Bradsher, K. 2004. 'Bangladesh Is Surviving to Export Another Day', *The New York Times*, 14 December 2004, Retrieved from http://www.nytimes. com/2004/12/14/business/worldbusiness/14bangla.html?pagewanted= 2&_r=0, accessed on 18 August 2013.

Chakma, M. K. 2010. 'The Status of Adivasi Hill Women in Light of the Chittagong Hill Tracts Accord', Bangladesh Nari Progati Sangha (BNPS), Muhammadpur, Dhaka.

Chapola, J. 2009. 'Labour Migration, Inter-ethnic Relations and Empowerment: A Study of Khyang Indigenous Garments Workers, Chittagong Hill Tracts, Bangladesh', MA Thesis. University of Bergen, Norway. Retrieved from https://bora.uib.no/bitstream/handle/1956/3524/Masterthesis_Chapola. pdf?sequence=1, accessed on 10 July 2013.

Dannecker, P. 2005. 'Transnational Migration and the Transformation of Gender Relations: The Case of Bangladeshi Labour Migrants', *Current Sociology* 53: 655–74.

Dewan, A. 2002. 'Woven Textiles as Art: An Examination of the Revival of Weaving in the Chittagong Hill Tracts', MA Thesis, Concordia University, Montreal, Canada.

Hale, A., J. Wills. 2007. 'Women Working Worldwide: Transnational Network, Corporate Social Responsibility and Action Research', *Global Networks* 7, 4: 453–76.

Hossain, D. M. 2013. 'Socio-Economic Situation of the Indigenous People in the Chittagong Hill Tracts (CHT) of Bangladesh', *Middle East Journal of Business* 8, 2: 22–30.

Hossain, N. 2012. 'Women's Empowerment Revisited: From Individual to Collective Power among the Export Sector Workers of Bangladesh', Institute of Development Studies 2012, 389: 1–40.

ILO. 2000. 'Traditional Occupation of Indigenous and Tribal Peoples: Emerging Trends'. Retrieved from http://books.google.com.au/books?id=_84Ggo5Bh YC&pg=PA102&lpg=PA102&dq=Numbers+of+Indigenous+workers+in+ factories+in+Bangladesh&source=bl&ots=q8siyfBd_P&sig=hCfY1Rf2J-G8cSPZK, accessed on 12 August 2013.

Kapeeng Foundation. 2013. 'Bengali Labourers Attack Indigenous Buddhist Labourers in Patenga', *EPZ*. Retrieved from http://www.angelfire.com/ ab/Jhumma/news2013/20130823_patenga_attack.html, accessed on 20 October 2013.

Khosla, N. 2009. 'The Ready-Made Garments Industry in Bangladesh: A Means to Reducing Gender-Based Social Exclusion of Women?' *Journal of International Women's Studies* 11, 18: 289–303.

Kumar, C. 2009. 'Migration and Refugee Issue between India and Bangladesh', *Scholar's Voice: A New Way of Thinking* 1, 1: 64–82.

Mitra, A. 2005. 'Women in the Urban Informal Sector: Perpetuation of Meagre Earnings', *Development and Change* 36, 2: 291–316.

Mohsin, A. 2003. *The Chittagong Hill Tracts, Bangladesh: On the Difficult Road to Peace.* Boulder, Co: Lynne Rienner.

———. 2002. 'Security of Indigenous Women', *Sarwatch* 3, 4: 41–47.

Nana, O. 2002. 'Gender and Migration: An Integrative Approach', Working Papers, Center for Comparative Immigration Studies, UC San Diego: 1–18.

Nath, T. K., M. Inoue, and S, Chakma, 2005. 'Shifting Cultivation (Jhum) in the Chittagong Hill Tracts, Bangladesh: Examining its Sustainability, Rural Livelihood, and Policy Implications', *International Journal of Agricultural Sustainability* 3, 2: 130–42.

North, A. 2013. 'Dhaka Rana Plaza Collapse: Pressure Tells on Retailers and Government', BBC, 14 May, Retrieved from http://www.bbc.co.uk/news/world-asia-22525431, accessed on 1 November 2013.

Paiewonsky, D. 2009. 'The Feminization of International Labour Migration'. Gender, Migration and Development Series Working Paper 1. Retrieved from https://trainingcentre.unwomen.org/instraw-library/2009-R-MIG-GLO-FEM-EN.pdf, accessed on 15 July 2017.

Paul-Majumder, P. and B. Begum. 2000. 'The Gender Imbalances in the Export Oriented Garment Industry in Bangladesh', Policy Research on Gender and Development: Working Paper Series No 12. Washington, DC: The World Bank. Retrieved from http://siteresources.worldbank.org/INTGENDER/Resources/trademaJhumder.pdf, accessed on 15 September 2013.

Research Initiatives and ILO. 2011. 'The Employment of Indigenous Women in the Urban Sector in Bangladesh'. Retrieved from https://www.academia.edu/6661873/The_Employment_of_Indigenous_Women_in_the_Urban_Sector_in_Bangladesh, accessed on 20 December 2014.

Richards, D. L., and R. Gelleny. 2007. 'Women's Status and Economic Globalization', *International Studies Quarterly* 51: 855–76.

Rock, M. 2007. 'Globalisation and Bangladesh: The Case of Export-Oriented Garment Manufacture', *South Asia: Journal of South Asia* 24, 1: 201–25.

Roy, C. K. 2000. 'Land Rights of the Indigenous People of the Chittagong Hill Tracts, Bangladesh', International Work Group for Indigenous Affairs (IWGIA), Copenhagen, Denmark, Document No 99, Retrieved from http://www.iwgia.org/iwgia_files_publications_files/0128_Chittagong_hill_tracts.pdf, accessed on 15 August 2013.

Roy, Raja Devashish. 2004. 'Challenge for Judicial Pluralism and Customary Laws of Indigenous People: The Case of the Chittagong Hill Tracts, Bangladesh', *Journal of International & Comparative Law* 21, 1: 113–82.

Schendel, W.V., W. Mey and A. M. Dewan. 2000. 'The Chittagong Hill Tracts: Living in a Borderland', *Sarwatch* 2, 2: 139–43.

Siddiqi, D. M. 2009. 'Do Bangladeshi Factory Workers Need Savings? Sisterhood in the Post-Sweatshop Era', *Feminist Review* 91, 1: 154–74.

Silvy, R. and E. Rebecca. 2003. 'Engendering Social Capital: Women Workers and Rural–Urban Networks in Indonesia's Crisis', *World Development* 31, 5.

Thompson, H. R. 2007. 'Bangladesh', in A. Simpson, ed., *Language and National Identity in Asia*, New York: Oxford University Press.

Ullah, A. K. M. A. 2007. 'The State of Female Migration Flow in International Labour Market: How Is Bangladesh Doing?' Retrieved from http://www. hull.ac.uk/php/ecskrb/GDP2007/Ullah.pdf, accessed on 20 June 2012.

United Nations 2015, 'International Migration Report 2015', Retrieved from http://www.un.org/en/development/desa/population/migration/ publications/migrationreport/docs/MigrationReport2015_Highlights.pdf, accessed on 15 June 2016.

Vinding, D. and E. R. Kampbel. 2012. 'Indigenous Women Workers with Case Studies from Bangladesh, Nepal and Americas', ILO's International Labour Standards Department (PRO 169), ILO Bureau for Gender Equality: 1–50, Retrieved from http://www.ILO.org/wcmsp5/groups/public/@dgreports/ @gender/documents/publication/wcms_173293.pdf, accessed on 20 June 2012.

Wazed, S. 2012. 'Gender and Social Exclusion/Inclusion: A Study of Indigenous Women in Bangladesh', PhD Thesis, University of Birmingham, United Kingdom. Retrieved from http://etheses.bham.ac.uk/3314/1/Wazed12PhD. pdf, accessed on 20 October 2013.

2

Dynamics of Female Migration in India: Issues and Concerns

SANDHYA R. MAHAPATRO

ECONOMIC LIBERALIZATION AND the ongoing socio-economic transformation that has taken place in India have noteworthy implications on the migration pattern, especially among females. According to Census 2011, migrants constitute 37 percent of the total population of the country based on the place of the last residence, and female migrants constitute 69 percent of total migrants, who outnumber their male counterpart. Further, female migration as a share of the total female population is more than half, which is 53 percent. The National Sample Survey estimates show that the proportion of women in the migration process increased from 35 percent in early 1980s to 47 percent in 2007–2008. The trend clearly indicates a feminization of the migration process since more women than ever before are leaving their place of origin.

Despite its significant and growing proportion, the role and recognition of women in India's migration studies are largely under-represented and remain invisible from the discourse of migration and development. The evidences from Census and National Sample Survey support this. According to Census 2011, around half of the migration of females is attributed to marriage followed by other reasons. Migration of males, its association with macro- and micro-level development, were the centre of discussion of many studies on migration in India (Hann 2000; Mitra and Murayama 2008). These studies view that women are mainly the associational movers as their migration is largely driven by marriage and family-related reasons rather than economic motivation. Such gender bias in the migration pattern is often explained in the context of prevailing socio-cultural norms that women play a secondary role to men in various matters including migration.

Owing to the male-centric conceptualization of migration, the dynamics of female migration and their economic significance in the migration process remain unexplored. Since female migrants are considered passive actors in the migration process, their movement to other places is also presumed to have no significant socio-economic implications for society at large and, hence, the individual economic contribution of females are often ignored (Agarwal 2006). Evidences from the secondary sources of data on migration show that female migration is mainly associated with marriage. However, one may reasonably state that the socio-cultural practices do not allow women to disclose the actual reason for migration. Familial reasons undermine their inherent economic motivation of migration in many instances. A study by Bhattacharya and Korinetk (2007) on female migrants working as construction workers in Delhi finds that strong societal norms may actually prevent women from acknowledging or articulating the true reasons for their migrations. In view of this biased view point, various economic and non-economic factors that motivate female migration remain largely unexplored.

An individual often migrates in response to needs generated by changes in the life-cycle and hence, her motivation to migrate changes accordingly. Though marriage remains the primary reason, an increased presence of females in employment after migration and higher mobility of the lowly placed socio-economic groups indicates the economic motivation behind their migration and, hence, the pattern of female mobility and forces that drive them are beyond marriage reasons alone (Mahapatro and James 2015). Apart from economic vulnerabilities, motivated by better opportunities due to expansion of education, training and technology, increased cost of living and changed social norms, more women also tend to migrate for employment (Philip 2002). In the recent times, economic changes intersecting with other socio-cultural and political changes are influencing female migration patterns.

The pattern of female migration in India in recent years, thus, encompasses an enormous economic and social diversity, and the migration decision of the female is closely linked to the development process of the country, although the underlying motives are not fully understood. Line studies have shown that creation of employment opportunities for women in the epoch of globalization, urbanization and modernization are the possible reasons for migration of females other than marriage (Arya and Roy 2006; Bhattacharya and Korinetk, 2007; Das and Murmu 2013; Ghosh 2002; Neetha 2004; Santhi 1991; Sundari 2005). However, the findings cannot be generalized for the entire population as these studies are not comprehensive in nature.

Given this scenario, it is pertinent to examine the pattern of female migration more closely to get a true picture of the female migration process rather than considering women as the passive actors of migration. The present study aims to understand the economic orientation behind female mobility and the factors associated with female migration.

DATA AND METHOD

For the purpose of analysis both the Censuses of India (1971–2011) and National Sample Survey (2007–2008) are used to understand the patterns and determinants of female migrants. For analysing the trends and patterns of migration, including reasons for migration, the study has used data till 2011. However, as all the migration tables of Census 2011 are still not available, the study is limited to Census 2001 for some of the analysis and also uses National Sample Survey data to supplement the argument. For instance, the district-level estimates were carried out using Census 2001, as district-level information is not available for Census 2011.

The Census of India is the largest source of information on internal migration. The studies on migration in India are mostly limited to the state level. However, 'District' is an important unit for capturing significant inter-district variation in the levels of development and their linkage to migration. A study by Mitra and Murayama (2008) carried out the analysis to the district level. It provides only an overview of the spatial distribution of rural–urban migration and its relationship with some urban characteristics. However, according to the Census data, a major proportion of female migration falls under the rural–rural category and what is important to note here is that over the years, women migrate for economic reasons. In this chapter, an attempt is made to carry out a district-level analysis, taking all the streams of migration into consideration. Further, to explore the economic motivations, pre- and post-work status of the female migrant as available in NSSO data is used.

The information on lifetime migrants is not ideal for comparison across periods as it is cumulative in nature and it does not capture the short-term fluctuations in migration trends. Thus, in order to have a better picture of the contemporary migration trends, only the migrants with 0–4 years have been considered for analysis in the present study. Ordinary least square (OLS) method is used for understanding the association between female in-migration rates and various socio-economic and demographic indicators at the district-level.

The dependent variable in the OLS model is the female in-migration rate for a given district which includes both intra-district and inter-district migrants. It is the gross migration inflow for a given district divided by its total population; the explanatory variables include the socio-economic and demographic characteristics of the district.

TREND AND GROWTH OF FEMALE MIGRATION

According to the 2001 Census data there were 453.6 million migrants comprising 312.7 million females and 140.9 million male migrants. This is nearly double the number of migrants (both male and female) as recorded in 1971. The migration trend from 1971–2011 shows except a slight fall in 1991 that it is increasing for both sexes (Figure 2.1).

Figure 2.1 clearly shows that the migration rate increases over the period irrespective of gender. While the overall migration trend has been increasing, a considerable gender difference in the pattern of migration is noticed. The migration rate of women is significantly higher than that of men in all census periods, implying the growth rate of the female migrant is higher than male migrant population. Along with marriage, socio-economic conditions such as extreme

Figure 2.1. Trends of Internal Migration in India, 1971–2011

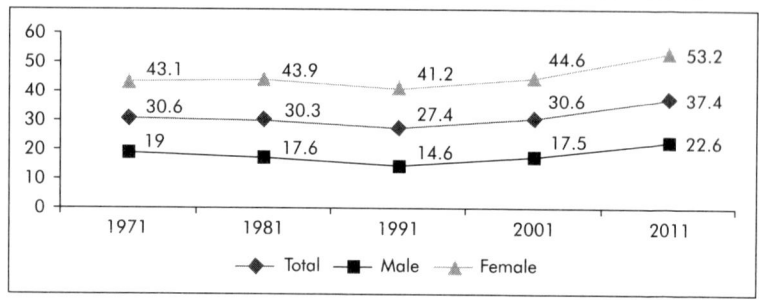

Source: Estimated from Census of India, 1971–2011.

poverty, mechanization of agriculture, environmental degradation, gender segregated labour market, and so on, are responsible for the increasing growth of female migration (Arya and Roy 2006; Shanti 1991, 2006; Sundari 2005).

RURAL–URBAN DISTRIBUTION OF FEMALE MIGRATION

Rural–rural migration is the most dominating trend, especially among females, and is explained in terms of marriage migration. The emerging migration pattern indicates an upward trend in the rural–urban and urban–urban flow for both genders, though the order of magnitude is relatively high for males. Because of the provision of hired wage employment opportunities and for attaining higher education, individuals migrate to urban centres of the developed states.

Category-wise migration and male–female break up are available in Table 2.1, which shows that there is a predominance of female in rural–rural stream followed by rural–urban. It is found that rural–rural migration declines over the Census period and become less significant for both male and female. From the table it is found that rural–rural flow between two Census periods declines from 64 percent to 54 percent among female migrants. On the other hand, urban–urban and rural–urban show an increasing trend over the period of time and the growth is higher in the urban–urban stream from 13 percent in 2001 to 20 percent in 2011.

Table 2.1. Stream-Wise Distribution of Migrants by Gender 1971–2011
(Duration Less than Five Years)

Total	1971	1981	1991	2001	2011
R–R	31.29	55.55	55.63	55.17	45.87
R–U	11.62	8.77	8.24	7.27	8.53
U–R	25.61	19.82	21.11	21.81	22.23
U–U	31.48	15.85	15.02	15.74	23.37
Male					
R–R	27.36	44.97	42.26	40.12	31.68
R–U	12.25	10.13	9.72	8.81	10.07
U–R	28.91	25.8	28.82	30.73	28.77
U–U	31.48	19.09	19.2	20.34	29.47
Female					
R–R	36.3	62.92	63.36	63.78	54.08
R–U	10.82	7.82	7.39	6.39	7.64
U–R	21.42	15.65	16.65	16.72	18.44
U–U	31.46	13.59	12.6	13.11	19.84

Source: Calculated using Census of India, 1971–2011.

The inferences drawn from the table are as follows:

(i) There is a preponderance of females in rural–rural migration stream. This is largely explained in terms of marriage migration. However, a few micro-level studies (Bardhan 1977; Teerink 1995) examined the rural–rural migration among females and brought out the significance of factors like changing agricultural practices, land and labour utilization patterns in determining the migration of women within rural areas. However, over time the rural–rural flow becomes less significant, irrespective of both the genders.

(ii) Unlike rural–rural migration stream, an increasing trend of female migration is observed in rural–urban and urban–urban stream. This increasing trend is explained in terms of commercialization and mechanization of agriculture in the rural areas, urban-oriented educational system, employment opportunities in urban area, social networking, development of communication factors like transportation and information technology.

These findings show that the pattern of female migration by streams of migration changed over a period of time. Rural–rural flow becomes less important while the other streams like urban–urban and rural–urban are becoming more prominent, attributed the socio-economic development of the country.

REASONS FOR MIGRATION

The reasons of migration are generally traced to various socio-economic, cultural and environmental determinants. Data presented in Table 2.2 show that marriage remains the major reason for migration among female. Nevertheless, as mentioned earlier, marriage as a reason for migration declines consistently over all Census periods. While in the 1991 Census, 60 percent of females who migrated in the last five years reported marriage as the primary reason for migration, it declined slightly to 58 percent in 2001. Between Census 2001 and 2011, marriage migration of women shows a tremendous decline from 58 percent to 51 percent in the 2011 Census.

Thus, marriage as the reason for migration is declining with time while employment and education as the reasons for migration increase.

Table 2.2. Distribution of Migrants by Reasons for Migration
(Duration of Residence <5 Year)

Reasons	Total			Male			Female		
	1991	2001	2011	1991	2001	2011	1991	2001	2011
Employment	13.31	16.19	12.58	30	36.78	27.78	3.67	4.19	3.63
Business	2.94	1.15	0.79	6.33	2.55	1.51	0.98	0.33	0.36
Education	5.75	4.49	4.30	11.31	8.49	6.76	2.54	2.16	2.86
Marriage	38.69	37.76	33.40	2.2	1.66	2.28	59.76	58.8	51.75
Moved after Birth	na	6.35	12.71	na	9	17.98	na	4.8	9.61
Natural Calamities	0.5	na	na	0.8	na	na	0.33	na	na
Moved with Household	24.7	22.62	23.18	29.98	24.54	26.55	21.64	21.5	21.20
Others	14.12	11.44	13.03	19.38	16.97	17.15	11.08	8.22	10.60

Source: Calculated from Census of India, 1991–2011.

Employment as the reason increases from 3.6 percent in 1991 to 4.2 percent in 2001 but it declines to 3.6 percent in 2011 which would be due to economic fluctuations and policy changes of the country. Education as the reason for migration is slightly increasing over the Censuses. Associational reasons: movement on account of accompanying parents or any other member of the family is elicited as the second most important reason among both male and female migrants. However, moved after birth as a reason for migration reveals a significant increase from 4.8 percent in 2001 to 9.6 percent in 2011.

Using marriage as the predominant reason for female migration, as observed from macro-level data, underestimates the actual motivation of their migration in the present context. As mentioned earlier, the persisting social-cultural norms restrict women's freedom to divulge the actual motivation of their migration in the household. Therefore, data on the reasons for migration may not help much in understanding the underlying motivation. To understand the economic orientation, the economic participation of female migrants is analysed in terms of the work participation rate in accordance with non-migrant, before and after labour force participation.

The subsequent section will be analysed using Census 2001 and NSS 2007–2008 due to the unavailability of Census 2011 data for other indicators like employment and labour force participation and district-level migration information.

PARTICIPATION IN EMPLOYMENT AND THE ECONOMIC MOTIVATION

This section will throw light on the economic orientation behind female migration. Since it is difficult to capture directly from the data the invisible economic motivation, an attempt is made to capture it by analysing their work profile in three parts: educational status of the employment-oriented migrants; work participation of the female migrant in comparison with the local female worker; and pre- and post-labour force participation rate.

Educational Status of Employment-Oriented Female Migration

An examination of the educational status of migrants who reported employment as a reason, not only helps to identify the motivations

Table 2.3. Educational Status of Employment-Oriented Migration by
Gender and Rural–Urban Status

Educational Status	Total		Rural		Urban	
	M	F	M	F	M	F
Illiterate	18.81	48.67	22.69	57.37	8.29	19.89
Below Matriculation	31.68	19.44	34.76	19.67	23.32	18.69
Below Graduate	27.02	14.00	26.30	11.38	28.98	22.65
Others	22.48	17.90	16.25	11.59	39.41	38.77

Source: Calculated from Census of India, 2001.

behind the migration, bur also helps to understand the direction of their movement, that is, whether they are migrating to the formal or the informal sector.

Table 2.3 reveals that Census 2001 shows that of the total employment-oriented female migration around half of the migrant female (48.67%) are illiterate and the share is substantially higher in rural areas (57%) whereas in the case of the male around 19 percent are illiterate. Structural reforms occurring in rural areas like mechanization, deforestation, privatization of common property resources and various developmental programmes resulted in loss of wage employment, especially among women and hence these people who were poor and of a low economic status prefer to move out to nearby urban areas for employment than to stay back in the village and face starvation.

Work Participation Rate of Female Migrant versus Non-Migrant

Although female migration for economic reasons seems to be limited, the transformation of employment structure, informalization of the labour market, particularly with opening up of gender-segregated labour market, a significant proportion of female migrants engage themselves in economic activity. In order to understand the economic orientation behind female migration, the employment participation of females in the labour market and the participation rate before and after is analysed. Table 2.4 shows the work participation rate of female migrant workers, and to explore the motivation, was compared with the non-migrant workers. It is found that migrants

Table 2.4. Work Participation Rate of Migrants and Non-Migrants
(15–59 Age Group)

Work Status	Total		Male		Female	
	Migrant	Non-Migrant	Migrant	Non-Migrant	Migrant	Non-Migrant
Total Worker	43.35	34.85	59.75	47.54	36.47	14.80
Main Worker	30.57	28.52	54.47	41.02	20.54	8.76
Marginal Worker	12.78	6.33	5.28	6.52	15.93	6.04
Not Working	52.22	61.03	36.16	48.66	58.97	80.60
Unemployed	4.42	4.11	4.09	3.80	4.56	4.60

Source: Calculated from Census of India 2001.

are more economically active than non-migrants and the difference is much higher in the case of females as compared to males. The work participation rate of female migrant workers is more than two times higher (37%) than non-migrants (15%). The same pattern is observed in the case of males also.

The findings as observed from the table are as follows:

(i) As the participation rate in the workforce among migrants is higher than the non-migrants. It reveals that unlike the local workers, the migrant workers have to keep on working even at lower wages as they migrate for survival reasons. As they do not have roots in the soil they have low bargaining power, so they are ready for work even at the low wage.

(ii) A significant gender gap is observed in the work status of the migrant. As compared to the male, the proportion of females engaged as marginal workers is high. Even though the work condition is deplorable or devalued, though they are the least paid, still a significant proportion of females are found as marginal workers. This indicates the importance of economic necessity behind the labour force participation of women.

(iii) The higher work participation rate of the female migrant compared to non-migrant shows that the economic condition of the migrant female is worse than the non-migrant's, especially those engaged in low paid jobs. The economic necessities of migrants push them to engage in low paid economic activity.

This indicates even that the low earnings of the women are crucial for family survival.

Pre- and Post-Labour Force Participation among Migrant Females

To understand how far the economic reasons are intertwined with other reasons behind female migration, the labour force participation of females by the pre- and post-migration status is analysed. Changes in labour market participation with migration might be able to give an understanding of the economic motivation of their migration.

Figure 2.2 shows that 20 percent of migrant women are currently in the labour force while it was 16 percent before migration. The increase is observed among married females as well. For instance, among married female migrants, the participation rate increased from 17 percent to 20.3 percent and for others, it increased from 10.6 to 15.7 percent. The small increase in the participation rate is also due to the fact that only migrants during the last five years are considered for the analysis to report recent changes. Even though the increase is not substantial it can be argued that better opportunities and intention to join the labour market to some extent intertwined with associational movement as well. These changes have significant implications to understanding the economic motivation for female mobility.

Figure 2.2. Labour Force Participation Rate of Female Migrants by Marital Status (Less than 5 Years)

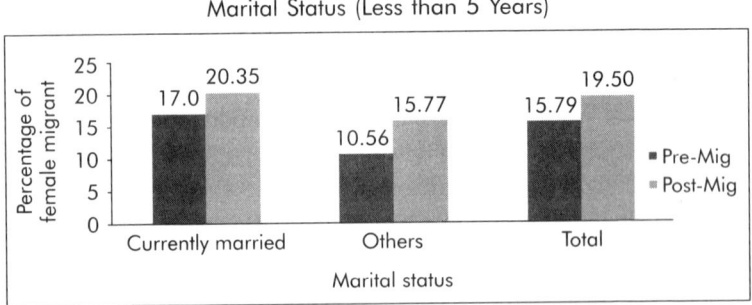

Source: Calculated using NSSO 64th round unit level data, 2007–2008.

REGIONAL PATTERN OF FEMALE MIGRATION

To understand the correlates of the inter-state variability of female migration, a glance on spatial analysis of female migration across the states is essential. The regional flow of female migration to different states shows that among the major states, migration is highest in Maharashtra (3.13 million) followed by Uttar Pradesh (2 million), Haryana (1.6 million), West Bengal and Rajasthan (1.1 million). On the other hand, out-migration is higher in states like Uttar Pradesh (4.32 million), Bihar (2.2 million), Rajasthan (1.5 million), Madhya Pradesh (1.3 million) and Maharashtra (1.28 million). However, a gain in in-migration over out-migration is observed in states like Maharashtra, Gujarat, Haryana, West Bengal, Karnataka, Jharkhand, and Madhya Pradesh (Table 2.5).

Table 2.5. Inter-state Net Female Migration Rates for the Major States of India, 2001

States	In-migration	Out-migration	Net migration rate
Andhra Pradesh	632,515	897,875	–0.70
Assam	182,952	431,777	–1.93
Bihar	1,394,325	2,211,222	–2.05
Chhattisgarh	520,502	521,464	–0.01
Gujarat	919,857	753,890	0.68
Haryana	1,601,921	1,175,633	4.36
Jharkhand	1,022,068	902,293	0.92
Karnataka	1,129,235	1,073,354	0.22
Kerala	220,091	512,858	–1.79
Madhya Pradesh	1,431,332	1,322,193	0.38
Maharashtra	3,134,462	1,281,334	3.99
Orissa	395,125	465,593	–0.39
Punjab	920,862	954,617	–0.30
Rajasthan	1,180,069	1,515,575	–1.24
Tamil Nadu	396,889	848,841	–1.46
Uttar Pradesh	1,999,663	4,324,799	–2.96
West Bengal	1,126,173	936,167	0.49

Source: Calculated using Census of India, 2001.

The spatial analysis of migration flows to different states shows that states like Maharashtra, followed by Haryana, attract more female migrants. Perhaps higher urban industrial concentrations along with well-developed educational institutions attract a large number of migrants to Maharashtra. Haryana is, however, an agriculturally developed state compared to Punjab, as the state has a diversified pattern of growth within the agricultural economy. The increasing rural income and agricultural development might be the possible reason for the growing flow of females into the state. Uttar Pradesh, Bihar, Tamil Nadu, Kerala and Punjab show a high-out migration rate. States like Uttar Pradesh and Bihar are not socially and economically developed. Hence, lack of employment opportunities, the absence of higher educational institutions induce females to migrate. Kerala though socially a developed state is not so economically. High population pressure and low per capita income in Kerala coincided with slow growth of employment opportunities, forced many people to migrate from Kerala to other states in search of employment (Kamble 1983). However, a survey conducted by (Zachariah et al. 2008), showed students constituted the highest number of out-migrants from Kerala, among them 38.1 percent are Christians. Higher out-migration of students from such a religious community indicates that most of the females migrate to other states for nursing education because of competition in the home state and also to get quick employment. Hence, the shrinking educational opportunities for young men and women, especially for those constrained by the reservation policies of the state, leads to out-migration.

Though various studies pointed out that like Haryana, Punjab is also an in-migrating state because of its agricultural development Table 2.5 shows that the state has a negative female migration rate (−0.3), which is not high. Possibly commercialization and mechanization of agriculture forced people to move out of agriculture due to lack of skills and demand for less workforce and hence agricultural labourers migrate to other states. Besides, with urbanization and modernization women also move for higher education and better employment to other states. In a nutshell, the inter-state variation in female migration rate suggests that the socio-economic development, especially the economic condition of the state influences the migration flow.

An examination of the trends, patterns and the economic characteristics of female migration in India, as discussed above, reveal that not only the magnitude of female migration has increased substantially over the years, but also the emerging migration pattern has taken different dimensions. Although marriage continues to be the predominant reason for the overwhelming presence of women amongst migrants, there is a clear indication of an increase in the migration of women seeking employment. Socio-cultural pressure, emphasized as it is a constraint, may not allow them to divulge the actual reason for their migration at the time of migration. However, with socio-economic development in terms of expansion of economic opportunities, set up of educational institutions, infrastructure development, social networking facilitate the sense of economic independence and desire for social advancement that are intertwined with the decision of associational movers. Thus, there is a need to understand the factors that are associated with female migration in India.

FACTORS ASSOCIATED WITH FEMALE MIGRATION

Although, migration of females for economic reasons seems to have been given less importance both in the Census and NSSO data, the economic characteristics of female migrants reflects their economic orientation. According to the latest NSSO (2007–2008) estimates migrant women constitute 68.5 percent of total employed women. This information indirectly indicates the significance of economic reasons behind female migration. The economic variables like work participation rate, unemployment, land holding, and infrastructure seem to have often attracted the attention of many studies. Classification of female migrants, according to the degree in the districts of the country depicts that for nearly 35 percent of districts the female in-migration rate is more than 8 percent, while for 10 percent of districts, the migration rate among males is above 8 percent (Table 2.6).

The migration rate of males falls substantially within the 6 percent range, while for females, the decline is found above 6 percent. A further analysis across states of India shows that states like Haryana, Maharashtra, Punjab, Madhya Pradesh and Gujarat have districts that exhibit a migration rate of 8 percent and above. In states like

Table 2.6. Female Migration Rate at the District Level
(Duration Less than Five Years), 2001

Migration Rate (in %)	Male		Female	
	No. of Districts	Percentage	No. of Districts	Percentage
Up to 2	173	30.19	24	4.19
2 to 4	177	30.89	38	6.63
4 to 6	119	20.77	151	26.35
6 to 8	48	8.38	162	28.27
8 to 10	30	5.24	132	23.04
More than 10	26	4.54	66	11.52

Source: Calculated using Census of India, 2001.

Bihar, Uttar Pradesh, Tamil Nadu and Odisha the migration rate ranges from 4 to 6 percent, while in respect of Karnataka, Kerala and Andhra Pradesh it ranges from 6 to 10 percent. This shows that the migration rate varies directly and substantially across the differing levels of development of the state.

To examine the relative importance of various socio-economic correlates with respect to on female migration, a district-level analysis was carried out. The dependent variable is the female migration rate while other socio-economic indicators of the district were taken as the independent variable. The economic variables considered for the analysis include female work participation, average size of land holding, irrigation, female unemployment.

Regression coefficients that represent the mean change in the response variable for one unit of change in the predictor variable while holding other predictors in the model constant. P-value represents whether the changes in the independent variable are associated with the changes in the dependent variable or not. An insignificant p-value (>0.010) suggests that changes in the independent variable are not associated with changes in the dependent variable.

The estimated results suggest that except land holding size, availability of electricity and health facility, other variables are associated with female migration. Work participation rate, an important economic indicator, is positively associated with female migration indicating with increase in work participation rate in the district, there is increasing

Table 2.7. Factors Associated with Female Migration

Variables	Coefficient	p–value
Average Size of Land Holding	0.069	0.014
Net Irrigated Area	0.05***	0.000
Female Work Participation Rate	0.013***	0.000
Female Unemployment Rate	−0.095***	0.000
Male Migration Rate	0.783***	0.000
Female Literacy Rate	0.029***	0.000
Proportion of Schedule Caste Females to Total Females	0.03***	0.000
Proportion of Schedule Tribe Females to Total Females	−0.031***	0.000
Child–Women Ratio	0.061***	0.000
Availability of Safe Drinking Water	0.043***	0.000
Availability of Electricity	−0.007	0.012
Higher Educational Institutions in a District	0.015***	0.000
Availability of Health Facilities	−0.006	0.013
Transport Facilities	−0.012***	0.000
Constant	−3.875***	0.000
N	481	

Source: Estimated from Census of India, 2001.

inflow female migration to that district (see Table 2.7). This explains the economic orientation of female mobility and availability of employment opportunities at the place of destination. The emergence of new developing markets in the context of globalization creates demand for female labourers in export processing zones, garment industries (informal labour market) acting as a pull factor for female migration in the process (Shanthi 2006). Besides, changing agricultural practices, depletion of natural resources in rural area, female losses in employment and fall into poverty result in migration to other areas (Arya and Roy 2006; Shukla and Chowdhry 1992), such as the urban area for employment. However, at the same time, there is a possibility of those females accompanying males also joining the labour force after the migration as petty workers in addition to managing their household activities. This could be one of the reasons for the work participation rate showing a positive effect on the female migration rate (Mitra and Murayama 2008). Thus, the higher work participation rate is both a determinant of female migration signifying their economic motivation and a consequence of their economic mobility.

Likewise, increased irrigated area under cultivation has a positive impact on the female migration rate, indicating higher the irrigated land in the district, there would be more inflow of female migrants to that district. This suggests employment acts as a major pull factor for females. Female work participation rate is highest in respect of irrigated area as compared to non-irrigated area (Sahu 1985). Unemployment has a negative impact on female migration. This implies that the possibility of unemployment in the destination place reduces the inflow of females. This supports the findings from other studies that poverty and lack of employment opportunity are fundamental push factors of female migration (Adhikari 1996; Kottegoda 2006; Seddon et al. 2001). The effects of work participation, irrigation and unemployment with female migration rate to destination areas suggest that like males, for livelihood females also migrate to other parts, leaving their place of origin than solely being marriage-driven.

An increase in literacy levels of females at the place of destination reflects not only the social development of a given district but also indicates the expansion of a highly skilled and better quality workforce. Increased education in the district encourages inflow of women to that district and the finding is supported by other studies (Mitra and Murayama 2008; UNESCAP 2003a). The percentage share of Scheduled Caste (SC) population has a positive and significant impact on the female migration rate, suggesting the presence of a substantial SC female population in a given place attracts a large number of female migrants through social networking. In this line a study on Tamil women migrants shows that the majority of the domestic workers who migrated from Tamil Nadu belong to the Scheduled Castes and the social barriers at origin force women from a backward caste to migrate to other places to work as domestic servants (Kaustri 1990; Neetha 2004). Another reason may be that SC women generally experience a low economic status that indicates a considerable proportion of female migration is due to poverty as well. However, on the other side, the percentage share of the Scheduled Tribes (ST), though statistically significant, have a negative effect on female migration. This means a large number of tribal women are concentrated in the hilly areas of the country engaged in traditional activities like forestry, the collection of firewood and other minor forest products that are meagre for maintaining subsistence level of living. This may not attract women to move for any livelihood opportunities to that area, hence reduces the inflow of female migrants. Further, in recent years there could be displacement of the tribal women located in hilly areas of the country especially from the eastern region because of developmental projects. This further reduces inflow of migration of females to those areas.

The positive association between child–women ratio and female migration, as evident from the results, is indicative of the fact that women with a large number of children are more likely to migrate in search of jobs so that they are able to meet the basic needs of their children. As expected, male migration rate at the place of destination has a significant and positive impact on the female migration rate. This finding corresponds to the findings of other studies that females are associational movers in the migration process in terms of accompanying their spouses and a proportion of female migration takes place for marriage reasons, which is also evident from the data. However, the significance of employment prospects as a determining factor of female migration even in respect of associational migration has been discussed by many micro-level studies (Chattopadhyay 2005; Kasturi 1990; Kaur 2006; Neetha 2004; Sharma 1986).

The availability of infrastructure in terms of higher educational institutions and safe drinking water in a given district has a significant and positive impact on female migration; thus reflecting better infrastructure base of the district attracts more females for better prospects and opportunities. Surprisingly, the transport and communication spread at the place of destination has a significant but negative impact on female migration. It is possible that with the mechanization of infrastructure development projects, the use of manpower and the creation of employment opportunities have largely reduced. Joshi (1997) observes that the underdevelopment and extreme poverty of a given area cannot be ascribed to the inaccessibility or lack of infrastructure. If this is the case, then without improving the resource base of an area and the creation of an infrastructure base there can have little impact on the development process.

CONCLUSION

The pattern of female migrations and the factors that are associated with female migration beyond the marriage reason are analysed. The study found a pattern of higher participation of migrant women in employment in relation to non-migrant women and higher work participation after migration. The empirical results suggest that the economic variables are significantly associated with female migration. The district-level estimates signify the importance of pull factors like increased availability of employment opportunities, a better infrastructure base and the social development of the destination has attracted a large number of female migrants to that place.

Findings from the above analysis suggest that the migration of females due to marriage has not been eliminated, gradually motivations of women to migrate are gravitating towards economic reasons, suggesting globalization and the associated changes have strong implications for their migration pattern. This can be understood from the relation between female migration and the socio-economic indicators in terms of work, employment and education. In this manner, these findings challenge the conventional viewpoint that female migration is only the outcome of marriage.

It has been observed that there are certain possible biases in exploring the economic aspects of female migration which needs to be addressed for better inclusion of female migration and its various dimensions in migration studies. The reasons for migration addressed both in the Census or the NSSO questionnaire allows individuals to state only one reason for migration. Considering that the respondents are required to give only one reason for migration, in the case of women, invariably the reason for migration is identified with marriage and the question is mostly asked to the household head and hence the issue of respondent bias also emerges. So even if a woman's movement from rural to urban or rural to rural is employment driven, the fact is that the ultimate goal is 'marriage' and as such, a woman's movement is always identified with marriage. Second, data on women participating in short distance migration as a seasonal migrant are grossly inadequate. Third, for district level estimates, the study has been limited to Census 2001 due to unavailability of Census 2011 data.

The discussion on the female migration has thrown up some of the issues that need further research for examining the gender-specific determinants of migration as a whole and more particularly the economic determinants, as the findings of the study suggest that economic factors play a significant role in determining female migration.

REFERENCES

Adhikari, Jagannath. 1996. *The Beginning of Agrarian Change: A Case Study in Central Nepal.* Kathmandu: TM Publications.

Agrawal, Anuja. 2006. *Migrant Women and Work*, vol.4, series editor, Meenakshi Thapan, New Delhi: SAGE Publications.

Arya, Sadhna, and Anupama Roy. 2006. 'Poverty, Gender and Migration', in *Women and Migration in India*, vol 2, series editor, Meenakshi Thapan, New Delhi: SAGE Publications.

Bardhan, Kalpana. 1977. 'Rural Employment Wages and Labour Markets in India: A Survey of Research'. *Economic & Political Weekly*, 12, 28: A34–48.

Bhattacharya, Sanghita, K., and Kim Korinetk. 2007. 'Opportunities and Vulnerabilities of Female Migrants in Construction Work in India', *Asian and Pacific Migration Journal* 16, 4: 511–531

Chattopadhyay, Basudha. 2005. 'Why do Women Workers Migrate? Some Answers by Rural–Urban Female Migrants', *Urban India* 15, 1: 34–43.

Das, Kailash Chandra, and Arunananda Murmu. 2013. 'Female Migration to Mega Cities and Development in India, International Union for Scientific Study of Population'. Retrieved from https://iussp.org/sites/default/files/event_call_for_papers/FEMALE%20%20MIGRATION%20TO%20MEGA%20CITIES%20%20AND%20DEVELOPMENT%20IN%20INDIA_IUSSP13.pdf; accessed on 04 July 2017.

Ghosh, Jayati. 2002. 'Globalisation, Export-Oriented Employment for Women and Social Policy: A Case Study of India', *Social Scientist* 30, 11–12: 17–60.

Government of India, Registrar General and Census Commissioner. 1971–2011. *Migration Tables*. New Delhi: Government of India, Registrar General and Census Commissioner.

Haan, De, Arjan. 2000. *Migrants, Livelihoods, and Rights: The Relevance of Migration in Development Policies. Social Development* Working Paper No 4. London: Department for International Development.

Joshi, Y. G. 1997. *Tribal Migration*. Jaipur: Rawat.

Kamble, N. D. 1983. *Labour Migration in Indian States.* New Delhi: Ashish Publications.

Kasturi, Leela. 1990. 'Poverty, Migration and Women's Status', in *Women Workers in India: Studies in Employment and Status*, Veena Majumdar, ed., New Delhi: Chanakya.

Kaur, Ravinder. 2006. 'Migrating for Work: Rewriting Gender Relations', in *Poverty, Gender and Migration*, Sadhna Arya and Anupama Roy, eds., New Delhi: SAGE Publications.

Kottegoda, Sepali. 2006. 'Bringing Home the Money: Migration and Poverty in Gender Politics in Srilanka', in *Poverty, Gender and Migration*, Sadhna Arya and Anupama Roy, eds., New Delhi: SAGE Publications.

Mahapatro, Sandhya R., and K. S. James. 2015, 'Understanding Female Migration Pattern in India: Exploring the Driving Forces', in *Gender and Migration: India Migration Report*, S. Irudaya Rajan, ed. New Delhi: Routledge.

Mitra, Arup, and Mayumi Murayama. 2008. 'Rural to Urban Migration: A District-Level Analysis for India', Discussion Paper No.137, Institute of Developing Economies.

National Sample Survey Organization (NSSO). 2007–2008. *Migration in India*, New Delhi: Government of India: National Sample Survey Office, Ministry of Statistics and Programme Implementation.

Neetha, N. 2004. 'Making of Female Breadwinners: Migration and Social Networking of Women Domestics in Delhi', *EPW* 39, 17: 1681–88.

Phillip, T. 2002. 'Impact of Women's Employment on Family and Marriage: A Survey of Literature', *Social Change* 32, 1&2: 46–57.

Sahu, M. K. 1985, 'Impact of an Irrigation Project on Labour force and Migration: A Case Study of Hirakud Project in Sambalpur District', PhD thesis, Institute for Social and Economic Change (ISEC), Bangalore.

Seddon, David, Jagnath Adhikari, and Ganesh Gurung. 2001. *The New Lahures, Foreign Employment and Remittance Economy of Nepal*, Kathmandu: NIDS.

Shanti, K. 2006. *Female Labour Migration in India: Insights from NSSO Data*, Working Paper (4), Madras School of Economics.

———. 1991. 'Issues Relating to Economic Migration of Females', *Indian Journal of Labour Economics* 34, 4: 335–46.

Sharma, Ursula. 1986. *Women's Work, Class and the Urban Household: A Study of Shimla, North India*. London: Tavistock.

Shukla, P. R., and S. K. Roy Chowdhry. 1992. *Poverty, Migration and Urban Unemployment*, New Delhi: Akashdeep Publishing House.

Sundari. S. 2005. 'Migration as a Livelihood Strategy: A Gender Perspective', *EPW* 40, 22–23 (May 28-June 10).

Teerink, R. 1995, 'Migration and Its Impact in Khandeshi Women in Sugarcane Harvest'. in L. Schenk-Sandbergen, ed., *Women and Seasonal Labour Migration*. New Delhi: SAGE Publications.

UNESCAP. 2003. 'Dynamics of International Migration from India: Its Economic and Social Implications', Ad Hoc Expert Group Meeting on Migration and Development, 27–29 August, Bangkok.

Zachariah, K. C., and Irudaya Rajan. 2008. *A Decade of Kerala's Gulf Connection Migration Monitoring Study*. Retrieved from http://www.cds.edu/overview.pdf, accessed on 6th July 2017.

3

Interface between Migration and Trafficking: A Case of Tribal Minor Girls from Jharkhand

GOMATI BODRA HEMBROM

THERE IS A STRONG interconnectedness between migration and trafficking. Though migration is related to human trafficking, it is not human trafficking itself. Domestic factors such as unemployment, poverty and low wages make people migrate to other places in search of better opportunities. The realities of tribal women and girls, trapped in distress migration and trafficking, differ according to specific contexts, reflecting the multi-faceted causes and consequences.

There has been a history of migration amongst the tribal/adivasi communities in the central and eastern regions of India. Migration of the tribal population from Jharkhand, Odisha and Chhattisgarh has been taking place since the last three centuries. In the eighteenth and nineteenth centuries, the migration was forced as the British employed tribal labour to work in the Assam tea plantations. However, since the latter half of the twentieth century, tribal people from these areas have begun to migrate voluntarily to earn their livelihood. In the last century a noticeable change was visible in the nature and pattern of tribal migration. Between the 1950s and the 1980s tribal people migrated to the rural areas of Bihar and West Bengal mainly to work as agricultural labour. But from 1980 onwards, they have started migrating to brick kilns and construction sites in bigger cities in search of employment. This is obvious from the large concentration of

47

tribal people in metropolitan cities like Delhi, Kolkata and Mumbai. Another new feature of the tribal migration from these states in recent years has been large-scale migration of single women to cities in search of livelihood which is autonomous and individualistic in nature (Jha 2005; Kujur and Jha 2008; Mazumdar 2016). Due to poverty and lack of employment opportunities, tribal families send unmarried daughters to cities in search of work. Single women and tribal girls are, however, prone to exploitation not only by employers, but also by anti-social elements. Migration is an important livelihood activity (Xaxa Report 2014).

In the last few decades, there has been a mass migration of single tribal women/girls, without reference to any male member, who migrate to Delhi to work as domestic workers, thus causing a sea change in the pattern of tribal migration (Jha 2005).These women and young girls migrate with the help of strong social networks; with the help of friends or relatives or through placement agencies or church-based organizations. Many of them are minors, therefore, unmarried. The majority of the tribal women who are live-in maids in the capital city of Delhi are from the states of Jharkhand, Odisha, Chhattisgarh and West Bengal (Jha 2005; Kujur and Jha 2008; Mazumdar 2016; Xaxa Report 2014).

In Delhi, Jharkhand has the maximum number of live-in domestics (51.82 percent). The other prominent feeding states are Odisha (12.73 percent), Madhya Pradesh (3.64 percent), Assam (3.64 percent) and West Bengal (1.82 percent). The source districts of these domestics are Gumla (79), Ranchi (16) and Palamau (5) in Jharkhand, Jaspur in Madhya Pradesh, Sundergarh in Chhattisgarh, Raigarh in Bihar. Unlike the live-out workers, live-in domestics are mainly unmarried girls (89.2 percent) belonging mainly to the age category of 15–20 (55 percent) and 21–25 (30 percent). Christians dominate live-in workers, accounting for 88 percent of the respondents. The tribe-wise distribution of live-in domestics shows that they are mainly Oraons, 55.3 percent, Munda, 25.3 percent, and the Kharias 12.1 percent and others 7.3 percent (Kujur and Jha 2008; Mazumdar 2016; Neetha 2004). The first World Day against Trafficking in persons was observed on 30 July 2014. Ruchira Gupta, founding president of Apne Aap Worldwide, an organization working in countering trafficking and helping women in prostitution, believes India is the epicentre of bonded labour in the world: India has the most numbers of slaves through debt-bondage and most prostituted children. Sometimes labour and sexual exploitation are interconnected. A person may be trafficked for labour and then may be sexually exploited as well.

It is very important for India to have strict laws against trafficking for labour exploitation. India has to make bigger legal changes. There is a UN Protocol against trafficking, which was passed in 2002. Also, while the law has changed, there are no budget allocations to provide legal, health, housing or capacity-building services to victims and survivors of prostitution. And on prevention, there is absolutely no policy at all. A holistic approach that links different departments, such as women and child, social welfare, education, police, is needed. Schemes need to be linked. The government must also identify those who are most likely to be trafficked and map them (Gupta 2014).

UNDERSTANDING MIGRATION AND TRAFFICKING

The International Organization for Migration (IOM) defines the term 'migration' as the movement of a person or a group of persons either across the border or within a country. It is a population movement encompassing any kind of movement of people, whatever its numbers, composition and causes, including migration of refuges, displaced persons, economic migrants and persons moving for other purposes. Migration from one area to another in search of improved livelihoods is a key feature of human history. The process of migration is influenced by social, cultural and economic factors and outcomes can be vastly different for men and women, for different groups and different locations. Migration encompasses enormous economic and social diversity. At the same time, it emphasizes the vulnerability and abuse of this migrant group, mainly woman. In terms of making a living, trafficking is seen as a frequent result of migration, forced and unforced.

Trafficking in women is a complex and extremely sensitive phenomenon, inextricably linked to poverty, migration, work, sex, money and violence. While the problem of human trafficking has captured widespread public attention in recent years, on the one hand, it has mostly focused on the impoverished women and girls trafficked into the sex industries, connected to organized crime (Kempadoo et al. 2016). On the other hand, considerably less attention has been devoted to the widespread practice of trafficking of women, men and children into agricultural work, construction work, domestic work or other non-sexual labour. Trafficking is a terrible crime of the sale of women and children for sexual exploitation and forced labour. Human trafficking is directly connected with modern-day slavery. Trafficking is a global crime and it is organized. It is a multi-billion-dollar industry that creates profits for those who are involved (ibid.). It affects millions of people, particularly in poor countries and poor communities. Generally unsafe migration leads to trafficking. Many children and women are being trafficked for forced labour, child labour, forced marriage, sexual exploitation and bonded labour.

Janet Henshall Momsen (1999) had intimately intertwined the three sets of processes that are gender, migration, and domestic work. According to her, domestic work is done by women, who are in some way 'different' from their employers (on grounds of race, class, origin, religion, citizenship), and this work is physically demanding, socially demeaning, and economically marginal. Yet, all over the world, women are leaving their own families (or, in some cases, moving with them) and are finding domestic service to be the only available employment. Women move from rural to urban areas within states, they move across nations, and they move in large numbers from their countries of origin to foreign shores, the commonality is that they move from poorer areas to richer areas, from periphery to core. First, the women tend to have few economic choices open to them, either at 'home' or in their destination country. Most of the women are very poor, come from regions under stress, and have migrated to find work and send remittances back to their families. Either there are no employment options for them at 'home' or the options are undesirable (farm work, factory work, or in some cases marriage). The apparent worldwide construction of domestic service (usually including cleaning, cooking, and laundry and often including childcare) as something of which women are capable merely by being women and the pervasive, essentializing construction of women as 'natural' domestic workers is across cultures and across borders. Momsen clearly mentions that a contradiction appears in that individual households employ domestic workers in order to 'free' the female householder from domestic labour. This arrangement enables middle-class women to avail various career opportunities, focus on children, or greater leisure without disrupting existing household gender divisions of labour. The labour of maintaining a household is still construed as naturally belonging to the woman, but she is able to deflect the actual work to another, lower-status woman by employing domestic help.

Momsen also discussed the multiple forms of oppression experienced by domestic workers, reflecting their positions on multiple axes of 'difference'. Domestic work is performed overwhelmingly by women, making gender a constant set of relations across diverse cultural and economic contexts. Class is inherently relevant as well, because domestic workers are almost by definition located in a lower social stratum than their employers. Beyond gender and class relations, however, their work offers many finely grained stories of the ways in which other differences play into local and individual situations: race, ethnic group, culture, nationality, place of origin, citizenship status, age, religion, and how unique combinations of difference shape the experiences of domestic workers and their employers. Employers often have preferences for certain domestic workers over others, based not on personality, experience, or skills but on where they come from. For example, Canadian employers prefer Filipinas, because Jamaicans are seen as too aggressive, urban Chileans want women from southern Chile to be their domestics because they are seen as innocent and trustworthy, British employers think Portuguese women are good at ironing and workers from New Zealand are good with children, and so on.

Most migrant women thus tend to be concentrated to a greater extent than their native peers in low-skilled personal service work. Globally, most women migrants generate income through jobs which are considered low-skilled, are poorly paid and often performed in the domestic and/or private domain or related to the expansion of the service industry, that is, the 3-d (dirty, demeaning and dangerous) jobs. Generally, such jobs tend to be looked down upon socially and devalued economically. Domestic and household work constitutes, together with nursing, the most female-dominated sector. The most widespread problems with domestic work are the low pay and long working hours, the inferior positions of domestic workers and highly personalized relationships with employers, which make it arduous for workers to receive their agreed pay or get time off. The health and safety situation for the domestic workers at home is seldom satisfactory, and if they are ill they do not get paid and also run the risk of losing their jobs. Psychological, physical and sexual abuses are very common. We can clearly observe the nexus between sexism and racism as these areas are not preferred by the native women because of the social stigma attached (Kempadoo et al. 2016; Sharma 2011).

Migration and domestic work in cities are closely related, owing to the ease with which migrants can enter this occupation and its gendered nature. Migration for domestic work, with deep historical roots, has been reinvented in the past two decades. Changes in the gender balance of the migratory stream, the migration of families as kinship units, have influenced the nature of domestic work. Domestic service has been the commonest and also normally the first occupation of women in almost all countries in the world, though the period varies across countries. Entry restrictions are almost zero in the case of domestic service, as the occupation does not demand any capital or skill. The decision to migrate was taken mostly in the context of the household, as, for many, it is part of the family survival strategies.

Poverty, lack of food and scarce job opportunities at the place of origin were found to be the most important reasons for migration to Delhi. Apart from unemployment and poverty, for the live-in workers, migration also meant a rite of passage that provided status, independence, training and savings for marriage on their return. Further, the search for personal freedom and the accompanying rejection of traditional gender roles were also found important. Living in cities is also seen as a step forward in social mobility and status. A few girls also admitted that the visits of domestics from Delhi tempt the aspirants. Yet another important form of migration for domestic work from the tribal pockets is the group migration of tribal girls. Girls organize themselves into groups which have as their leader one person who has either worked in Delhi as a domestic worker or is known to someone working as a domestic worker or has some information about the city and its employment opportunities. Tribal girls come to Delhi in large numbers by train during January-March looking for employment. Most of these workers migrate under the influence of old workers who have visited their native place during Christmas and other tribal festivals. Added to the money income, the charm of the city also attracts many workers, who are the main source of workers for private agencies. About 12,000 girls migrate to Delhi every year as groups (Kujur and Jha 2008; Mazumdar 2016; Neetha 2004).

Let us analyse the emergence of a new phenomenon of nexus between distress migration and trafficking of women and minor tribal girls in Jharkhand. There is a rise of distress migration among young single, unmarried women. But in recent times, young girls are trafficked and taken to metropolitan cities like Delhi, Mumbai and sold and coerced to work as domestic maids. The causes of trafficking lie in poverty coupled with negligible development, rural–urban migration, Maoist violence, failure in implementation of social security schemes. The social context of this intersectionality of migration with trafficking is the prime focus of this chapter. At the same time, it focuses on both the supply side as well as demand side of trafficking. Theoretically, critical feminist theory has been used to look at the problem of female distress migration and trafficking in the Jharkhand region, based on secondary data, relevant literature and personal observations.

THE PROBLEM OF TRAFFICKING OF MINOR TRIBAL GIRLS FROM JHARKHAND

Trafficking of girls is common in Jharkhand's hinterland. According to the state CID, every year 207 minor (who are mostly tribal girls) are being trafficked from state to metropolitan cities like Delhi. Acute poverty coupled with negligible development and failure in implementation of social security schemes are reasons behind this unending migration and trafficking of girls (*Hindustan Times* 2015, October 15).

Most portrayals depict trafficking as an act or series of acts of exploitation and violence, perpetrated by traffickers and suffered by desperate and poverty-stricken victims. While accurate in some respect, such depictions are incomplete. The problem of trafficking and distress migration lies not with the traffickers themselves, but the conditions that caused their victims to migrate under circumstances rendering them vulnerable to exploitation. Human trafficking is but 'an opportunist response', trafficking lies at one extreme end of migration continuum, where the migration is for survival: that is, escape from economic, political or social distress, as opposed to opportunities seeking migration that is merely a search for better job opportunities (Chuang 2006; Kempadoo et al. 2016). Contrary to the popular, sensationalized image of a trafficked person as either kidnapped or coerced into leaving her home, more often than not the initial decision is a conscious one. Yet the decision to uproot oneself, leave one's home and migrate elsewhere cannot be explained as a straightforward 'rational choice' by a person who accesses the cost and benefits of relocating rather than having an understanding of this decision, and it must account as a macro factor that encourages, induces or often compels migration.

NEXUS OF TRAFFICKING AND MIGRATION

Trafficking perhaps becomes most complicated by its links to migration. Research (Kempadoo et al. 2016; Mazumdar 2016; Nuimai 2016; Sen 2016; Sharma 2011) shows that most of the women who are trafficked have a strong desire to migrate and are thereby abused during the process of migration. As poverty disproportionately affects women (along with their children), they are more likely to be stirred to migrate hoping to improve the economic situation both for themselves and their families. Out of 1.3 billion absolute poor in the world today, 70 percent comprises women and their minor dependents. Further, restrictive regulations which reduce legal female migration lead to a rise in illegal migration. This multiplies the risk of exploitation of female migrants as it might result in trafficking in order to avoid deportation. Trafficking is increasing rapidly not only due to rising demand but also as a result of larger and varied sources of supply due to precarious life conditions in many parts of the developing countries. Conducive conditions are found in the rural areas of the developing world where the peasantry has been hit by agrarian crisis or in societies afflicted by violent conflict or ravaged by natural calamities. As mentioned earlier, a substantial amount of trafficking occurs not only for commercial sex work but also for use as slave labour in factories and other economic activities such as domestic or informal service sector work.

Many times trafficking is not by coercion but out of oppressive or abusive or extreme poverty conditions at the home place. The traffickers are also involved into luring females by false promises of high paying jobs, fraudulent marriages, and so on. The majority of women who migrated through trafficking systems were aware of the conditions they would work in but for them the prostitution contract was a part of the bigger migratory project. Discrimination against women in the labour market, growing unemployment and a lack of skills and training contribute to their willingness to search for improved living conditions and career opportunities via unorganized routes, ultimately falling into the hands of the traffickers (Kempadoo et al. 2016; Mazumdar 2016; Nuimai 2016; Sen 2016; Sharma 2011).

The movements of population have continued under the forms of both voluntary and involuntary migration. Traditionally, women migrated as part of the family or as a dependent migrant accompanied by men, from one rural area to another. A study of tribal migration shows that migration has changed from the rural–rural migration of the pre-1980s, to rural destinations in Bihar and West Bengal, to rural–urban migration to faraway metropolises such as Delhi, Kolkata and Mumbai (Jha 2005; Kujur and Jha 2008).

A UNDP research paper (2012) states that some 20 million people (mainly women and girls) migrate for domestic work to Mumbai, Delhi and other large cities from the eastern states of Jharkhand, Odisha, West Bengal and Chhattisgarh. These girls are mostly illiterate, semi-literate and school dropouts. During the last few years, tribal girls have been trafficked by agents in cities for domestic work. Young tribal women and girls from Jharkhand, Odisha and Chhattisgarh are being brought by private recruiting agencies and Christian volunteering agencies to be employed as maids in daily households. Approximately, there are more than 100,000 tribal domestic women workers in Delhi (Kujur and Jha 2008). It is believed that domestic service does not need any special skills. Most instances show that they come from remote tribal areas, are extremely poor and have no acquaintance with the ways of city and city people. There are multiple factors due to which tribal women migrate to cities and work as domestic workers. A 2013 report by the Geneva-based International Labour Organization (19th ICLS, Geneva Report-II, 2013) found that the number of domestic workers in India ranges from 2.5 million to 90 million. And despite being the largest workforce in the country, the workers are unrecognized and unprotected by Indian law (*Business Standard*, 18 March 2015).

GLOBALIZATION, MIGRATION AND WOMEN TRAFFICKING

According to Saskia Sassen (2000) due to economic globalization, in the developing countries a variety of circuits has emerged which she also termed as counter-geographies. These circuits are enormously diverse, but share one feature: they are earning a living, profit or revenue making, on the backs of the truly disadvantaged. These include the process of migration and illegal trafficking. These circuits could be considered as indicator of feminization of survival because it is increasingly on the backs of the women. The notion, feminization of survival, refers to the fact that households and whole communities are increasingly dependent on women for their survival. Sassen tries to make an analytical effort to uncover the systemic connections between low income individuals, who are often represented as a burden rather than a resource and what are emerging as a significant source of profit and government revenue enhancement, partly in the shadow economy. Prostitution, labour migration and illegal trafficking in women and children are growing in importance as profit-making activities. Women are by far the majority group in prostitution and in trafficking and they are becoming a majority group in migration for labour. Another impact of economic globalization in a developing economy, which is also stagnant, struggling and shrinking, is that it had to implement new policies and accommodate new conditions such as structural adjustment programmes, opening their economics to foreign firms, the eliminations of multiple state subsidies. These conditions created enormous costs for certain sectors of the economy and the population, such as the growth in unemployment, the closure of many firms in often traditional sectors oriented to local or national market, the promotion of export-oriented cash crops which have increasingly replaced survival agriculture and food production for local and national markets. Economic globalization leads to a systematic growth of high unemployment, poverty, bankruptcies of a large number of firms and shrinking state resources to meet social needs. Increase in government debt has detrimental effects on women and children, as there is severe cost cutting in education and health care. Increased unemployment of both men and women in their households added to the pressure on the women to find ways to ensure household survival. Shrinking economic opportunities resulted in the increased use of illegal profit-making enterprise such as trafficking. Trafficking of poor women and children has become a profitable business.

Globalization has a profound effect on human trafficking. It has increased the economic gap between countries and also between regions and communities within a country. Tribes in a developing country like India experience the threat of globalization, specifically those living in a poor state like Jharkhand, as the investment on public welfare has started to decline during this period. Though the growth rate of Gross Domestic Product (GDP) has accelerated since 1990, the major part of foreign investment which flowed into India after liberalization gets invested mostly in developed states like Delhi, Gujarat, Tamil Nadu, Karnataka and Maharashtra, whereas poor states like Jharkhand, Bihar, and so on, received far less, on account of their adequate infrastructure. These poor states are usually dependent on central grants, which declined due to fiscal constraints (Munshi 2012; Rath 2006; Sunder 2016). This shows that the international capital that flowed through globalization contributed less to the welfare model of development, and the internal investment made by the state also declined. In this whole process the position of tribal population becomes highly vulnerable.

Globalization has accelerated the process of industrialization and the gradual erosion of tribal rights over natural resources like land, forests, and commons. There is a constant decline in the tribal working population hence increase in unemployment. At the same time agriculture and forest-based work, which is the main source of income, remained in a stagnant position even in the days of economic reforms because tribes were unable to break from their traditional sources of employment or diversify their occupations (ibid.). Ironically, due to lack of professional education or skill building, adivasis are unable to get jobs in the various industries, mining projects, government and private jobs in their states. So, agriculture and forest resources continue to form their primordial economic activities, but these barely provide food for six months. Thus migration becomes a survival strategy and tribes mostly work as labourers in the construction sites, brick kilns and other informal sectors. Because of poverty and also because they are innocent and semi-literate, they are severely exploited.

On the other hand in metros like Delhi, as a result of globalization, the realignment of social and cultural relations and radical changes in the labour market, more and more women, who were traditionally confined to the homes, are now seeking alternative, preferred and more viable livelihood options elsewhere, as in the IT sector or multinational companies. The globalized world is experiencing a rapid transfer of goods, service and social aspirations. In the post-reform era the number of women in paid employment has risen. If women in Delhi make a career for themselves and devote a great deal of time to demanding professions, their maids and helpers arrive as a result of the increasing demand for help at home which has become a veritable industry.

According to Janie Chuang (2006) more often than not, trafficking is labour migration gone horribly wrong in our globalized world. Notwithstanding its general economic benefits, globalization has bred an ever widening wealth gap between countries and between rich and poor communities within countries. This dynamic has created a spate of 'survival migrants' who seek employment opportunities as a means of survival as jobs disappears in their place of origin. The desperate needs to migrate for work, combined with high demand for cheap labour, in destination cities like Delhi, render these migrants, specifically women, highly vulnerable to trafficking. The tools of globalization are beneficial to traffickers. For instance, technology is helping them use all kinds of devices, which make it easier for traffickers to operate their trafficking networks, keep in touch with each other, and find out where girls can be sold cheaply. The business of human trafficking became desirable because of least risk, high profits and large demands.

Women's lack of rights and freedom are further exacerbated by certain micro-level globalization trends that have produced an environment. A certain trend is the shift in the structure of power at the international level, that is, the rise in the power of international market focused institutions such as MNCs, the IMF, the World Bank and the WTO, relative to those that are more people-centred and concerned with sustainable human development such as ILO, many UN agencies and Non-Governmental Organizations. These global restructuring trends have harsh effects on women in developing countries: either fostering exploiting conditions for women working in the formal sector or pushing women directly into work in the informal sector (my observations based on research).

Another one is the structural adjustment policy mandated by the IMF and the World Bank as a condition for loans, requiring a government to open its markets to further financial and trade flows and to undertake austerity measures which falls heavily on the poor, particularly on women. Structural adjustment policies add to the pressure on women to migrate in search of work. These policies, which require governments to cut programme and reduce expenditure on social services, cause woman to take on additional income-earning activities in order to maintain their family's standard of living as government decreases benefits in housing, health care, education, food and fuel subsidies. This often pushes women to work in the unregulated, informal sector, contributing to the rise of gender–labour networks: prostitution or sex work, domestic work and low-wage production work. Women often migrate in search of jobs in these largely unregulated sectors, rendering them all the more vulnerable to traffickers. Compelled to leave their home in search of a viable economic option, previously invisible, low-wage earning, migrant women are now playing a critical role in the global economy. The pull and push factors of migration are directly related to the process of globalization and eventually with trafficking.

TRAFFICKING AND ILLEGAL PLACEMENT AGENCIES IN DELHI

Most minor girls who ended up as domestic helps in cities were lured to leave their villages by a neighbour or relative or friend who had already worked outside, specifically in Delhi. These girls accompanied these known persons to their destination, mostly to Delhi. Most of them took this decision without parental consent. The girls were mainly motivated by the desire for a better life and more money. They are bought to Delhi on the pretext of jobs, free and good education or even of marriage. They were passed on three or four times before reaching Delhi, which points to the existence of a trafficking racket. Most of the time, they are being, raped and tortured during their journey by traffickers.

In Delhi, a large number of illegal placement agencies are involved in trafficking of minor tribal girls and selling them as domestic slaves. For years, the agencies have flourished in this way. These agencies liaise with natives of remote villages, mostly from the eastern part of India like Jharkhand, who, as local agents, carry out the first step in the trafficking process. The agents sell them for about ₹20,000 to ₹22,000 each to a domestic worker placement agency. The agency then re-sells her to a family as domestic maid, charging between ₹50,000 to ₹70,000. The girls are made to work 14 to 16 hours per day and do all household chores, from cooking, cleaning, to baby-sitting. They are paid almost nothing. Often their monthly wage is paid to the agencies—not to them. Most of the girls get trapped in this vicious cycle forever. Unaware and often illiterate, they have little knowledge of their rights and no clue of how to return home. The traffickers and agencies make the most of their vulnerability and for years move them from one household to another. Many are also sexually exploited (Sur 2013).

Most of the placement agencies which recruit domestic maids to different households are not registered and are illegal. The agents act as middlemen who handle the employment of these migrated tribal girls. They take hefty amounts from the employers as commission to provide a maid and on the other hand take away the tribal domestic worker's salary in the name of safety and give a meagre amount to her. This way these placement agencies have made it a huge money-minting business. In Delhi, these illegal placement agencies are run by both tribals and non-tribals. Kujur and Jha (2008) have mentioned around 200 placement agencies in their work, but according to Piyali Sur (2013) there are around 5000 such illegal agencies only in one neighbourhood, Sakur Basti. One thing is clear that all of the agencies in different periods of time send their agents (both men and women) who have kinship ties in the village, so that they can traffic more minor girls. Lately these agencies have realized that selling of young minors as domestic helps is a lucrative business and also a safe one without any police hassles. One prominent NGO, Bachpan Bachao Andolan, has rescued many minor girls working as domestic maids, most of whom were trafficked and given jobs through placement agencies in Delhi. Now the placement agencies have increased their commission from ₹20,000 to ₹60,000 from employers, which reflect their growing demands for domestic workers. According to the chairman of this NGO, the agents now work through cell phones and do not operate from offices. They tell their employers to give the salary of the workers to them and don't allow the girls to talk to their parents.

SUPPLY SIDE OF WOMEN TRAFFICKING

The supply is always an important factor to examine when we intend to show the market of a certain commodity. In order to understand the whole dynamic of trafficking in Jharkhand, we need to look at the factors which prepare the base of supply of girls from Jharkhand to Delhi:

(i) Abject poverty, lack of employment opportunity at home, lack of quality education, vocational training and skill training which lead to high dropout rates from school and colleges. There is a negative impact of education as educated youth feel ashamed to work in the forest and fields and yet often lack the necessary qualification to get white collar jobs.

(ii) At the social level, the tribal community system is breaking down due to the increasing individualism created by the money economy. The complete disappearance of traditional institutions such as youth dormitory, *akhara*, *tabenjom*, *bitlaha* has led to dis-orientation and unrest among tribal youth in villages and failed to safeguard the position of women, which deteriorates. Alcoholism is another problem which leads to break down in the family and also a continuing breakdown of the rural joint family structure.

(iii) The failure to improve the state of the tribals in the tribal areas
has been the result of the complex interplay of economic and
political processes and many maladies in the administrative
machinery. The disparity in the level of living of the tribal is
seen in terms of unequal distribution of land and livestock, lack
of subsidiary occupation and other socio-cultural inequalities.
The use of modern agricultural equipments, use of fertilizers,
pesticides and improved seeds is rare among tribals. There is
no irrigation facility in these areas. The tribal areas are hardly
covered by any cooperative societies or government's welfare
networks. There is a lack of proper implementation of many
pro-poor policies in tribal areas and corruption in tribal
districts. Development-induced displacement due to big dams,
mines, industries and infrastructure projects have permanently
displaced large tribal populations from their land. Women are
the worst sufferers because in the traditional division of work, it
is their duty to provide the basic necessities like food, water and
fuel. Mechanization and industrialization leads to overdrawing
of natural wealth and deforestation. It throws women out of
their natural and traditional sources of livelihood. Wealth gets
concentrated in a few and the gap between rich and the poor
widens. In the contemporary scenario many tribal families are in
debt because of loans taken from moneylenders and often to the
extent that they even mortgage their land.

(iv) Another issue is the Naxal conflict in tribal areas, as often the
police and the paramilitary force abuse and exploit adivasis in
the name of combating operations; on the other hand, the
Naxalite outfits also pressurize the youth to join their organization. In such a situation there is a grave security threat to young
tribal women.

(v) Though urban migration has started as an economic compulsion,
lately it has also become a trend. Urban life appears attractive
because of the new style and ways of speech of these adivasi
domestic workers, who almost become a role model for the young
girls in rural areas. At the same time, the agents of placement
agencies, well equipped with motor bikes, cell phones, cameras,
are also able to lure many poor tribal girls in the name of jobs,

love or marriage. These agents have agreed to earn more money and become rich by taking a hefty amount of registration fees from the employer as well as depriving the domestic worker of her hard earned wages.

DEMAND SIDE OF WOMEN TRAFFICKING

The demand side is equally important to evaluate the exact situation. Using Delhi as the site of demand, the following consequences are:

(i)   As mentioned earlier, there is a very high demand for cheap labour in the form of domestic helps in Delhi. Feminization of labour defines not only the objective aspects of the quantitative increase in the active female population around the world, but increasingly underlines qualitative and constituent character of these phenomena. Saskia Sassen (2000) postulated the idea of the existence of a systematic relationship between globalization and feminization of paid work. In the post-reform era, the number of women in paid employment has risen. For middle-class career women in Delhi, their maids and helpers arrive as a result of the increasing demand, which has become a veritable industry. The upwardly mobile middle classes, for status enhancement, have withdrawn their women from domestic work, which let them pursue higher education, skill training and acquiring different professions. Domestic work is a class issue between low-paid maids belonging to poor classes and their middle-class employers. To reiterate, this consumption of labour of the women of poor classes allows the middle-class women to pursue high income jobs and profession, to engage in social work.

(ii) The high growth in demand for cheap labour generates, promotes and perpetuates trafficking. This is a vicious cycle which includes the exploitative employment practices. The upper- and middle-class mentality to consider domestic work as degrading and dirty and low means they like to engage very young minor tribals (the age group of 12 to 15 are in very high demand). Adult, experienced and literate women are mostly

rejected. As these girls are outside the caste system so the notion of impurity is also not attached to them as in the case of dalits, so they are easily allowed to work inside the house and kitchen. The employers are specifically looking for minor girls as they come cheap, complain less and remain tight-lipped while being exploited. And at times it is also possible to hold them in captive as modern-day slaves inside the household. These tribal girls are being reportedly ill-treated at work. Insufficient and stale food is given to them and they are made to sleep in bathrooms and balconies. One girl complained that she was made to sleep in the rooftop room which had a water tank and every morning she used to get wet as the tank overflowed. These girls worked for 15 to 16 hours per day; often beaten and injured very badly with sticks, iron rods, brooms, and burnt with hot tawa or griddle and iron. They were being sexually assaulted by their employers or other male relatives in that house or by other male workers like drivers, watchman. A recent case arose in Vasant Kunj, an affluent neighbourhood, where a lady executive working in an MNC tortured and injured her domestic help who was a tribal teenage girl.

(iii) It is seen that the illegal placement agencies actively participate in trafficking of tribal minor girls. The existing laws do not provide protection to domestic worker's needs. It is well known that as there is no system of social security on which they can fall back upon, many of these tribal domestic workers have become contemporary slaves; many women and children are trafficked and exploited by the placement agencies, which operate openly without any form of restrictions and regulations. In the last decades there has been a tremendous growth in the demand for domestic workers which has led to the trafficking and other forms of exploitation of millions of tribal young women and girls and to meet this growing demands, there has been a spurt of hundreds of placement agencies, providing domestic workers in Delhi, remaining outside the purview of any legislative control.

(iv) There is very strong government apathy in relation to trafficking of minor tribal girls. There are around 100,000 full-time domestic workers in Delhi and many more part-time helps. However the lack of laws leaves these workers, mostly women and girls, at the mercy of employers and placement agencies (*Times of India*, 30 October 2013). The Domestic Workers Welfare and Social Security bill, 2010, is still pending before the government. At the same time the Delhi Private Placement Agencies (Regulation) bill, which is being drafted to regulate placement agencies is yet to be placed before the state assembly, while most of the minor domestic helps come from Jharkhand, the government has not filled an action-taken report in more than one and half years after the National Commission for the Protection of Child Rights directed it to do so (*Times of India*, 21 July 2014).

SITUATION IN JHARKHAND

Jharkhand has a vast reservoir of natural resources in terms of forest areas as well as minerals. This immense potential, however, has not been utilized properly and is thus counted among the backward states in the country. At the same time, the adivasis have suffered the most due to the process of industrialization, urbanization, globalization and modern development, which has resulted in severe problems of poverty and hunger, exploitation and social exclusion. Jharkhand is beset with many socio-economic problems and extreme poverty in the region facilitates both distress migration and trafficking of women and girls. More than 70 percent of tribals live below the poverty line. There is widespread illiteracy, especially among women. Displacement, land alienation, deforestation, detribalization, alcoholism, declining status of tribal women, exploitation by middlemen, ill health, unbalanced demography, tribal–non-tribal tension problems related to rehabilitation of those displaced and those who have been the victims of development programmes are only a few of the cost in the name of state–tribal development in Jharkhand. Even though most these problems have existed prior to state formation, with the rapid pace at which development is taking place some of these problems have accelerated. Many developmental programmes have adversely affected the tribal community (Munshi 2012; Singh and Jha 2004; Sunder 2016; Xaxa Report 2014).

Adivasis in Jharkhand, lead deprived and impoverished lives. Their economy is excessively dependent on agriculture and forest-based activities but these are seasonal in nature. The seasonal nature is due to lack of irrigation facility and thus they are heavily dependent on rain which if inadequate ultimately leads to a severe situation of food insecurity. Land plays a very important role in their survival but most of them have very small landholdings. At the same time, the forest too is under threat because of considerable deforestation for activities such as mining, construction and other purposes. Food insecurity is directly related to massive malnutrition among them. Their agricultural output is not sufficient to feed them during them lean season and inadequacy of funds many a times reduces their purchasing power even for buying from the Public Distribution System (PDS) that runs ration shops. In this situation, migration becomes the only survival strategy. Most of the rural families experience great difficulty in trying to sustain themselves. While the deteriorating social-economic conditions affect all members of society, women in particular are vulnerable to trafficking and distress migration because of the discrimination they face in household decision-making matters, and the constraints they face in their households with regards to viable opportunities for earning a living. Families vulnerability to the trafficking of their female members is a symptom of the desperation that exists in their lives. Socio-cultural pressure marginalizes women from birth onwards.

The impact of 'development' has been felt to a greater extent by women than men since the tribal forest economy is essentially a 'women-centred' economy. Women are responsible for subsistence and survival: for collection, management and distribution of food, fuel, fodder and water resources within the family as also within their community. Women now walk long distances in order to search for forest products, food, firewood, fodder and water (Fernandes 2006). With so-called state development, these natural resources are becoming rare, forcing tribal women to seek alternative sources of income to supplement the family income. This ultimately leads to migration of tribal women in search of livelihood. Tribal women are equal partners in the traditional tribal economy. They are laborious and docile. They can be easily manipulated. Hence there is the fear of exploitation by middlemen who lure them on the pretext of fetching jobs in the cities. Most of these women are illiterate, unconscious of their rights and privileges and hence vulnerable. Because of these factors, there is a clear-cut preference for tribal women in certain occupations such as in the domestic world. Another noticeable trend in migration is the exodus of semi-literate and even girls who are matriculates. Most of these girls who migrate are single and unmarried. They desperately try to help their parents, say, for marriage or to contribute towards the education of their brothers and sisters back home. At times, it is sheer economic need to be free of mortgaged land (that is, they need to pay back the loan) that is responsible for migration. At the other times, it is the desire to explore the world or breakdown in family relations that induces migration (ibid.).

Traffickers often used relatives and close friends of targeted women and girls to lure them and avoid detection by authorities or communities. Traffickers manage to convince and lure these girls to go the metros, promising a good job or marriage without informing her family. Most of the victims are drawn from rural and still very traditional backgrounds where kinship ties are still strong. The elder male or female relative is still regarded with respect and authority. This adds to the victim's dependent state and strengthens the trafficker's control over her. The youngest known victims are just 12 to 17 years, often have not completed their schooling.

SYSTEMATIC DISPOSSESSION: DECLINE OF THE STATUS OF TRIBAL WOMEN

Gender is not a fixed unchanging entity that is naturally derived but is intimately linked to particular social and historical contexts. Generally at a disadvantage, a woman's position is dependent on the interplay of various social factor such as age, caste, class, ethnicity, race and her capacity to negotiate with the system. Whenever these factors singly or jointly mediate unequal gender relations, women's subordination gets sharply accelerated.

The status of women in a society is a significant reflection of its level of social justice. Women's status is often described in terms of their level of income, employment, education, health and fertility as well as their roles within the family, the community and the society. In tribal communities, the role of women is substantial and crucial. They constitute about half the total population but in tribal society women are more important than in other social groups, because they work harder and the family economy and management depends on them. Unlike other communities, among adivasis there are no restrictions on women's participation in the cultivation process as well as forest-based activities. In agriculturally backward areas, women are forbidden to touch the plough; other than that, a tribal woman can participate actively in all agricultural operations. Women provide sustenance to the family and community by their judicious use and management of natural resources or ecology. Women are consumers, producers, educators and caretakers of their families, playing an important role for a sustainable eco-system in the present and the future.

Adivasi women are breadwinners, dependent not on their menfolk for survival, but on the common property resources (CPRs: common land, forest, grazing grounds, water bodies). Traditionally, agricultural land was communally held by the whole lineage group, divided equally among the various households in the village. Men were the owners (corporate ownership), but women certainly had life-interest in land (as widows) and the right to maintenance (*khorposh*). Their traditional societies are patriarchal, women are not equal to men, but they do have higher status than their high-caste counterparts. Tribal women own their relatively high status to both the abundance of resources and a clear division in their societies between the family and the social spheres. The men represent their families in the society and the women are the main decision-makers in the family economy, production and social relations. But this was possible as long as the natural resources were CPRs. Alienation from these resources results not merely in economic deprivation but also in deprivation of the social support, that is, weakening of their community system. Downward mobility follows this process (ibid.). The breakdown of traditional sources of livelihood and institutions of social control and conservation of ecology continues to generate an emerging gap on gendered role expectations and economic resources of the family as well as of the community. Later due to structural change in the social, economic and cultural context of tribal societies, there is a complete disappearance of these women's rights to land which provided a safety net as well as higher status.

The dominant perception is that tribals are more present-oriented, they work for subsistence, do not have a work ethic and have a weakness for music, dance and alcohol. On the other hand the non-tribals are considered to be more achievement- and future-oriented. Apart from the universal disadvantage of being a female, women in tribal society also suffer from the problems related to their economic and social backwardness and the geographical and political isolation of their habitat, which are common to most tribes. The rich resource-base of tribal areas has further added to the problems of tribal woman. Attracted by the economic prospects of the region non-tribal people have entered into these areas in large numbers and are indiscriminately exploiting their natural resources to convert them into industrial raw material and consumer goods for the urban market. These processes have a direct repercussion on tribal woman, as given their subsistence level of production and dependence on the forest, the incursion of the micro-economic process has adverse impacts on their livelihood. Economic disposition is but only one side of the coin. Non-tribal colonization has also exposed tribal women to the most degrading form of exploitation in which non-tribal men exploit their sexuality in order to gain access to the tribe's social and economic resources. This venal objectification of the tribal woman has not only contributed to the degradation of the tribal culture it has also fuelled the resurgence of ethnic politics in which women have to bear the brunt of increasing male chauvinism and control. Thus, trapped by the stereotypes of development policies on the one hand and their social and economic backwardness on the other, their subjugation is reinforced.

The cultural construction of femininity among young adivasi women has been found to be significantly different from that among mainstream Hindu and Muslim women. They have been shown to be more autonomous and oriented to work, earning a livelihood, freely interacting with men, than their non-tribal counterparts. In the present situation due to extreme poverty, ethnic discrimination and migration, there is an over-representation of young tribal women in the informal unorganized sector, for example, in the construction industry, brick kilns and as domestic workers in metro cities. Today in India adivasis are considered as a 'radicalized labouring class' and subjected to the worst forms of violence.

ISSUES OF SUSTAINABLE LIVELIHOOD

Agricultural produce is seasonal in nature, and, as mentioned earlier, the output is not sufficient in the lean season. Most tribals own land, but it is usually a small plot and soil quality is not good without any irrigation facilities. Generally they are marginal farmers (*ekfaslikisan*: one-crop farmer). During this period they are entirely dependency on forest products for food and livelihood. However decreasing forest cover in present times has added to their miseries. Another aspect is related to purchasing power to buy food. Inadequacy of funds reduces their purchase even from the PDS shops. At times there is no proper functioning of PDS due to corruption. So there is both shortage of food and work. Sustainable livelihood at the tribal regions for their dignified survival is not available. There is a lack of supplementary source of income for women and women-headed households. Sustained availability of work at the grass root level, such as community works, conservation of forest resources, revival of traditional water supply system that could increase productivity, does not exist.

Women Self Help Groups (SHGs) should be a strong unit of a social safety net. But SHGs in these areas are not sustainable and so women are not able to earn a decent amount throughout the year from the SHG activities. At the same time, the members are not being given intensive capacity building, thrift credit, training of members, marketing linkage facilities still today; tribal women are the major gatherers of Non-Timber Forest Products (NTFP), but supplementary income facilities from these are again not strengthened through cooperatives and other state authorities. So women get severely exploited by the middlemen in the market. This is also true for farm-based produce and livestock. Protective legislation like Panchayats Extension to the Schedule Area Act 1999 (PESA), poverty alleviation programmes, such as Mahatma Gandhi National

Rural Employment Guarantee Act 2005 (MNREGA), Integrated Child Development Scheme (ICDS), Public Distribution System (PDS), and other health, education schemes/programmes are not being effectively implemented in the tribal regions. Again there are lack of employment opportunities, particularly self-employment opportunities at the village level. Wage facilities are also not available within the locality for 8 months. And even if these exist there, like the informal/unorganized sector, there is a huge wage disparity on the basis of gender. Moreover people are not at all aware about the various social protection schemes (rural banking, for instance), even if they are; the process of accessing the benefits of such schemes are not simplified, easy and transparent. Common Property Resources such as forests, land, fodder and water gave the women some control in as much as they were in charge of the family income and production. Generally tribals lack legal titles (pattas) to these commonly owned recourses. The legal system in India neglects such collective group's rights which lead to development-induced displacement and alienation from Community Property Resources.

GENDER DISCRIMINATION WITHIN TRIBAL SOCIETY

Tribal women are marginalized in their own society. They are deprived of inheriting landed property of their fathers and husbands and their contributions to the economy are never acknowledged. The patriarchal social organization greatly favours the male gender. Women live a very hard life and are being treated as economic assets, as valuable property and their labour is often exploited. They are deprived of education and skill training as compared to men. Pervasive social discrimination contributes further to crimes against women such as forced migration, domestic violence, trafficking, rape, and so on.

Moreover, tribal society never had the practice of female infanticide and foeticide, dowry, veiling. There was a custom of bride price, right to choose their life partners, freedom of physical movement and earning money were marks of high status. But again a custom branding of women as witches and killing them still prevails. The discrimination of tribal women is in a very subtle way. They are being deprived of education and skill-training. Moreover the

low quality education which is available to the tribals is inadequate
to ensure a sustainable livelihood. These days, increasingly, the
parents of young girls feels that with a minimum level of education
like up to class 4 or 6, these girls could be sent to Delhi to earn
lots of money. Pervasive social discrimination contributes further to
women's trafficking.

The tribal population in eastern India faced the worst of historical
negligence and exploitation through both state action and inaction in
the colonial period, which continues after Independence. In the case
of the tribals, much of the larger contexts of structural violence are
provided by the process of state formation, nation building, political
and economic development in the postcolonial period. Development
as a conscious practice, as a set of policies, alters gender relations in
the favour of men; shifting resources to the male sphere of control
and making women more vulnerable to violence. Such structural
violence has created these circumstances, causing the status of tribal
women to decline and subjecting them to the worst forms of violence.

THROUGH THE LENS OF CRITICAL FEMINIST THEORY AND FEMINIZATION OF POVERTY

Critical feminist theory takes gender as a focus of analysis and
reconstructs social structure which has devalued and marginalized
women. Deborah L. Rhode (1990) has explained that critical feminism aspires to describe the world through women's experiences and
thus demands fundamental social transformation for the equality of
the genders. It rejects the existing ideological and institutional structures that position women as the second sex and challenges the existing
distributions of power. It also questions the gap between legal understanding and social experiences of the problem. Critical feminism has
its basis in pragmatic philosophical traditions and techniques of consciousness rising in contemporary feminist organizations. It draws its
practices from deeper understanding of experiences and integrates its
experiences into theories. Thus the critical feminist perspective explains
that the trafficking of women cannot be seen in a vacuum. It has its
basis in gender relations, political situations and economic conditions
of women. Critical feminist theory is particularly useful for this study

because it recognizes the importance of the historical context in order to challenge policies and practices that affect women. Women are differentially discriminated against depending on the interests of the dominant group, and depending upon the intersections of their identities (Mackinnon 2004; Sandoval 2004; Selgas 2004).

As mentioned earlier, trafficking and distress migration can also be explained by the concept of the feminization of poverty (Sassen 2000). The feminization of poverty means that women have a higher incidence of poverty than men and their poverty is more severe than that of men and that poverty among women is on the increase. Poverty affects women the most because patriarchal society does not give enough opportunity to girls to study, which leads to economic dependence. The feminization of poverty is a phenomenon commonly understood as the general disproportionate over-representation of women in poverty globally. Lack of income seems to be an important by product of the vicious cycle of inadequate access to resources perpetuated by global patriarchal practices. By examining and targeting socio-cultural factors associated with the feminization of poverty, advocates may spur changes that will address policies and social traditions that trap women and their children in a state of economic disadvantage (Abercrombie and Hastings 2016).

Moreover, in India now there is a shift from ideas of the welfare state to a neo-liberal state (post-1991 economic reforms) which is based on capitalist market economy. Now the state outsources aspects of human development indicators such as health care, education and livelihood to private organizations like NGOs. There were government jobs for tribals in the public sector, but now in the private sector there is no reservation). Market driven forces add to widespread poverty and unemployment rates among women. Traffickers being opportunity seekers by nature, simply take advantage of the resulting vulnerabilities to make a profit. Because women are over-represented among survival-migrants, it is not surprising that women comprise the vast majority of trafficked persons. This gender disparity is often attributed to the feminization of poverty arising from the failure of existing social structures to provide equal and just educational and employment opportunities for women. While women migrate in response to economic hardship, they also migrate to flee gender-based repression. Women will accept dangerous migration arrangements in order to escape the consequences of entrenched discrimination against women, including unjust or unequal property rights or unemployment, gender-based violence and the lack of access to resources for women.

Migration has both positive and negative consequences for migrants. While it saves them from starvation at home, it exposes them to appalling living and working conditions at construction and other work sites. Additionally, migrants also do not have access to pro-poor schemes such as subsidized food, health care and schooling and must pay for everything. On the positive side, migration has given tribal people an exposure to the outside world, including new skills. Their remittances have helped the family in consumption, repayment of loans, fulfilling social obligations and to finance working capital requirements in agriculture as well as investment in better housing and purchase of consumer durables. On the negative side, they suffer from family and social disorganization, harsh and unhygienic living conditions at work sites and physical and sexual violence in the case of female domestic workers. Empirical evidence collected by case-studies in tribal areas of central India indicate that women domestic workers on their return to the village are viewed with distrust, as they show signs of having been influenced by an alien culture. Such women workers are exploited and harassed, when they migrate and are regarded with suspicion when they return. Comparison made between tribal families who migrate and those who do not reveals that the non-migrating families own more land and are in a better position to access and benefit from various development schemes available for them and so are able to improve their standard of living and educate their children. On the other hand, migrating tribal families have less land, lower level of literacy and on migrating, suffer from exploitation and harassment and low wages. They are able to stave off starvation, but do not earn enough to improve living standards. Moreover, their children do not get education and so the future of the next generation is equally bleak. Added to this, is the tendency of the unskilled youth to prefer employment in non-agriculture sectors, as farming does not give adequate returns. This is a challenge for both rural and urban planners (Xaxa report 2014).

CONCLUSION

It is clear that poverty and illiteracy are often seen as root causes of distress migration and trafficking. Tribal girls are more vulnerable as they come from poor, socially neglected ethnic groups. The assurance from the recruiters and brokers of earning lots of money, good jobs, of long-term love and married life, free education and similar false promises raise in these girls hope of escaping from their current existence. However, rising unemployment, poverty, a turbulent situation caused by Naxal conflict and a weakened social structure have resulted in the newly formed state of Jharkhand to become the latest target for the recruitment of minor tribal girls into modern-day slavery of domestic work and as indentured servants and silent slaves. There is absolute no political will from the elected tribal representatives to tackle this issue of distress migration and trafficking.

In fact, all cultural practices that challenge the sexual integrity and equality of women create an environment that lends itself to distress migration and trafficking of women and girls. Both female migration and trafficking are complicated by their location at the intersection of a number of major social and structural categories. The issues involved in distress migration and trafficking include deeply entrenched stereotypes, ignorance and bias against domestic workers, migrants, racial and ethnic minorities, women and poor people. So, one must consider the complicated and interrelated factors that contribute to the problem in order to understand it. It is important for the government to view trafficking and distress migration in the broader background of poverty, discrimination and gender-based violence rather than as just a law and order problem.

REFERENCES

Abercrombie, H. Sarah, and Sarah L. Hastings. 2016. 'Feminisation of Poverty', in Angela Wong et al., eds. *The Wiley Blackwell Encyclopaedia of Gender and Sexuality*. Retrieved from https://doi.org/10.1002/9781118663219. wbegss550, accessed on 12 June 2018.

Banerjee, Paula. 2016. 'Criminalising the Trafficked: Blaming the Victim', *EPW* 2, 45 & 46 (5 Nov).

Chuang, Janie. 2006. 'Beyond a Snap Shot, Preventing Woman Trafficking in Global Economy', *Indiana Journal of Global Legal Studies* 13, 5.

Fernandes, Walter. 2006. 'Development Induced Displacement and Tribal Women', in Govind Chandra Rath, ed. *Tribal Development in India*. New Delhi: SAGE Publications.

Gupta, Ruchira. 2014. 'Interview by Anuradha Sharma', *The Diplomat*, 21 August 2014. Retrieved from https://thediplomat.com/2014/08/interview-ruchiragupta, accessed on 23 August 2015.

ILO. 2013. *Nineteenth International Conference of Labour Statisticians*. Report-II, Geneva, 2–11 Oct. 2013, Statistics of Work, Employment and Labour Underutilization, Geneva: ILO.

Jha, Vikas. 2005. 'Migration of Orissa's Tribal Woman: A New Story of Exploitation', *EPW* 40, 15 (9–15 April).

Kempadoo, Kamla, Jyoti Sanghera, and Bandana Pattanaik, eds. 2016. *Trafficking and Prostitutions Reconsidered*. New York: Routledge.

Kisleya, Kelly. 2013. 'Vasant Kunj Maid Could Be Face of Anti-Trafficking Drive in Jharkhand', *Times of India*, 30 October 2013.

Kujur, J. M., and Vikas Jha. 2008. 'Tribal Domestic Workers', New Delhi, Indian Social Institute.

Mackinnon, Catharine, A. 2004. 'Feminism, Marxism. Method and State towards Feminist Jurisprudence', in Sandra Harding, ed., *The Feminist Standpoint Theory, Reader, Intellectual and Political Controversies*. New York: Routledge.

Mazumdar, Indrani. 2016. 'Unfree mobility, Adivasi Women's Migration', in Meena Radhakrishna, ed, *First Citizens: Studies on Adivasis, Tribals and Indigenous People in India*. New Delhi: Oxford University Press.

Momsen, Janet Henshall. 1999. ed. *Gender, Migration, and Domestic Service* (Routldge International Studies of Women and Place). New York: Routledge.

Munshi, Indra, ed. 2012. 'Introduction', in *The Adivasi Question: Issues of land, Forest and Livelihood*. Hyderabad: Orient BlackSwan.

Neetha, N. 2004. 'Making of Female Breadwinners: Migration and Social Networking of Women Domestics in Delhi', *EPW* 39, 17 (24–30 April).

Niumai, Ajailiu. 2016. 'Unspoken Voices of Trafficked Women and Children in Manipur', *EPW* 2, 45 & 46 (5 Nov).

Pandit, Ambika. 2014. 'Jharkhand Haat, Melas Hotbeds of Traffickers', *Times of India*, 21 July 2014.

Press Trust of India 'India doesn't Ratify ILO Convention on Domestic Workers', *Business Standard,* 18 March 2015.

Rath, Govinda Chandra. 2006. *Tribal Development in India*. New Delhi: SAGE Publications.

Raza, Danish. 2015. 'What Makes Jharkhand the Hunting Ground of Human Traffickers', *Hindustan Times*, 15 October 2015.

Rhode, Deborah. L. 1990. 'Feminist Critical Theories', *Stanford Law Review* 42, 3 (Feb 1990): 617–38.

Sandoval, Chela. 2004. 'U.S. Third World Feminism: Theory and Method of Differential Oppositional Consciousness', in Sandra Harding, ed.,

The Feminist Standpoint Theory, Reader, Intellectual and Political Controversies. New York: Routledge.

Sassen, Saskia. 2000. 'Women's Burden: Counter-Geographies of Globalization and the Feminization of Survival', *Journal of International Affairs* 53, 2 (Spring 2000), ABI/INFORM Global: 503.

Sen, Samita. 2016. 'Impossible Immobility: Marriage, Migration and Trafficking in Bengal', *EPW* 2, 45 & 46 (5 Nov).

Selgas, Fernando, and J. Garcia. 2004. 'Feminist Epistemologies for Critical Social Theory: From Standpoint Theory to Situated Knowledge', in Sandra Harding, ed., *The Feminist Standpoint Theory, Reader, Intellectual and Political Controversies.* New York: Routledge.

Sharma, Rashmi. 2011. 'Gender and International Migration: The Profile of Female Migrants from India', *Social Scientist* 39, 3–4 (March–April): 37–63.

Singh, Vinita, and K. N. Jha. 2004. 'Migration of Tribal Woman from Jharkhand: The Price of Development', *Indian Anthropologist* 34, 2.

Sunder, Nandini, ed. 2016. 'Introduction' in *The Scheduled Tribes and Their India: Politics, Identities, Policies and Work.* New Delhi: Oxford University Press.

Sur, Priyali. 2013. 'Silent Slaves: Stories of Woman Trafficking in India'. Retrieved from http://www:blog dated 30 Dec 2013, accessed on 14 January 2015.

United Nations Development Programme. 2012. 'Synthesis of Important Discussion on Livelihood, Microfinance, Issues of Domestic Workers'. New Delhi: United Nations Development Programme.

Xaxa Report. 2014. *Report of the High-Level Committee on Socio-Economic, Health and Educational Status of Tribal Communities of India.* New Delhi: Government of India, Ministry of Tribal Affairs.

4

Places of Migrants' Hope: Bosnian Women in Migration

SANELA BAŠIĆ

INTRODUCTION: WHO ARE THE BOSNIAN MIGRANTS?

Bosnia is a country situated on the Balkan Peninsula. It stretches over 51.129 sq. km, and official estimates indicate that its multiethnic and multi-religious society amounts to 3.831 million inhabitants. Since the fall of communism in 1989, Bosnia has gone through profound economic, political and social changes, experiencing the triple challenge of transition from communist rule to democracy, from political conflict to peace, and from a planned economy to market capitalism. Indeed, migration seems to be a constant feature of its vibrant history. Either because of forced displacement of the population in the times of armed conflicts (Balkan wars, First and Second World Wars, the wars in the 1990s) or voluntary migration in periods of peace and stability triggered by an escape from poverty and lack of opportunity, Bosnians were in movement.

From a current point of view, three major migration waves are clearly identifiable in the last century: pre-war socialist migration, war displacement (1992–1995), and post-war migration. According to UN data, nearly a million Bosnian immigrants—a fifth of the entire population—lived abroad in 1990 (2012). Beyond a number of political dissidents who left the country because of disagreement with the communist regime, pre-war migration was primarily economically motivated. Despite the communist party rhetoric and formal commitments towards economic and social progress, people faced considerable challenges in securing a normal livelihood. In his recent work *The Book of My Lives*, an American writer, a refugee from Bosnia, Hemon Aleksandar (2013) describes the consequences of the overall lack of opportunities for highly educated young people: resignation, apathy and hopelessness in 'our sad socialist society where it is quite normal to grow old and still live with your parents, forever unemployed'.

Therefore, a lack of jobs and prosperity made emigration an exit option, with the promise of rescue from unemployment and its attendant low quality of life for diverse parts of the population, especially those with poor education as well as those with university degrees. The most common pattern of socialist migration was called Gastarbeiter-migration. A literal translation of this German term in English denotes a guest worker—a migrant who settled in West Germany for work. Many low skilled workers from all parts of Yugoslavia moved to West Germany in the early 1970s within the frame of the formal guest worker programme. It was the time of the so-called German economic miracle: fast growing industry sectors needed workers, while migrants from poorer countries from Europe's periphery needed jobs. In order to match demand and supply on the labour market, the government of West Germany subsequently signed bilateral recruitment agreements with Italy, Spain, Greece, Morocco, as well as Yugoslavia (in 1968). The new opportunity was highly attractive to growing numbers of Bosnians who could not take advantage of the socialist economic miracle by the end of the 1960s.

The second wave of migration occurred after the fall of socialism and was triggered by conflict over the country's independence from a common Yugoslav state. Genocidal by its nature, the war resulted in massive displacement of the population: 1.2 million people fled the country, while another million were displaced within the country. The former entered into world's refuge population, and the latter became known as Internally Displaced Persons. The peace agreement was signed by the end of 1995 in Dayton, Ohio, USA. However, the consequences of war displacement in social and demographic terms were dramatic: once an ethnically mixed and intertwined society became more or less an ethnically divided society. Ethnic over-emphasis permeated also a new political and administrative profile of the country and influenced its post-war economic development. By stipulating the right to return to former places of residence to refugees and internally displaced persons, the Annexure 7 of the Dayton Peace Agreement created a mechanism for reversal of the effects of displacement. However, the process of post-war repatriation which took place between 1996 and 1999 run counter to these expectations. Instead of returning to their pre-war places of residence, about 800,000 returnees were repatriated to the localities where their ethnic community was a majority. Many factors contributed to this outcome, but the most compelling seems to be the fear of renewed violence in light of the suffering experienced during the war (individual and mass killings, torture inflicted in concentration and rape camps).

In the post-war period, continuing political and economic crisis in conjunction with revived nationalistic rhetoric prolonged existential fears and insecurities for a traumatized population. Indeed, the developmental model proposed by the key international players (International Monetary Fund, World Bank and European Union) in the context of war-driven devastated infrastructural, institutional, social and human resources pushed the country into extreme impoverishment. The new model provided a constant economic growth (as measured by GDP per capita) and macroeconomic stability, at least until the last economic crisis in 2008. Nevertheless, growth was accompanied by a constant increase in unemployment: in 2018 for example, the aggregate unemployment data was 18.4 percent, with youth unemployment (young people aged 15–24) being 57.7 percent (BHAS 2018). The prolonged crisis resulted in a new wave of migration, which could also be described as 'brain drain'. The migration data from 2005 onwards show higher emigration rates among tertiary educated persons (IOM 2007). As the results of a study on youth conducted in 2014 shows, this trend will probably continue to plague the country with 49.2 percent of respondents aspiring to leave the country if given the opportunity. The hierarchy of motivating factors reflects the economic and existential fears of a young generation: 67.8 percent would migrate to secure a better living standard, an additional 14.6 percent for better employment opportunities and 6.8 percent because of the not beneficial situation in the country (Žiga et al. 2015).

Currently, according to the 2016 figures of the BIH Ministry of Human Rights and Refugees, the total number of persons in the diaspora originating from Bosnia-Herzegovina is at least 2 million which makes 56.6 percent of the total population in Bosnia-Herzegovina (MHRR 2016). The largest migrant communities of Bosnian expatriates live in Europe: Croatia (which is home to one third of Bosnian emigrants), Germany, Austria, Switzerland and Scandinavian countries, whereas about 200,000 have settled in the USA, Australia and Canada. Their contribution to the home country in the form of remittances is immensely important. According to the data from BIH Central Bank remittances amounted to 2,396.8 million BAM in 2016. Including all transfers from abroad (foreign pensions) totalled to 3,608.4 million BAM. The World Bank data for the same year point to even higher levels of remittances, 3,338.4 million BAM (World Bank 2016). According to the World Bank, this translates into remittances contributing to 11.1 percent of the GDP in 2015 (MHRR 2016).

The yearly produced 'BIH Migration Profile' does not segregate data on migrants according to socio-demographic characteristics (age, education, employment, and so on) and therefore it is difficult to give a clear socio-demographic profile of migrants. However, in relation to the composition of migrants with regard to gender it is clear that women account for slightly over 50 percent of Bosnian emigrants. The Bosnian migration pattern appears to be relatively constant, stable, and gender-balanced, portraying migration as predominantly family issues. More detailed information on migrants was provided in the first study on BIH migration profile conducted by the International Organization for Migration in 2007 and clearly showed the pattern of the brain drain.

The footprints of the brain-drain that were first recorded in the study on BIH migration profile conducted by the International Organization for Migration in 2007 showed the following:

- Skilled Emigration: 28.60 percent
- Emigration rate of tertiary educated persons 28.66 percent (2005)

- Emigration of physicians 821 or 12.76 percent (2005) (IOM, 2007).

Since 2015, circular emigration waves of skilled work force have intensified.

Although the last war in Bosnia-Herzegovina (1992–1995) caused dramatic migration flows and completely changed the socio-demographic profile of the country, and the post-war brain drain will probably have long-lasting effects, the issue of migration provoked limited interest in researchers until very recently. The majority of existing studies have concentrated on the issues of the return of internally displaced persons and the peace-building process (Eastmond 2006; UNDP 2007) identity and the effects of remittances on economic development, particularly poverty reduction (Emirhafizović et al. 2013; Kukanesen 2003). In spite of its global relevance, a gender perspective on migration, however, has remained on the margins of mainstream research. This chapter, therefore, attempts to move the gender analytical framework closer to the centre of migration studies by exposing how migration affects the empowerment of Bosnian women.

DOING RESEARCH ON THE EMPOWERMENT OF WOMEN THROUGH MIGRATION: THEORETICAL, ANALYTICAL AND PRACTICAL FOUNDATIONS

Empowerment is simultaneously a popular, powerful and contested concept, a (desired) state and path-breaking process, well-developed discourse and analytical tool. Since its inception in late 1970s, a huge amount of literature concerned with developing and/or expending its epistemological foundations, as well as establishing theoretical frameworks for analytical purposes has been published. Its popularity stems probably from its central component, enhancing people's ability to expand their choices (Sen 1993), transform choices into desired actions and outcomes (World Bank 2005), or expand people's ability to make strategic life choices in a context where this ability was previously denied to them (Kabeer 2001). In short, being empowered is about gaining control over external factors (actions, resources) which affects one's well-being. In that vein, Gita Sen (1993) defines empowerment of women as altering relations of power which constrain women's option and autonomy, and adversely affect health and well-being, whereas Keller and Mbwewe (1991) conceptualize empowerment of women as a process whereby women become able to organize themselves to increase their own self-reliance, to assert their independent right to make choices and to control resources which will assist in challenging and eliminating their own subordination. In line with the given conceptualization, for the purpose of the present study, the empowerment of women is pragmatically defined as possession of the following qualities:

- Having access to and control of relevant information and resources
- Having a range of options from which to make choices
- Having decision-making power (use of choice)
- Having the capacity to achieve desired outcomes (achievement of choice).

On the international level, there is a wide range of theoretical and empirical literature on the impact of migration on the empowerment of women (Aysa and Massey 2004; de Haas 2005; de Koning 2008; Duflo 2012, Fargues 2006; Gunnarson 2006; Hadi 2001, Menjivar and Agadjanian 2007, Stevenson 1997; Saeed 2001; Taylor 1984). Without going into detailed discussion of its findings, from the available studies it might be concluded that the effects of migration on the position of women within the family occur at the following levels: economic (better employment and earning opportunities), socio-cultural (changes in gender roles), and interpersonal (family structure, household decision-making). Moreover, the existing studies also show that the linear relationship migration-empowerment of women cannot be taken for granted, as migration-driven experiences prove not to be always beneficial and empowering to women.

In order to explore more specifically the life narratives of migrant women in an attempt to understand and shed light on how the migrant process and status affect the economic and social position of women, empirical research has been done. Given its exploratory nature, qualitative research approach has been applied. Focus group interviews were conducted to gain insights into women's perceptions of the role of migration in their position within families. Based on the existing knowledge of the linkages, migration-empowerment of women, the position of women in the family is conceptualized in terms of control of *economic resources* (e.g., possible changes in access to paid employment and its effects), *relative degree of autonomy* (mobility, value system, freedom to choose one's own lifestyle) and *relative degree of decision-making power*. Correspondingly, the topic guide used in the focus group interviews was divided into three modules analyzed at the household level. The participants of the focus groups were selected primarily based on their migration experience. In that respect, three groups of women were targeted: *women with own migration experience* (migrant women), *women with experience of migration in the family* (male out-migration or other) and *women with no migration experience* (control groups). Additionally, sampling included heterogeneity of focus groups participants in relation to education, employment and civil status, as well as rural/urban divide. In total, six focus groups were conducted: two focus groups with women without migration experience (rural and urban area), two focus groups with women with own migration experience (rural and urban area) and two focus groups with women with migration experience in the family (rural and urban area). The data has been collected in spring in fall 2013. In total, 37 women participated in the research with which contacts have been established through women's networks in a given area.

ECONOMIC (DIS)EMPOWERMENT OF WOMEN AFFECTED BY MIGRATION

Women's perceptions of their employment status, for example, participation in the labour market and, if available, their status in jobs and job satisfaction, have been used to arrive at conclusions that are related to the changes in the economic position in the family due to migration. Research findings suggest that there is a plurality of women's experience of migration-related economic empowerment that depends on a complex interplay of other factors, such as educational level, pre-migration employment status and place of residence.

The highest degree of empowerment in economic terms is found in the non-migrant urban women (the urban control group). All of the participants in this group have formal employment by which they generate income and, by doing so, to a large extent contribute to the family budget and to family well-being. They are highly educated, live in the capital of the country and share many commonalities with regard to their worldview and lifestyle. If economic empowerment is measured by the working status of only the participants, the economic position of women in the non-migrant rural group appears to be less advantageous. Among this group of women, there is an apparent polarization between women who work in formal employment and unemployed women.

The possible effects of their own (female) migration and male out-migration on the economic position of women have been investigated through the stories and experiences of women who have migration experience. Empirical evidence suggests that migration can con-tribute to both economic empowerment and disempowerment of women, as well have no impact at all. Based on the women's views, three different modalities that link migration and its empowering or disempowering economic outcomes for diverse types of women can be identified: empowering, disempowering and a neutral pattern.

First, the experiences of the urban migrant women do not support the positive causality of migration to the economic empowerment of women. In contrast, in the case of urban migrant Bosnian women, migration appears to have contributed rather to their disempowerment. Prior to migration, the majority of women had already experienced economic emancipation: they had some form of tertiary education, a stable, recognized professional engagement, and displayed relatively high job and life satisfaction. The migration was involuntary, war-related and as such a difficult burden to be borne. Yet they decided to leave, and they found refuge in Western European countries. Their husbands were more often left behind. Those who were at a productive working age reported that their economic position worsened while living abroad because they could work solely in less paid, less rewarding and less attractive jobs:

> Yes, I worked. I cleaned.... Before the war, I worked in Jugo bank. I have a high school degree in accounting. (I, 1)

> I shortly lived in Serbia, and then I moved to Germany where I lived
> for five years…. I worked in the restaurants, hotels, everywhere…. Before
> the war, I worked in 'Magros'. (I, 6)[1]

Interestingly enough, none of these women expressed the wish to
migrate again. Only a young woman who was a child while living
abroad had plans to settle abroad again.

The opposite pattern is observed in migrant women from a rural
background. Although sharing the same war-related motives for
migration, rural migrant women perceive the impact of migration
on their economic position to be quite positive. They appear to have
economically benefited from migration, and their experience reveals
its beneficial outcomes. Perceived positive changes are related to
the availability of paid employment, as well as better educational
opportunities for the children. For the first time in their entire lives,
these women had the opportunity to earn their own money, be in
charge of decision-making, broaden the educational alternatives for
their children, and financially support their relatives in Bosnia. Unlike
their urban counterparts, they were visibly impressed by newly gained
earning opportunities and not worried at all because they worked in
precarious jobs:

- I left during the war. I was a young girl. There I got married
  and gave birth to my first daughter. I returned because our
  refugee status was abolished. As peace agreement was signed,
  we had to come back. In Germany everything is easier … life
  is easier. It was easier to get a job, to go to school…. I worked
  …. I was able to support my parents…. It was difficult to find
  job as we came back. We were abroad, and priority is given to
  people who stayed here…. My God, so is the law…. (V, 3)
- Life in Germany has brought nice changes into my life, even
  though it was difficult for me to accommodate. For three
  months, I did not unpack our baggage. I wanted to come back,
  but it was not possible. So, I stayed. My husband changed a lot.
  Here, he worked a lot and also spent his earnings on alcohol,
  friends, in the bars…. As he realized what is life about in
  Germany, he calmed down and life got much better…. Here,
  teachers said that we should not send our son to school after

he finished elementary school. In Germany, he performed well. He even finished high school. (V, 4)

It is important to note the interaction of migration with other factors that are at play, such as the educational level and pre-migration working status. Rural migrant women tend to be less educated not only in comparison to urban migrant participants but also in comparison to participants in both of the control groups. Furthermore, all the women declared themselves to be housewives. Additionally, there are important variations in the contexts from which and into which rural women migrate. The most common pattern was that a woman migrated together with minor children for war-related reasons, leaving her husband behind. Only in a few cases, rural women migrated together with their spouses. None of them reported not being allowed to take up or search for employment. However, the 'golden age', which is the frame migration period, ended up upon return because almost all of them 'continued' to live as they did before migration and now contributed to the family income by running a small agricultural production and performing daily household work.

If judged from the perspectives of the urban and rural women who have the experience of migration in the family, the impact of migration on their economic position appears to be rather neutral. For the urban women who have migration experience, this impact is possibly related to the fact that the migrating person is not the husband or partner living in the same household. In most cases, the brothers or sisters of the participating women have migrated abroad. Because all of the five participants had paid employment in conjunction with being highly educated and having an urban background, it is no wonder that they display a higher degree of economic independence, as is found with women in the urban control group. They do not depend on cash remittances from their relatives who are living abroad. The majority of women mentioned 'presents' as the most common form of exchange between migrant and non-migrant relatives:

- By the beginning of war, my sister left for Serbia and from there to Canada. She lives with her husband and children. They do not intend to return. There is no need to regularly

send me money, but every time they come here for vacation
they bring some gift. (II, 2)
- My brother lives in Canada. He studied philosophy…. He is
  not sending money, there is no need for it. When visiting us,
  he always brings presents. (II, 3)

The situation of rural women who have migration experience is
somewhat different but is also neutral in relation to economic
empowerment. The major difference from its urban counterparts is
that here we must address typical male out-migration that is motivated
by rural poverty and limited employment opportunities in rural areas.
It is typically the husband who permanently or temporarily works
abroad. Women left behind are relatively educated but they are mostly
unemployed and housewives. In comparison to rural migrant women,
women affected by male-out migration do not engage in agricultural
production. It is attributed to having demanding parenting and
household duties. Again, if judged solely by their position in the labour
market, it can be concluded that their economic position is vulnerable
as, in fact, they are economically dependent on the income that is
generated by their spouses. However, they do not comfortably fit into
that disempowered image. Relatively higher self-esteem of rural left-
behind women can be probably explained by their appreciation of
the contribution they make in the absence of their spouses in terms
of parenting and household work, but also as a primary visible actor
towards diverse social institutions:

- I contribute to the family budget as well … by doing household
  and taking care of children. (VI, 1)
- By taking care of household I do contribute to family budget
  … and I know well how to distribute money which my
  husband brings home. (VI, 5)

Socio-cultural Empowerment of Women Affected by Migration

Socially, empowerment is conceived in terms of woman's relative
autonomy, freedom, and independence in relation to issues related
to marriage and sexuality (reproductive) health, children's schooling,

woman's role as caregivers, and so on. Participants in the focus groups were asked to share their thoughts, feelings, values and behaviours regarding perceived degree of autonomy and freedom to live as they wish, child rearing and education and ownership rights.

Freedom and Autonomy

Generally, women feel free to live as they wish and be autonomous. However, subtle feelings of uneasiness have been observed among participants in the focus group with male out-migration in the rural area. Their perceptions are diverse. Some women feel free to live as they wish:

- My husband has been working in Germany since 1980. I got used to this kind of life.... I feel free and I live as I wish. I do not care what people are saying. People always have something to talk about. (VI, 6)

Some participants feel less secure when left alone:

- My husband works in Austria and I feel more secure when he is here.... I feel responsibility when he is absent ... and our environment is as such. Women are being watched over if they are alone. (VI, 2)
- I do not feel free. I feel better when he is there ... as a woman .... It is difficult to raise children without a husband. (VI, 5)

Apparently, male-out migration aggravates vulnerability of rural women in relation to external and internal social demands and expectations. On the one hand, they might experience more strict indirect control by community members as to what they do, where they go and how they live. In a traditionally conservative and less open-minded environment any behaviour considered inappropriate for a (married) woman left alone might make her an easy target of rumour and gossip. On the other hand, some women might feel overburdened with growing responsibilities. The absence of another parent implies tripling of the duties mothers must take over in household, in child rearing and education, as well as in relation to the public domain.

Child Bearing and Education

Given that education is rightly associated with positive life outcomes, participants have been asked about their attitudes and actions related to education of their children. The research shows that there are almost no differences in approaches to parenting, child rearing practices and relationship to their children among women in all six focus groups. Women seem to share the same gender-friendly beliefs and values with regard to their roles as parents and often primarily as caregivers. However, while generally admitting that they do not agree with the statement that there should be any differences in rearing between son and daughter, urban women with migration experience in the family mentioned, give privileges to girls rather the boys:

- My husband and me were not giving more privileges to boys as compared to girls. But, I do give privilege to girls. And my son, too. That is how I raised him probably. (II, 1)
- I have four children. Ideally, I would have had five.... We have planned our family, my husband and me. We pay more attention to our daughters and we have same standards for boys and girls. (II, 3)

Similar line of thoughts is found in rural women affected by male out-migration. They prefer to pay 'more attention' to girls:

- I have only a son as of now, but I think they should be raised in the same manner and get the same level of education. (VI, 4)
- I raise my children in the way to help them become honest, dedicated, educated persons. I think both girls and boys should receive same conditions, so that they alone can decide what they want. I know lot of girls who did not want to continue with education. They had choices.... For my own daughters; I wish them to be as they are, to think with their own head, to get educated and economically independent. (VI, 1)

In all groups, participants admit striving to provide the highest possible level of education to their daughters. They place strong emphasis on girl's education, understanding the way in which education might influence life opportunities as well as life choices. The social change that might also be observed in the rural population is also embracing the same value attached to girls' education. Participants of rural background, with and without migration experience, stress the devastating role of economic (in)capacities of parents in rural areas to educate their children:

- I think daughters should be given more attention, educate them. In our environment/surrounding there are still a lot of girls with only elementary education. Parents do not have money to educate them. If they have both a girl and a boy, they give preference to the boy. I do not agree with that. (V, 2)

Inheritance and Ownership Rights

A similar attitude was prevalent when the participants were asked about inheritance customs in their social environment. All, regardless of their migration status, do support the idea that daughters should receive the same share as male family members. Discussion among the rural participants who did and did not have migration experience showed that there was social change underway because in the past female family members were expected to give up their shares on behalf of the male members:

- It was not like this before here. Sisters usually withdrew on behalf of the brother(s). Now it is different. (V, 1)
- My parents are still alive, so did not share anything. My younger brother lives with our parents, and his wife often says she will do this or that if we give them a house.... I will not give up my parcel of land as it was a custom before—sister gives up for brother. I want to have my own parcel of land, so that whatever I want I can do with it. (VI, 2)

The practice of having a male succession line has been considered to be one of the most important features of traditional, patriarchal pre-industrial Bosnian society and has been a sign of women's subordination. Today, this practice can be interpreted from another perspective. Prior to the Second World War, Bosnian society was an agricultural society that had a high proportion of the peasantry living on the land. Land ownership was important for survival. Male ownership and inheritance practices appeared to be more an issue of survival than an intended humiliation of women. Women were expected to marry and be cared for by the husband. Because divorce was rather rare and it was socially stigmatized, women were expected to live throughout their lives under their husband's auspices. During socialism, the situation began to change. Socialist industrialization (and urbanization) attracted many former peasants to the city who started working in the industrial sector. They were no longer dependant on the land and agricultural production as a source of living. As a result, the traditional norms that were based on male inheritance became less meaningful. Women started challenging these norms and obviously had success in changing traditional patrimony patterns:

> Daughters should be given same share in family patrimony ... for now, I did not regulate it. If death does not take me away, I will take care of it. (V, 4)
> Family patrimony should be equally shared among sons and daughters. In the past, son would have a priority. But, currently situation has changed a lot. (VI, 6)

Interpersonal Empowerment Affected by Migration

The third element relates to having a say in the domestic decision-making process, that is, having the capacity to decide and act upon their own decisions in relation to a wide range of domestic issues, such as household purchases, household work, money borrowing, spending related to education and the health of children, in addition to other choices. In what follows, the perspectives, attitudes and experience of the participants will be mapped with the aim of gaining insight into eventual migration-related changes with regard to a variety of aspects.

The key findings of the present study support the idea of high levels of decision-making power in Bosnian women, regardless of age and education, employment or migration status as well as the urban/rural dichotomy. Decisions on important domestic issues are commonly made by partners, or together with other family members (those living with parents and/or sisters/brothers). There is a tendency to include children in the domestic decision-making process. Thus, one participant in the urban control group states:

- We negotiate and take decisions together. And we share work. It is considered to be normal in our environment. And this is how we raise our children to do the same. (III, 5)

Additionally, a participant in the rural control group states:

- Together. Especially on larger investments, such as what changes are required in the house. For smaller things, it is not important to discuss. We both know what is needed. (IV, 4)

The same answers are given by the participants in the other groups. For example, urban and rural migrant women stated, regarding their husbands' help in the household:

- I cannot quote precisely how much my husband assisted me in doing household work in number of hours. But, he was helping me … he was supportive and helpful even more as the children were smaller. I think men and women should share household responsibilities … both should participate in doing household work. It is something I have passed to my son. I raised him to be helpful in the household. (I, 3)
- Our husbands behave differently. We have had good education, so women have changed. It was not always as it is now. For example, my father contributed in the house as much he wanted, and the rest he used to spend in the bar. (V, 2)
- I cannot be silent. My husband allows me to decide everything. I do not know is it because he is freeing himself from responsibility or is he really admitting that I am better in organizing things. (V, 3)

Urban women with migration experience in the family briefly answered '*We decide together*' (4, 5, 6,). The experience of rural women with male out-migration is in a similar way democratic: while the husband is absent, the woman decides alone. There is also an unwritten, common rule or practice of informing the absent partner on every important issue. Decisions are made together, when he is present:

- I decide on my own. When he is here, we decide together. (VI, 1)
- At home, we decide together about everything. Even children can participate in the discussions on important issues. I do care about their opinion. When he is absent.

Some women stress the fact that their husbands do not expect them to report everything they have done and allow them to decide alone:

- My husband is letting me decide on everything. He says I know better how to manage the money, evaluate our needs, etc. I keep account on our spending, and when I try to show it to him he does not want to look at it. If I bring something new in the house, he is positively surprised. (VI, 5)

When asked to relate the influence of migration on the possible changes in attitudes and values, women in this group mention the following:

- Those living abroad are more modern then men who have never been abroad. They better understand and value women. (VI, 6)
- Living abroad has left positive effects on our men. In many situations and in many things, they think and behave differently than our neighbours. In respect of child raising, education.... They give us full freedom to decide. (VI, 2)

CONCLUSION

Over the past two decades migration flows drastically affected the demographic, socio-economic and development profile of Bosnia-Herzegovina. However, little is known about the effects of migration on the life situation of the migrants and their families. I have provided a deeper understanding of the complex intersections of gender and migration. Returning to the three areas of inquiry referred to in the conceptual framework, the empirical evidence brings together further information to the understanding of how migration impacts the empowerment of women at the household level, and how women cope with the migration-related changes.

First, research evidence suggests that migration in combination with other background factors, such as educational level, pre-migration employment status and urban/rural characteristics, contributes to both empowering and disempowering the outcomes in the economic positions of women. Notably, the empowering effects of migration positively correlate with the prior non-working status, low education and rural background. In the present study, the most profound positive change in the economic position of women is found in the less educated, rural migrant women who never worked in paid employment prior to migration. Unfortunately, these empowering effects proved to not be long-lasting. Upon return, women usually conform to their role as housewives again because their rural context is marked by poverty and no employment opportunities. The opposite pattern is observed in urban migrant women, who are highly educated and had paid employment prior to migration. Being forced to take up less rewarding, less demanding and poorly paid jobs, this group of women experienced a severe negative change in their own economic position as a result of migration. Furthermore, research findings suggest that the experience of migration in the family has no significant impact on the economic emancipation of women. Rural women, who are left behind, despite being relatively well educated, tend not to work, whereas urban women with the experience of migration in the family appear not to depend on cash or other remittances from family members who are living abroad.

Second, empirical findings suggest that despite variations in the degree of power and the autonomy of the women in the present study, women's perceptions do not support the idea that women are subject to male domination in their families. Quite the contrary, participants overvalue girls over boys, they are committed to enable the highest possible education level for their daughters. In addition, they are in favour of girls' rights to have the same share in the family inheritance. And apparently, they lean more towards making effective choices in this regards, as well as to translate their choices into desired actions and outcomes.

Third, in terms of migration dimensions, there are no considerable differences among participants in the sphere of domestic decision-making. The nuclear family model dominates, and the research results create an image of empowered Bosnian women who do have a strong say in the domestic decision-making process. Although women and men are both included in the process of decision-making, some evidence of male subordination to women in the domestic area is noted. As a result, women do exercise a high level of control over their domestic resources, for example, decisions regarding child rearing, health and education as well as household expenditures. In the case of male out-migration, the decision-making powers have been transferred to the women.

Fourth, one of the most striking findings from the study is the powerful image of emancipated, self-aware and empowered Bosnian women. Thus, might observed findings be instructive in making generalization about the position of (migrant) women in the society as a whole? And how we can explain it? Indeed, the results of the present study should be viewed with some caution for a compelling reason: the women's perceptions of empowerment were examined for the level of household only. And, in spite of the socialist heritage of egalitarianism, on the one hand, and the constant struggle between neoconservative and liberal changes of gender regimes of present transition, on the other, the position of women at the household level is commonplace, an archetype of being female.

In the time of socialist emancipation, Bosnian women experienced that greater participation in paid work would not be compensated by a decrease in their responsibility in domestic work. The access to paid work was opened through massive integration into the labour market and employment-based system of social security, including highly gendered childcare benefits and leave schemes. However, the work-related emancipation resulted in a double-burden: paid work contributing to family income in public and unpaid household work in private. The collapse of the socialist welfare state in transition contributed to the revival of a triple-burden, as once socialized child-care was transferred to the family, notably female responsibility. Ultimately, the underlying idea is that the domestic sphere is regarded as women's 'natural' environment. Therefore, it appears 'natural' that women as an 'extension of nature' also assume their 'natural' tasks: unpaid household and care work. From this perspective, gendered views on the private (domestic) sphere translate into a relatively high degree of bargaining and decision-making power for women. If the analytical framework were expanded to include political, legal and psychological dimensions, as well as the perceptions women hold of their (migration-related) empowerment on the community and wider society level, and these elements were put under scrutiny, the observed image of empowered Bosnian women would likely be less pronounced.

NOTE

1   'Magros' was a relatively large textile producer during the socialist period.

REFERENCES

Aysa, M., and D. Massey. 2004. 'Wives Left Behind: The Labour Market Behaviour of Women in Migrant Communities', in Jorge Durand and Douglas S. Massey, eds., *Crossing the Border: Research from the Mexican Migration Project*. New York: Russell Sage Foundation, 131–44.

BHAS. 2018. Labor Force Survey. Retrieved from http://www.bhas.ba/temats kibilteni/LAB_00_2018_Y1_0_HR.pdf, accessed on 19 December 2018.

De Haas, H. 2005. 'International Migration, Remittances and Development: Myths and Facts', *Third World Quarterly* 26: 1269–84.

De Koning, M. 2008. Return Migration to Bosnia and Herzegovina. Monitoring the Embeddednes of Returnees', Center for International Development Issues, Radboud University Nijmegen.

Duflo, E. 2012. 'Women Empowerment and Economic Development', *Journal of Economic Literature* 50, 4: 1051–79.

Eastmond, M. 2006. 'Transnational Returns and Reconstruction in Post-War Bosnia and Herzegovina', *International Migration* 44, 3: 141–66.

Emirhafizović, M., E. Ćosić, A. Osmić, and V. Repovac-Pašić. 2013. 'Migration from Bosnia and Herzegovina', Faculty of Political Sciences and Ministry of Human Rights and Refugees, Sarajevo.

Fargues, P. 2006. *The Demographic Benefit of International Migration: Hypothesis and Application to Middle and North African Contexts*, World Bank Policy Research Working Paper 4050. Washington DC: The World Bank.

Gunnarsson, B. 2006. 'Influence of Male Migration on Female Resources, Independence and Development in Gambian Villages', MA thesis, Malmo University.

Hadi, A. 2001. 'International Migration and the Change of Women's Position among the Left Behind in Rural Bangladesh', *International Journal of Population Geography* 7: 53–61.

Hemon, A. 2013. '*Knjiga Mojih Života* (The Book of My Lives)'. Sarajevo: Buybook.

IOM. 2007. 'Bosnia and Herzegovina: Migration Profile 2007'. Geneva: International Organization for Migration.

Kabeer, N. 2001. 'Reflections on the Measurement of Women's Empowerment', in *Discussing Women's Empowerment—Theory and Practice*, Sida Studies No. 3. Stockholm: Novum Grafiska AB.

Keller, B., and D. C. Mbwewe. 1991. 'Policy and Planning for the Empowerment of Zambia's Women Farmers', *Canadian Journal of Development Studies* 12, 1: 75–88.

Kukanesen, R. 2003. Female-Headed Households: Bosnia-Herzegovina Report. New York: United Nations.

Menjivar, C., and V. Agadjanian. 2007. 'Men's Migration and Women's Lives: Views from Rural Armenia and Guatemala', *Social Science Quarterly* 88, 5: 1243–62.

MHRR. 2016.' *BIH Migration Profile*. Saravejo: Ministry for Human Rights and Refugees of Bosnia-Herzegovina.

Saeed, K. E. 2001. 'The Impact of Male Out-Migration on Women's Role and Status in Sudan', *The Ahfad Journal* 18, 1: 62–73.

Sen, G. 1993. 'Women's Empowerment and Human Rights: The Challenge to Policy'. Paper Presented at the Population Summit of the World's Scientific Academies, October 24–27, New Delhi, India.

Stevenson, Thomas B. 1997. 'Migration, Family and Household in Highland Yemen: The Impact of Socio-Economic and Political Change and Cultural Ideas on Domestic Organization', *Journal of Comparative Family Studies* 28, 2: 14–40.

Taylor, E. 1984. 'Egyptian Migration and Peasant Wives', Middle East Research and Information Projects, Working Paper no. 124.

UNDP. 2007. 'The Silent Majority Speaks. Snapshots of Today and Visions of the Future of Bosnia and Herzegovina', Sarajevo: Oxford Research International and United Nations Development Program, Office of Residential Coordinator.

United Nations Department of Economic and Social Affairs Population Division. 2012. 'Trends in International Migrant Stock', The 2012 Revision CD-Rom Documentation.

World Bank. 2005. 'What is Empowerment?' Chapter 2, in *Sourcebook on Empowerment and Poverty Reduction*. Retrieved from http://siteresources, worldbank.or/INTEMPOWERMENT/Resources/486312-1095094954594/ draft2/pdf, accessed on 29 January 2013.

——. 2016. 'Migration and Remittances Factbook 2016'. Retrieved from https:// siteresources.worldbank.org/INTPROSPECTS/Resources/334934-1199807908806/4549025-1450455807487/Factbookpart1.pdf, accessed on 19 December 2018.

Žiga, L., A. Osmić, L. Turčalo, S. Bašić et al. 2015. 'Youth Study in Bosnia and Herzegovina', Sarajevo: Friedrich Ebert Foundation and Faculty of Political Sciences.

5

Violence, Forced Migration and Vulnerability of the Adivasi Women in Western Assam

NAZIMUDDIN SIDDIQUE

ASSAM, A STATE situated in the northeastern part of India, can rightly be termed as being on the periphery of the South Asian country. Post-independent Northeast India, in general, and Assam, in particular, has been perennially witnessing violence in many forms. The intensity of recurrent violence and the magnitude of forced migration are given in Table 5.1. Forced migration is not a new phenomenon in Assam or for that matter in India. It has been a recurrent phenomenon in colonial and postcolonial Assam. The state of Assam is inhabited by several socio-religious communities (henceforth SRCs) which include people from various religious and ethnic tribal groups, with many of them having their own language, writing system, traditions, and so on. Post-independent Assam has lost a significant part of its territory in the form of newborn states: Mizoram, Nagaland, Meghalaya, NEFA (present day Arunachal Pradesh) after substantial bloodshed in the region. The partition of the state was largely a result of Assamese 'irredentism', and identity assertion of the diverse tribes.

Assam is in deeper turmoil today than ever before. 'Apodictically, an obvious truth, the society in Assam has transformed very distinctly into a notoriously violent one without any tangible sign of abnegation. Violence has been an inseparable part of Assam's social and political development since independence' (Hussain 1995: 1154). Through a

Table 5.1. Number of People Currently Living in Displacement in
Northeast India

Situation	Reported Numbers Originally Displaced	Reported Numbers of IDPs as of 2011
Western Assam, displaced October 1993	More than 18,000	More than 10,000
Western Assam, May–June 1996	More than 200,000	More than 16,000
Western Assam, May 1998	Almost 315,000	Almost 20,000
Mizoram–Tripura, October 1997 or November 2009	More than 35,000	More than 30,000
Assam and Meghalaya, December 2010–January 2011	50,000	Unknown
Total	More than 830,000	More than 76,000

Source: Internal Displacement Monitoring Centre of Norwegian Refugee Council, November 2011.[1]

gendered prism, this essay attempts to view a particular aspect of a conflict which occurred in an area that geographically falls under western Assam. The entire western Assam has witnessed perennial violence since 1987, a major concern for the people of this region and beyond, and the violence has significant gendered dimensions. 'The connections between conflict and gender have been the subject of a growing interest, over the last two decades, in particular, in academic, policy, and humanitarian and development circles' (Bushra and Gardner 2004: 14). Though all the communities of western Assam have been deeply suffering from conflicts, the focus shall be limited to the conflict which occurred between Bodos and adivasis, in a particular geographical region: the Bongaigaon district.

In the context of Assam and particularly western Assam, violence is a usual and quotidian phenomenon. There are various causes of the conflicts of Assam and of the Northeast, among them ethnicity is the most potent factor (Goswami 2013). If we go deeper into these conflicts, a strong impact of tacit communalism, which is deeply rooted, can be sensed from the underlying currents. Additionally, a close observation into the conflicts portrays that the victims always belong to one or another marginalized communities. The Northeast in general and Assam in particular has a population that is multi-lingual, multi-cultural, multi-religious, multi-ethnic and hetero-geneous. Therefore, to comprehend the concept of ethnicity in the context of Assam in general and western Assam in particular bears much significance. Though many scholars argue ethnicity to be the only responsible factor, it needs mentioning here that ethnicity is not solely responsible for the eruption of violence. It is asserted that the competition for scarce values and material goods is exactly what propels people to see themselves as members of distinct ethnic groups whose interest conflicts with those of other ethnic groups (Horowitz 1985). The difference between ethnic conflict and vio-lence is very narrow but distinguishable. As Varshney (2002) argues, ethnic conflicts are a regular feature of ethnically plural democracies, for if a different ethnic group exists and freedom to organize is avail-able, there are likely to be conflicts over resources, identity, patronage, and policies. Violence occurs when massacres are carried out, riots break out, atrocities, kidnappings, extortions take place. Conflicts can be categorized as religious, racial, linguistic, sectarian.

A section of scholars argues that the ranges of ethnic-conflicts are limited only to those conflicts which are racial in nature and at best can be extended to linguistic conflicts. Varshney held that exponents of the broader usage disagree with such distinctions. 'Existing traditions of inquiry into ethnic conflict can be classified into four categories: essentialism, instrumentalism, constructivism and institutionalism'. Out of these four categories constructivism and institutionalism are of recent origin and have the edge over the other two.

'The basic intuition of essentialism is that ethnic conflicts today can be traced back to older animosities between groups; the key prop-osition of instrumentalism rests on the purely instrumental use of ethnic identity for political or economic purpose by the elite, regard-less of whether they believe ethnicity' (ibid.: 27). Instrumentalism is based upon the view that ethnic conflict is manipulated by either the relationship between economic desires—greed and grievance—or the active manipulation of ethnic identities by political leaders for their political gain (ibid.).

The idea of primordialism and its connection to ethnic conflict can be traced from the works of Clifford Geertz (1963).[2] What he suggests is that ethnic 'ties' are inherent in us as human beings; that we have deep, 'natural', connections that link us to some people and that lead to natural divisions with others, whether based on race, religion, language, blood, custom or location. Thus division caused by natural 'ties' has been referred to as 'ancient hatreds' (Toft 2003; Varshney 2001). The 'primordialist' position came under strong criticism by Eller and Coughlan (1993) 'for presenting a static and naturalistic view of ethnicity and for lacking explanatory power' (Hutchinson and Smith 1996: 8).

'Over the past ten to fifteen years, the study of ethnicity has been profoundly influenced by constructivism' (Varshney 2002: 31). Exponents of constructivism argue that ethnic conflict is a consequence of historical processes over time that result in divergent ethnic identities and hostility between them. 'With respect to postcolonial societies such as India, the principle constructivist claim is that the major contemporary ethnic cleavages were a creation of colonial power and, given the immense power of colonial masters, such division has endured and will last for a long time' (ibid.: 33).

THE BACKGROUND

Bodo is the name of a tribe, an offshoot of the Tibeto-Burman linguistic family which primarily inhabits the plains of the Brahmaputra Valley of Assam. Members are found in Nepal and Bangladesh, though in meagre numbers. The Bodos migrated to Assam from Tibet a long time ago. This tribe constitutes about 4 percent of the total population of Assam, inhabiting areas which can be geographically marked as western Assam.

'Ethno-nationalist identities are important categories of identity formation in Northeast India' (Barbora 2005: 198). Most of the ethnic groups of Northeast India have been agitating to preserve their identity and protect their rights (George 1994: 878). Similarly, Bodos too started a movement popularly known as the Bodo movement. We will not discuss the entire Bodo movement in micro detail till date; rather an attempt would be made to keep our prime focus on the impact of the movement on the adivasi population of western Assam, on the adivasi women to be precise.

Bodos, the single largest tribal community of Assam, were oppressed by the hegemonic Assamese political leaderships for decades. As a result of this long drawn oppression, alienation, marginalization, and backwardness—in socio-economic and political terms—surfaced as the Bodo movement. The movement draws its reference from the infamous and 'proto-fascist' Assam movement which started in the 1979 and ended in 1985 (Guha 1980). The demand was for an exclusive homeland for the Bodos, in the form of a state, to be carved out from the territory of Assam. Though the movement is known to have started in 1987, the struggle of the Bodos for a separate state had begun decades ago. At an initial stage, an organization was formed in 1967, namely, the Plains Tribal Council of Assam (PTCA). It demanded the formation of a separate state of 'Udayachal' on the north bank of the Brahmaputra for the plains tribes (Baruah 1999). However, the demand did not gain ground and could not materialize as well. Though PTCA failed, the demand of a separate state remained alive, and subsequently it was started again with renewed vigour. Therefore on 2 March 1987 a new student organization, the All Bodoland Student Union (ABSU), came into being. Since the very inception of the ABSU, the demand for the separate statehood got intensified and the student organization opted for extreme violent ways to realize the target—a separate state exclusively for the Bodos.

The renewed demand under the fresh banner started substituting the demand of 'Udayachal' with 'Bodoland'. In the consecutive months, a major section of ABSU members shifted their allegiance from the ABSU to opt for more violent methods and as a consequence, two ruthless armed extremist groups got splintered from the organization: Bodo Volunteer Force (BVF) and National Democratic Front of Bodoland (NDFB). In the later period the BVF reconstituted as the Bodo Liberation Tigers (BLT). Both the armed organizations had been mainly and largely targeting non-Bodos, in an extremely ruthless and violent manner.[3] In 1987, the demand for a separate state with the slogan 'Divide Assam 50–50' was pushed fiercely under the banner of ABSU. The most significant disadvantage of the Bodo chauvinist group was that the territory they were demanding as 'Bodoland' or as the exclusive state for the Bodos, had a population of diverse communities where Bodos constituted only about 27 percent of the total population.

Apart from Bodos, the other major communities who belong to the region are: adivasis, Bengali Hindus, Koch-Rajbanshis, Muslims and Nepalis. As Bodos are numerically in the minority in 'Bodoland' in comparison to the non-Bodos, a major section of the Bodo leaders has been in a constant endeavour to build a majority and this has been violently spearheaded by the Bodo terrorists. The majority building of the Bodo population is essential for the Bodo political organizations as it will put more weight to their bargaining with the government for a separate state: 'Bodoland'.

This idea has been the driving force behind the ruthless 'ethnic cleansing' by the Bodo militants, aimed at forcing 'other' communities out from the territory of 'Bodoland'. 'Cleansing' of non-Bodo communities by the Bodos, through plunder, arson, massacre and persecution, has forced a large number of non-Bodos to flee.[4] This heinous act which resulted in massive forced migration, has been executed purely by the Bodos in order to gain political mastery in the area. Bodo political organizations have been making staunch territorial claims on land. They have been demanding the demarcation of land through violent ways and at the cost of non-Bodo lives. In the early phase of the movement, open threats were issued to non-Bodo communities to quit the Bodo-dominated areas. This was followed by severe clashes as the leaders of the Bodo movement adopted more violent means and their prime target was the non-Bodo communities. During 1989–1991 large numbers of linguistic Assamese and Koch-Rajbanshis were forced out of the area through incessant violence, exploitation and threats. Further, it continued through 1991–1993 and a large number of Nepali- and Hindi-speaking people were also forced to leave the area. Severe attacks on Bengali Hindus were unleashed in 1994–1995 which followed a horrendous attack on adivasis in 1996. The clashes between the Bodos and the adivasis were severe and lasted for years in the region, and many adivasis were killed. In 1998 clashes between the Bodos and adivasis further deepened which led to the internal displacement of thousands of people. Many of the adivasi people displaced during these prolonged clashes continue to live in camps even today.[5] There are several dimensions to this conflict but the major underlying cause is the political motive of the Bodos to establish their tribe as the numerically majority community in the area.

The history of Assam is a history of migration. 'Assam has been a region of in-migration, hosting new generations and collections of settlers each century, from prehistoric times to the present day' (Ludden 2003: 6). The history of the adivasis in Assam began with the creation of tea plantations in the state by the British. These adivasis were originally from Jharkhand, Bihar, Odisha and Madhya Pradesh. As Hussain (1993) puts it, 'They started to migrate to the Assam and North Bengal tea gardens in the latter half of the nineteenth century, after they had been alienated from their traditional lands by non-tribals under the patronage of the colonial state'. Another noted scholar of the region, Hiren Gohain (2007: 113) observed:

> Adivasi of western and central Assam districts … live in isolated villages mired in poverty and squalor, forgotten by the rest of Assam, particularly by the state government, and in tea gardens owned by the Marwaris, Sindhis, Punjabis, foreign multinationals and Indian big business houses. They have little contact with the Assamese. During colonial times the British had lured them in lakhs from Chotanagpur, Bengal Presidency, even Andhra, and forced them into a terrible state of servitude marked by low wages, restriction on free movement, and denial of right to education and near total absence of medical care. Following independence, the pharisaical humanitarianism of the Indian National Trade Union Congress (INTUC), sheltering behind the Assam Plantation Act, modelled on a central act, left the labour force to the tender mercies of the garden management. Even when epidemics raged, the district administration could not intervene to rush medical supplies to areas under law-abiding management. The management took necessary care to preserve this vast army of cheap labour unspoilt by modern temptation.

THE VIOLENCE

'From the very beginning the Bodo movement was marked by extensive violence' (Bhaumik 2009: 125). In the violence propagated by the violent section of Bodos, the worst sufferers have been the Muslims and the adivasis. It is so because they are very easily considered as soft targets. 'Needless to say, the Muslims have emerged today as the softest target for collective political violence in India' (Hussain 1995: 1155). In 1996, a severe conflict took place between the Bodos and the adivasis. The clash started in the Kokrajhar district and soon it spread like wildfire to Bongaigaon district and other areas of western Assam and was severely violent. Misra (2007: 13) observes 'there were severe clashes between adivasis and Bodos which left scores killed and hundreds injured, while over a lakh of people were uprooted from their homes'. This violence was a part of the series of the above discussed violence, attributed to the infamous Bodo movement. We will now discuss a particular violence, which is a part of the series of the violence of 1996 itself, which occurred in the southern foothills of Bhutan, under the territory of the Bongaigaon district of Assam.

The area in question falls in the Indo-Bhutan borderland under the present Chirang district of Assam. Prior to these, sporadic clashes between the adivasis and Bodos occurred in the Bongaigaon district. In 1996, adivasis of Amteka, Koylamoyla, Oxiguri, Malavita, Patabari of the present Chirang district came under deadly attacks from the Bodo terrorists,[6] executed with sophisticated weapons by the Bodo militants. Many villagers were brutally killed on the spot, while the rest escaped in order to save their lives, leaving behind everything they had earned in a lifetime. Villages were burnt to their entirety, and, attacks were accompanied with looting. These clashes led to massive 'ethnic cleansing' and drew very little or no attention of the local media let alone national media.

This particular attack can be put under the third phase of 'ethnic cleansing' by the Bodo militants. The first phase and the second phase of 'ethnic cleaning' were administered on Muslims and on Bengali-speaking Hindus, respectively. In 1989 thousands of Rajbanshis too were forced out of different places of western Assam at gunpoint. It is noteworthy to mention that Muslims were severely attacked, in the same areas, and were forced to leave their homes, villages in October 1993. The attack on Muslims left many killed and thousands were rendered homeless. Had the government learnt from the attacks on Muslims, and had it taken preventive measures, the attacks on the adivasis and other communities could have been prevented. But the government learnt absolutely nothing from the earlier massacres, thus creating a conducive milieu for the terrorists to carry out further devastation of life and property. It needs to be mentioned here that these deadly attacks on the marginalized communities are still continuing in the region (Siddique 2014: 2015).

Post-conflict, most of the affected people fled to the makeshift camps set up in the Deosri forest village.[7] These Internally Displaced People (IDPs) received meagre or no humanitarian assistance from the government. IDPs are people who 'escape human rights violations carried out by government forces, rebel groups, and other civilians that are caused by political, civil, and ethnic unrest as well as economic, environmental, and other forms of dislocation' (Veney 2007: 4). Norwegian Refugee Council (NRC) (2006) segments the causes of Internal Displacement as: *(i)* political causes, including secessionist movements; *(ii)* identity-based autonomy movements; *(iii)* localized violence; and *(iv)* environmental and development-induced displacement. However, the cause of the internal displacement in question falls under the second category, that is, 'identity-based autonomy movements', of the fourfold division devised by the NRC.

WOMEN AND MAKESHIFT CAMPS

Violence brings extreme misery to all, but the sorrows are more intense for women in comparison to their male counterparts. Most of the affected women happen to be poor, and, violence further brings extreme poverty to them, 'poverty implies being hungry, lacking shelter and clothing, being sick and not cared for, and being illiterate and not schooled' (Holtzman and Nezam 2004: 13). Poverty often pushes the women to sell even the ornaments at extremely low prices, provided they succeed in saving those from the attackers. Makeshift camps, locally known as relief camps or refugee camps, are places of extreme human suffering. The problem exacerbates for women who are not accompanied by males of their families. This situation arises as many women lose their husbands or family members in the conflict. Veney (2007: 191) argues,

> Whether women are accompanied or unaccompanied in the camps, they encounter particular challenges in their efforts to obtain water, firewood, employment, and health care in the areas of reproductive health and STDs.

Due to certain conditions found in refugee camps such as overcrowding that puts strangers in close proximity to one another, idleness on the part of male refugees who often do not have employment opportunities, high rates of alcoholism and other drug use, gender-based violence that affects women tends to be prevalent.

The living condition in such camps are always unhygienic, insecure, extremely uncomfortable, and the difficulty increases manifold for the women. The safety and security of women and children remain elusive, for, such camps are highly insecure for them. Human trafficking too, takes place from such makeshift camps. Heartbreaking pain due to untimely loss of husbands, family members or close relatives presents extreme mental setbacks to women. Fear and insecurity in camps loom large. Losses compounding with lives and property make lives of women extremely painful and unbearable. During the stay in the makeshift camps, women do not get access to any paid work; therefore, their lives are pushed further to the margin. In such a scenario they only remain reliant on government aid or humanitarian assistance, which is always inadequate in quantity and poor in quality. The makeshift camps intrinsically are overcrowded and the living conditions are significantly miserable. The camps, per se, do not provide the women even the minimum privacy they require in their daily lives. No such camps come with proper toilets; therefore, defaecation is a major issue for the womenfolk, in places surrounded by men. Situations become worse for pregnant women during the stay in such camps. It is immensely unbearable for them to stay in relief camps, wherein, many a time childbirths do take place, in the absence of medical facilities, care, unfortunately even in the absence of the minimum required privacy.

Women are vulnerable, both, during conflict and post-conflict situations. Crisp, in his study on the Kenyan refugee camps, derives a fourfold typology of violence: 'domestic and community violence; sexual abuse and sexual violence; armed robbery; and violence both within and between national refugee groups' (Crisp 2000; Pickering 2005: 26). The presence of similar violence cannot be denied, and at least the first three types of violence are common in the makeshift camps of Assam. Even cases of harassment by a section of opportunistic male inmates in the makeshift camps are also commonplace occurrences.

THE LIMBO

The violence in question undoubtedly induced a massive forced migration, and created a significant number of homeless people. These people stayed for years in the makeshift camps, and received almost no assistance from the government to get rehabilitation. The affected women could not return to their homes for 'security concerns, destruction of property, occupation of property by others' (Holtzman and Nezam 2004: 5). Even the government did not encourage them to return, and, the displaced people thus continued to remain displaced. In the absence of the intervention of the government in the form of rehabilitation, they had no option but to encroach on parts of Chirang reserve forest, adjacent to the Deosri forest village, in order to start their lives again. As a result, a series of encroached villages have emerged in the area: Mohanpur, Aye Puwali, Nagdalbari, and so on.

Settling on a new site, that too after clearing heavy jungles, is an extremely arduous task and women, in particular, bore the brunt of this heavy burden. Clearing of the forest, compounding with other human atrocities on the forest, invited a serious degradation of the environment and adversely affected the ecology of the region. However, it must be mentioned that these encroachments on the forest could take place because of the violence inflicted on the Adivasi people. The affected population was dependent on agriculture; for that reason, on land. In their new site of settlement, the women got meagre or no access to land to carry out their agricultural activities, in a full-fledged manner. In these processes of displacement from one place to another, women play a very significant role in nurturing the family. 'Displacement has increasingly meant women have become the main breadwinners', and in many cases shared more responsibilities than its gendered counterpart (Pickering 2011: 22).

TOWARDS A CONCLUSION

On 10 February 2003 a Memorandum of Settlement (MoS) was signed between the Assam government, the Union government and the Bodo Liberation Tigers in New Delhi and thus the Bodoland Territorial Council (BTC) surfaced.[8] It was created under the Sixth Schedule of the Constitution of India and was expected to bring sustainable peace in western Assam; moreover the expectation was that the theatre of violence in the belt, would come to an end for once and for all. But time has proved the model to be severely flawed, and it has numerous discrepancies. The model is highly unrepresentative in an ethnically, culturally, linguistically and religiously plural region. The BTC 'comprising the four districts of Kokrajhar, Baksa, Udalguri and Chirang, covering an area of 27,100 sq. km (or 35 percent of Assam's area) was awarded to the Bodo tribe—which, according to the 2001 Census, had 1,296,000 members, or 5.3 percent of Assam's population (Barooah 2013: 50). Time has come to review such a severely faulty model of governance, and transform it to a more representative and democratic one.

The IDPs under discussion are still living a life full of uncertainty. Many factions of Bodo terrorists are still active in the zone. The villages, where adivasi women are living presently, are encroached entities, which virtually means that the government can in any given time evict them. The affected women are hapless victims, but they are fighting back towards survival. The women are actively participating in income-generating micro projects. Participation of women in farming and raising animals is contributing significantly towards their survival in a life of extreme destitution. The government must take the initiative to address the multi-dimensional grievances of these women, their men and children, and the role of civil society will remain very crucial to pressurize chronically lenient governments.

NOTES

1   Retrieved from http://www.internal-displacement.org/assets/publications/ 2011/201111-ap-India-this-is-our-land-sum-country-en.pdf, accessed on 6 December 2015.
2   The term was first used by Edward Shils (1957) and popularized by Clifford Geertz.
3   In western Assam, people not belonging to communities other than Bodo are known as non-Bodos, e.g., adivasis, Bengali Hindus, Koch-Rajbanshis, Muslims, Nepalis.
4   See 'A profile of the internal displacement situation', 9 February 2006. Retrieved from www.internal-displacement.org, accessed on 6 December 2015.

5   The author visited an adivasi camp at Srirampur check-post under Kokrajhar district on 5 May 2014. This particular camp has about 150 families. There are many other Santhal camps of this kind.

6   During the violence, these places were under Bongaigaon district. In 2003 Chirang district was curved out from the erstwhile Bongaigaon district.

7   Deosri is a forest village under Sidli subdivision of present-day Chirang district (during the violence it was under Bongaigaon district). This area is situated hardly a few kilometres away from the international border of India and Bhutan. The forest village is situated in the Chirang reserve forest.

8   BTC is also known as Bodoland Territorial Area District (BTAD).

REFERENCES

Barbora, Sanjay. 2005. 'Autonomy in the Northeast: The Frontiers of Centralised Politics', in Ranabir Samaddar, ed. *The Politics of Autonomy: Indian Experiences.* New Delhi: SAGE Publications.

Baruah, Sanjib. 1999. *India against Itself: Assam and the Politics of Nationality.* Philadelphia: University of Pennsylvania Press.

Bhaumik, Subir. 2009. *Troubled Periphery—Crisis of India's North-East.* New Delhi: SAGE Publications.

Borooah, Vani Kant. 2013. 'The Killing Fields of Assam: Myth and Reality of Its Muslim Immigration', *EPW* 48, 4 (26 January).

Bushra, Judy, and Judith Gardner. 2004. *Somalia—The Untold Story: The War Through the Eyes of Somali Women.* London: Pluto Press.

Crisp, J. 2000. 'A State of Insecurity: The Political Economy of Violence in Kenya's Refugee Camps'. *African Affairs* 99, 397 (October 2000).

Eller, Jack, and Reed Coughlan. 1993. 'The Poverty of Primordialism: The Demystification of Ethnic Attachments', *Ethnic and Racial Ties* 16, 2.

Geertz, Clifford. 1963. 'The Integrative Revolution', in Clifford Geertz, ed., *Old Societies and New States.* New York: Free Press.

George, Sudhir Jacob.1994. 'The Bodo Movement in Assam: Unrest to Accord', *Asian Survey* 34, 10 (October 1994).

Gohain, Hiren. 2007. 'A Question of Identity: Adivasi Militancy in Assam', *EPW* 42, 49 (8 December).

Goswami, Uddipona. 2013. *Conflict and Reconciliation: The Politics of Ethnicity in Assam.* New Delhi: Routledge.

Guha, Amalendu.1980. 'Little Nationalism Turned Chauvinist: Assam's Anti-Foreigner Upsurge, 1979–80', *EPW* 15, 41: 1699–1720, Special Number (October).

Holtzman, Steven B., and Taies Nezam. 2004. *Living in Limbo: Conflict-Induced Displacement in Europe and Central Asia.* Washington, DC: The World Bank.

Horowitz, Donald. 1985. *Ethnic Groups in Conflict.* Berkeley, CA: University of California Press.

Hussain, Monirul. 1995. 'Ethnicity, Communalism and State Barpeta Massacre', *EPW* 30, 20 (20 May).

———. 1993. *The Assam Movement, Class, Ideology and Identity.* New Delhi: Manak.

Hutchinson, John, and Anthony D. Smith. 1996. *Ethnicity.* New York: Oxford University Press.

Ludden, David. 2003. 'Where Is Assam? Using Geographical History to Locate Current Social Realities' (*CENISEAS Papers 1*: Sanjib Baruah Series Editor), Guwahati: Centre for Northeast India South and Southeast Asia Studies, OKD Institute of Social Change and Development.

Misra, Udayon. 2007. 'Adivasi Struggle in Assam', *EPW* 42, 51 (22 December).

Norwegian Refugee Council/IDMC. 2019. 'India: Tens of Thousands Newly Displaced in North-Eastern and Central States. A Profile of the Internal Displacement Situation, 9 February 2006. Retrieved from https://www.refworld.org/docid/44031ac44.html, accessed 11 September 2019.

———. 2011. 'This Is Our Land: Ethnic Violence and Internal Displacement in North-East India' (November).

Pickering, Sharon. 2011. *Women, Borders and Violence Current Issues in Asylum, Forced Migration and Trafficking.* New York: Springer.

Shils, Edward. 1975. *Centre and Periphery: Essays in Macrosociology.* Chicago, IL: University of Chicago Press.

Siddique, Nazimuddin. 2015. 'Massacres Recoiled in Assam: Adivasis this Time', *Mainstream* 53, 11 (7 March).

———. 2014. 'Massacre in Assam: Explaining the Latest Round' *EPW* 49, 22 (31 May).

Toft, M. 2003. *The Geography of Ethnic Violence: Identities, Interests, and the Invisibility of Territory.* Princeton, NJ: Princeton University Press.

Varshney, Ashutosh. 2002. *Ethnic Conflict and Civil Life: Hindus and Muslims in India.* New Delhi: Oxford University Press.

———. 2001. 'Ethnic Conflicts and Ancient Hatreds,' in N. Smelser, et al., eds., *International Encyclopedia of the Social and Behavioural Sciences.* Oxford: Pergamon.

Veney, Cassandra R. 2007. *Forced Migration in Eastern Africa: Democratization, Structural Adjustment, and Refugees.* New York: Palgrave Macmillan.

6

Towards Emancipation or Bondage? Rohingya Women's Narratives from Bangladesh Refugee Camps and Indian Jails

SUCHARITA SENGUPTA

*Imagine there's no countries,
It isn't hard to do.
Nothing to kill or die for
And no religion, too.
Imagine all the people
Living life in peace …*
—John Lennon

IMAGINING A WORLD without boundaries is impossible especially when marking and securitizing boundaries constitute the heart of international relations and politics. People on the peripheries or migrants are ignored mostly, but the undeniable truth is that to understand the core of nation formation in South Asia first the people must be considered (Samaddar 1999). The study of the nation no longer assumes a crucial place of significance; instead, 'governing the mobile' and messy flow of population has become the centre of our political understanding (Samaddar 2015). This is linked with a broader context, that is, the processes of globalization. It is now increasingly being argued that capitalism and the processes of globalization will give rise to new global geographies and increase all manner of links (cultural, political, economic, informational) across

113

boundaries' (Paasi 1998). Although transnational population flow/migration/forced migration as categories are distinct, the difference in their meaning often gets blurred in practice. These can neither be branded as fixed or watertight categories nor situations of exception or banality, specifically in the context of South Asia. To stress on the bit of exception, following Agamben (2015), would therefore mean ignoring concrete colonial and postcolonial conditions in countries like India where conditions of exception are integral to the socio-political history of this region (Samaddar 2016).

At this juncture, a crucial question could be invoked in studying the cross-border migration between India and Bangladesh: could migration in this specific historical and geographical context ever be 'free'? There is always some kind of a force in the form of ethnic violence, domestic tensions or sheer economic compulsions that propel continuous movement of people across the Bengal Borderland.[1] Thus drawing from a point made by B. S. Chimni at a conference in Cairo in 2008 and expanded further by Mezzadra (2013), migration is almost never 'voluntary' or 'free' and the margin between people *willing* to cross the border and *forced* to do so often gets annihilated. The vulnerability of women migrants across the Bengal–Bangladesh border or another key border, the Myanmar–Bangladesh one, is revealed when knowingly or unknowingly they have illegally crossed the demarcation line between the two territories and landed in danger in camps in Bangladesh and also in prisons in India. Most of these are Rohingya women who hail from a very low economic background with an absence of any formal education.

In 2019, despite apparent peace and better security of lives in the 34 Rohingya camps (with redrawing of maps, this number changes) in Bangladesh, it is impossible for one to ignore the hopelessness that clouds conversations occasionally in the camps. It will not be accurate to say everything in my rounds of conversations with the camp dwellers, especially women, was absolutely grim and dark, that there were no hope, no quest or no dreams. In fact their zest often surprised me. Despite that, the poignancy of being stranded is undeniable. For instance, it is two years since Jasmine with her family have come to these settlements in Ukhiya. I met her at Balukhali, which is numbered as Camp Number 9. Her father lives in Saudi Arabia. She has studied till class seven in Myanmar and hails from an economically well-established family. That has helped her to get a relatively better location inside the camp. Her cousin sister's husband, at the time of this field study, was the Majhi of their block and Head Majhi of the entire Camp 9. A camp is divided into several blocks and each block is headed by a leader who is known as the Majhi. All the Majhis are under the Head Majhi, who is the chief leader or representative of the entire camp and directly interacts with the Camp-in-Charge (CIC) regarding any issue whatsoever inside the camp. Even a marriage within the camps can take place only if the Majhi takes permission from the CIC. The Majhi is not elected but selected. Usually, the Majhis are men and are better educated than most within the community. As a result, they get a position of prominence.

> We do not have any problem here. We can at least sleep peacefully, pray, and eat with our lights on. This is something we could never imagine in Myanmar. Yes, I do miss my own home and the life we had there.... There are still many problems ... but not like there.... 13-year-old Jasmine[2]

Jasmine comes across as a shy, pretty and cheerful young girl who is both interested in education, like her cousin Sulaima, and is quite positive about getting married off in Australia, but she remains silent when asked the reason for such a belief. Both Jasmine and Sulaima were confident in their communications, albeit shy. Sulaima, aged 22, wife of the Head Majhi, and mother of three, had studied till class ten in Myanmar and used to work with the UNHCR there. She proudly showed me all her work certificates. Interestingly I did not understand every word that they were saying, but Sulaima could communicate with me directly in her broken English. There were, thus, empowered women like Sulaima and a young girl like Jasmine who oscillated between hope and despair. Class privileges set them apart from the teeming toiling mass of women inside most of the camps. Most are shrouded in obscurity and are not even aware of the right to have rights, or the voice to express choice. Most often, they were not allowed to speak without the presence of a male member of the family.

The following anecdote helps in understanding the gender dynamics that prevail in Bangladesh, especially the district where the camps are based. It was 9 pm on a warm March evening in Ramu, a subdistrict under Cox's Bazar, Bangladesh, when I returned from my day's work to my rented accommodation.[3] It took me roughly four to five hours daily by public transport to commute to and from the Rohingya camps situated in Ukhiya, in the district of Cox's Bazar. That day, it took longer because I left the camps at 4 pm to go to Cox's Bazar to meet an NGO worker, based in the main town area. All big NGOs and International NGOs (INGOs)[4] working on providing humanitarian assistance to Rohingya refugees in the camps of Bangladesh are based in the main town area of Cox's Bazar. This journey took one and a half hours and the discussion took another two hours, by which time it was 8 pm, and I got back to my room after another hour.[5] I was stopped by my landlady who wanted to alert me that one or two neighbours had complained about my work timings. I was perplexed and could not understand what that was supposed to mean, as Ramu is in itself a tourist area, though quiet, not desolate, and shops and the main market close to my room are open till very late. As an outsider, a non-citizen of Bangladesh, my work in the field was not only about interviews but also to understand the lives of the people, to witness their living process as much as I could, to observe and spend time with them and to build a relationship of trust. The landlady insisted that my neighbourhood was not used to women solo travellers, and returning so late in night gave rise to a number of speculations as to the nature of my work. Explanations of the geographical realities were futile.

This was a defining moment when I realized the clear distinction between being a researcher interested in ethnographic research of forced migrants or refugees and being a woman researcher, interested in the same set of things. Starting from unwritten rules that a woman is expected to conform to, to being weary of implications pertaining to meeting male interviewees without any aid, there were multiple moments of helplessness and anger during the research. I realized the gendered nature of ethnography and the vulnerability that characterizes women belonging to people with major social constraints, especially for refugee women. It is interesting how many female researchers 'decide' or rather get compelled to 'move to women' and make them the core respondents because of feeling 'discomfort' in their respective fields of research.[6]

The questions of security or protection in many instances were just used as pretext in concealing patriarchal subjugation.[7] Bangladesh has been termed as a country with 'classic patriarchy'. Social life there is still characterized by extremely restrictive gender roles. There is prevailing rigid gender segregation, 'and a powerful ideology linking family honour to female virtue. Men are entrusted with safeguarding family honour through their control over female members; they are backed by complex social arrangements which ensure the protection —and dependence—of women' (Kabeer 1988).[8]

Thus within the general situation of Bangladeshi women, refugee women represent a figure of the doubly marginalized. In particular, women among the Rohingyas hardly enjoy autonomy to make choices or take decisions. They led a closeted life in Myanmar, with denial of basic rights like education. My primary aim was thus to locate whether a voice of dissent was slowly rising in a more closeted, yet 'open' existence as that of a camp.[9] Or was the subjugation fiercer than ever before? While the narratives of victimization are not very hard to gauge, this piece will try to throw light on the courage and valour of some women that I have met in ten camps who are not mere victims or silent spectators but survivors in the truest sense of the term. Their resilience and courage defying all odds might not be successful every time but their everyday struggle and quest for survival are revealed through snippets of conversations and narratives.

This account is largely based on my field experience in the Bangladesh Rohingya Refugee Camps in Ukhiya and Teknaf in the first half of 2019. This essay is divided into three parts. In Part I, I have written about the women I have met in the camps and the current situation. I have also narrated my experience and interactions with NGO employees working with women in the camps. Many awareness sessions are organized inside the camps in order to educate the women on reproductive health and to provide psychological assistance in case of harassments or sexual advances. Interaction with female NGOs working in this context is particularly interesting as their experiences often reinforce gender biases and the thwarting of voices across communities and continents. In Part II, I have tried to sketch a historical background of the Rohingya in Myanmar and their historical persecution and flight to countries like Bangladesh and India in search of asylum. In Part III, I discuss the situation of Rohingya women held as illegal migrants in Indian prisons.

I THE CURRENT SITUATION IN BANGLADESH

Bangladesh has been housing the Rohingya since the 1970s. In 1978 almost 200,000 Rohingya refugees fled to Bangladesh. By April 1992, another 300,000 had joined them. At that time 20 camps were built and later dismantled. Only two had remained: Nayapara camp near Teknaf and Kutupalong camp in Ukhiya, housing 21,621 refugees. The rest were repatriated.[10] These two camps are the only two official refugee camps administered by the UNHCR. The influx, however, continued informally, and after a fresh exodus, a massive influx of Rohingya, an estimated 745,000 Rohingya (as of January 2019) started from 25 August 2017. This date is now termed by the Rohingya living in Bangladesh camps as 'genocide day'.[11] As a result, Bangladesh is now hosting 1 million Rohingya in formal and informal camps, creating the world's largest refugee settlement and a humanitarian crisis in Bangladesh. This has evoked a humanitarian response and the involvement of a number of international and local non-governmental organizations with UNHCR and the International Organization of Migration (IOM) at the helm. The humanitarian response platform has in particular given importance to preventing sexual violence on women and children and to create a safe environment for them within the camps. Prospects of employment have also increased. Although there is no system of formal education in the camps, there are sessions organized by UN women in collaboration with local NGOs. Many local NGOs too have separate programmes of safe centres for young girls and women.

According to a UN report in collaboration with the humanitarian assistance platform created to respond to the Rohingya crisis in Bangladesh, published in February 2019, 52 percent of the total refugee populations are women and girls and 16 percent of families are female headed. Girls (57 percent) represent a larger and more vulnerable group as they are more exposed to sexual abuse, child marriage, child trafficking, abuse and neglect. The report mentions that though initial aid from the government to resettle the refugees after August 2017 was swift, there still remain numerous gaps, especially relating to the gender protection sector. One of the key recommendations made by the report was to include and train men and adolescent boys 'to promote positive masculinities and gender equality as a strategy to end gender-based violence' (UN and UNHCR 2019). In order to promote leadership among women, and equal representation within the camps, various women's groups and men's groups are being formed in the camps to make them audible on protection issues. There are active initiatives to involve Rohingya women as volunteers in the following:

- Health Sector as assistants in health facilities and as assistants to midwives and doctors.
- The Sector of Wash, as hygiene promoters to generate awareness regarding safe drinking water, use tube wells and promotion of latrine use.
- Protection Sector, as team members in the Protection Emergency Response Units, to provide basic first aid, search and rescue.[12]

Despite measures like these, implementation and involvement of women have been daunting tasks. There are both external and internal restrictions. External being sufficient income opportunities have not been created for women. For instance, Anwara (24), housed in Camp 9, Balukhali, said,

'I know sewing and have a machine too [that I could see], but I mostly stitch our own clothes. Why doesn't she sell the products? She said, 'I want to but I do not have resources to make something in order to sell. I have asked a few NGO workers to help many times but no one has helped so far. I send my daughter to the skill training sessions that the NGOs organize here, but she says they don't do skill training. Sometimes there are workshops but that will not help us. Even if we know what to do the question is how to do it. We are not used to working outside or to make things for sale.'

What I could understand by talking to her and getting many such similar accounts is that child marriage and early pregnancy resulting in big families, without even basic education, mark the lives of most

Rohingya women, if not all. Low levels of literacy particularly within women and gender norms that restrict many women from public spaces or from taking a public role, pose the biggest challenge for women to work inside the camps even if there are more opportunities now than what they used to get in Myanmar. Many of them even face difficulty in accessing the latrines because they are built far from home. Most women I met confirmed that there were more opportunities in the camps for them to work as compared to Myanmar, but most often they were not allowed to explore these by the male members. Even now, when they are trying to earn to help the male members in the family, they do not get assistance or support. While some do manage by teaching in schools or with INGOs like the UNHCR or IOM, there are internal restrictions from the families themselves.

Ali Aham (52 years) has six daughters. They are a family of eight members, including his wife. He is extremely poor and illiterate, for which reason he has not managed to get any work in the camp, unlike some of his neighbours. They are dependent only on the ration provided by World Food Programme. I wanted to talk to his daughters on their lives inside the camps, but it was Ali who kept on answering on their behalf. They hail from Maungdaw in Myanmar, Rakhine state. His elder daughters are twins, aged 18 years, and the youngest daughter is four. He had a business of dry fish in Myanmar, but after they left the country in a rush, penniless, following the major crackdown in 2017, he has not been able to start afresh in Bangladesh. Unlike many Rohingyas living in the camps, Ali had not been to Bangladesh before; hence he has no contacts with anyone who could help him with capital to resume work. Additionally, he is extremely worried as he does not have a son who could support him and the daughters 'are gown up, already passed the age of marriage but I am unable to get them married off without arranging for dowry the groom asks for'. I was surprised. Since everyone had to leave behind their resources in Myanmar, how would he arrange for any money and gifts like gold that they usually give when a daughter gets married in Myanmar?

> They do not understand, Didi. So many prospective grooms and their fathers have come to see my daughters but because I am poor and cannot arrange anything at the moment, apart from the marriage ceremony, they are not willing to take my daughters. How can I arrange for gold and cash

when I am not even able to provide adequate food to the family? The ration is not enough as we get only rice, dal and sugar. You tell me how someone can survive without vegetables or fish and meat which we are used to having. Is it possible to eat rice and dal every day? Others here earn money somehow or the other or they sell off their extra packets of rice and dal to buy vegetable or fish and meat but the ration that I get is not even sufficient.

I asked why doesn't he let his daughters work then? There are so many opportunities in the camps now for young girls and women to get informal education or work.

My daughters are not educated and I will never allow them to study. Our religion does not allow that. I will not even let them go out, especially the eldest ones as they are quite grown up and should stay indoors, covering themselves well. Our women are not allowed to go outside or earn money; that is prohibited in our religion.

My attempts to talk to the girls were not much successful as although they kept staring at me with eager eyes, their father was strict and vigilant to make sure they did not talk. One of the daughters, aged seven, was eager to talk, and I asked her whether she goes out to the women friendly spaces—one was built right next to their shelter— which prompted me to ask the question. 'I and my younger sisters go there. We really like going there. The women teach us, allow us to play, we can sing too there.' At this point Ali snubbed her by asking her to stop. Then he told me,

I have till now allowed three of my daughters to go to this centre because they are not adults yet but I will not allow them to continue as I am already receiving threats from our maulavi, who does not want the daughters to step out. The camps are filled with many outsiders. There are so many male NGO workers. Often, they try to be friendly with our daughters, marriages are taking place. But, I will never let my daughters go out and be friends with men. I am a god-fearing person and cannot allow something that our religion does not permit.[13]

While there are many families like this in the camp where the men in the family do not allow the women to go out on pretext of religious restrictions, in other instances there are threats from outside. People were scared to name the 'outsider' but I met a brave girl, Arifa (name changed) who told me how members of Arakan Rohingya Salvation Army (ARSA) will not allow girls to go out and work. Opinions regarding the role of ARSA within the Rohingyas are very divided. While most activists who believe in democracy and restoration of peace and even most Rohingyas are not supportive of ARSA,[14] the latter does still enjoy considerable support. Arifa was teaching Burmese in a school built by a local NGO, close to her home. My interaction with some of the NGO workers on their work in the education sector led me to Arifa (17) who has studied till standard nine in Myanmar. Arifa belongs to an educated family and her elder brother is also working with an NGO. Her family was supportive when she got the job in school for 8000 Bangladeshi taka. But after few months, she said,

> My father started getting threat calls to stop me from working. Then one night a group of four or five men came and told my father if I do not stop working the consequences would not be good. I was still adamant of not leaving work as security is much better in the camps, but then I got a call recently and the man told me if I still continue to work then they will kidnap and kill me. On hearing this, my parents and brother got very scared and that is when I left my job. I have told this to my school authority but reporting to the administration will be risky as they might harm me or my family. Although there is security in the camps, after 5pm till the next morning there are no guards or protection. That is when all incidents take place in the camps.[15]

Despite incidents like the ones mentioned above, Rohingya activist and Human Rights lawyer Razia Sultana grew up in Bangladesh and founded the Rohingya Women Welfare Society. She is a member of a number of voluntary groups within the camps. She received the International Women of Courage Award 2019. Razia hails from a rich and influential family in Myanmar and has citizenship status in Bangladesh. She has drawn flak from a few within her community and some gender-based organizations in Bangladesh. She has emphasized on the need for education among the women and awareness regarding family planning. She presented me with two of her reports on serving rape victims in the camps by counselling and emotionally supporting them. She argued,

Systematic use of rape has been organized by the Myanmar Army as a weapon against the Rohingya over the years and especially in August 2017. My own research and interviews provide evidence that government troops raped well over 300 women and girls in 17 villages in Rakhine state. With over 350 villages attacked and burnt since August 2017, this number is likely only a fraction of the actual total number of women raped. Such scale and breadth provide strong evidence that rape was systematically planned and used as a weapon against our people. As you might be aware, the life of the Rohingya women in the camps is quite difficult. They not only face the general hardship of insufficient food, shelter and healthcare for their families, but also face their own specific problems relating to reproductive health and gender-based violence. Since the authority in the camps is exclusively men, the specific needs of women are never prioritised.

There are some small centres like women friendly spaces but their functioning is extremely limited. They do not focus on building skill as most NGOs do not get funds for the same. The most important issue that hardly gets enough attention is the psychological trauma that many rape victims are still facing. The daily hardship of trying to survive in the overcrowded refugee camps is compounding this trauma. Specific programmes are needed to provide the women, not only victims, but all of them, with an environment of freedom where they can be free to voice out their own difficulties. The issue of privacy for the women in makeshift camps is another major area of concern. In their eagerness to break free and find a better place to live, they are falling prey to traffickers on tropes of marriage, job, and so on. Especially, the camps are not secure for young girls as despite stringent rules by the Government of Bangladesh, child marriages and prostitution are taking place. I have been also organizing campaigns to generate awareness on reproductive health and birth control measures, but even if some women are convinced and willing to accept pills, there is a dearth of supply.[16]

She added that often she has received questions from the men of her community; to quote her again, 'You are a Muslim woman, why are you doing these things? It is written in the Quran that women should not do these things.' To which I asked them to show me where is it written? I think they are interpreting it differently and I believe that women work even in Saudi Arabia, so why cannot we work?[17] Rohingya women leaders like her, she added, 'fight dowry, child marriage, domestic violence, polygamy, as well as conflict-related sexual and gender-based violence in order to overcome barriers as Rohingya girls and women and fight for promotion of their rights to justice, decision-making and economic opportunities'.[18]

On 16 July 2019, UN Women Bangladesh in partnership with Oxfam and Action Aid along with several other organizations collaborated to invite the UN Resident Coordinator and organized a gathering of Rohingya women leaders from new and old camps, representing their different networks and self-help groups in order to discuss common challenges, issues, demands and how to create a woman's platform or network to address these issues in order to foster gender equality and the empowerment of women and young girls.[19] These initiatives indicate how despite odds and barriers Rohingya women in the camps are better off in terms of their awareness of rights, as compared to what it was like in Myanmar. Some of them are trying hard to break away from their shackles.

The women whom I met in Camp 14, Hakimpara, embody emancipation. Hakimpara in Camp 14 is a widow block. I heard about Shaufika (24),[20] a woman leader of the widow block, and went to speak with her. I was surprised by her grit and strength. She is not a widow. Her husband is incarcerated in a prison of Myanmar and has sent her two letters to the camps with help from the Bangladesh Red Crescent Society. She had to flee Myanmar with her two children, with her neighbours, after the exodus in August 2017. That was when her husband was arrested and others of her family were killed. Shaufika is not educated but is learning new skills now. She was a housewife in Myanmar and never had to bother about feeding her family or about earnings. The changed situation has not caused her to break down but rather to take an active role in starting a new chapter of her life here. She has become the leader of the widows in her block, trains them on her sewing machine and earns money by selling hand-knitted garments like dresses and shawls, to make lives better for her children. Many like Shaufika dream of getting their children out of the camps to get educated and live a different life than theirs, be it in Myanmar or inside the camps.

Sipping my tea made by Shaufika and chatting with her and other widows from Hakimpara over biscuits and warm hospitality, I was impressed by the courage and strength of these women. Most of the young widows in the block have lost their husbands in the 2017 crackdown in Myanmar, but still they have not lost hope or surrendered to their fate by living only off the rationing provided by the government. Rather, many of them are striving to earn so that they can keep capital for their children and make their future secure outside the camps. One of them recently told me how they can now write their name or count numbers.

> We never got any opportunity in Myanmar to educate ourselves, but now that we are getting the chance here and NGO leaders and activists are trying to help us, we are extremely happy as this is the first time we are feeling important. We now feel we have a role too in making choices or take decisions and bring our children up in the absence of our husbands or any male figure in the family. This is a boon in disguise for us. Many men inside the camps are unable to accept this but since the NGOs are helping and providing protection to us, we have got the courage to come out and be leaders ourselves,' one of the widows from Hakimpara told me.[21]

The men and the community believe strange myths regarding the women spaces in the camps. Generally, my experiences with INGOS and NGOS working on the Rohingyas have been that they do not share any data on the services they are providing to and for women, especially the services rendered within a 'women friendly space' are kept guarded, maybe for protecting the victims. So in a way it is difficult for a researcher to elicit any information from any INGO/NGO representatives on this, especially on the services being provided to women who have been victims of sexual and gender-based violence (SGBV) in Myanmar. I felt that they could have at least easily shared the community services they provided.

I first tried speaking to the representatives in Camp 9, Balukhali 1, 'women friendly space' by a local NGO called DAC. But the woman in charge said she could not interact owing to official policy. She was courteous enough to invite me inside while she discussed with her seniors based in Cox's Bazar, whether she could speak to me; the response was a denial. There was a kitchen inside and through informal chitchats I learnt that the camp inmates cooked and often ate together or took back food to their families. So an ambience of relaxation and harmony was being attempted in order to promote community programmes. Since I could not talk to the representative or the women inside the space, I tried speaking to some of the women and girls in the neighbourhood who might be going to the place.

I could talk to three (young girls between 7 to 12 ages, approximately) from the same family who shared that they are taught how they can protect themselves from eve teasing inside the camps and take measures in case they are attacked or touched inappropriately. So measures to combat are being offered apart from psychological counselling.

In Camp 7, I went to another women-friendly space by the NGO Pulse and IOM. Here, the IOM representative who was also the safe space supervisor or woman in charge spoke to me because my interpreter was a close friend. She said this space was meant to provide relaxation and rest to women and children. They taught the women handicraft, IT and sewing. I was shown some beautiful handicrafts and bags made by the camp inmates. Under IT, the women were being taught basic computer skills. There was also a television set inside one if the rooms, I even saw it, but the person in-charge denied it, saying the sound was coming out from a nearby place. They also provided snacks and thami[22] to new Rohingyas. She said around 60 to 70 women visited this place on a daily basis. There were also awareness programmes on trafficking, art therapy, dance and music sessions. However, male resistance continued in the sending of women to these spaces. Patriarchy, fear of religion and the military regime in Myanmar too have contributed in limiting the role of women. Their mobility was restricted to save them from being kidnapped or raped by the military. It is imperative at this juncture to delve briefly on the history of the Rohingyas in Myanmar and their persecution in order to understand the dilemmas of a completely deracinated community.

II BRIEF BACKGROUND: WHO ARE THE ROHINGYA?

In contexts like that of South Asia, as mentioned earlier, often the existing categories of transnational population flows/migration/forced migrations/asylum seekers/economic migrants as categories get blurred in practice. How do we address the question of law in this context that incarcerates the 'illegal' migrant most often than the trafficker? How do we deny the agency of migrants who want to cross borders posing a 'threat' to nation states and ignore the historical or geographical contexts of such drives? Can we ever solve the paradox that states in trying to securitize their borders de-securitize their borderland residents, viewing them as suspects as if confining them in a panopticon?[23] Can we address or offer a solution to the plight of millions fleeing home, both in Europe and in South Asia, for instance, the Rohingyas, living a precarious existence for being 'stateless' through a domestic law in Myanmar? The root cause of Rohingya persecution stems from their lack of citizenship in Myanmar and the colonial history of partition dividing territories and loyalties.

Burma, as the earlier name of Myanmar under British rule, is the largest of the Southeast Asian states. It is located strategically, flanked by an economic giant like China and growing economies like India, Thailand and Malaysia. A former prime minister, U. Nu, had thus remarked once, 'We are hemmed in like a tender gourd among the cactus' (Steinberg 2010: 3). Historically, and before the great partition, Indians and Chinese were economically very powerful, which had made them dominant over the indigenous people, causing resentment among most Burmese. The vast natural resources in Myanmar have been a major source of attraction to the neighbouring countries, triggering often regional rivalry. China's deep influence in the country has been a bone of contention for India, since India has been trying to establish trade relations with the Southeast Asian countries, for which Myanmar is crucial.

The thousand-year history of Burma has proved to be the bedrock of the unfolding current scenario. Azeem Ibrahim writes that until 1784, the histories of Arakan and Burma were largely separate. This history is important to understand the contemporary situation of persecution, basing on who lived in Arakan when it was conquered by the British in 1826 (Ibrahim 2016). However, he contends that it should not determine the basis of exclusion or violence which has compelled the Rohingyas to flee to neighbouring countries. Population settlement in Chittagong in the late eighteenth century was managed by the East India Company. The population that was to be settled was termed in revenue records as 'Arakanese Refugees'. The settlement of these refugees by the company was a 'mix of military and economic combinations of viewing space predicated on ideas of usefulness and peculiarities of refugee labour' (Sen 2015: 1). After 1784, the Ava kingdom (i.e., Myanmar–Kon-Baung dynasty) expanded into Arakan and refugee influx had escalated to a great degree. This continued throughout the last years of the eighteenth century, when around 30,000 to 40,000 people 'streamed into Chittagong in these three years' (ibid.). Chittagong had been under the Marak U. dynasty since the sixteenth century. It became a frontier unit of Bengal in 1761. Throughout the late eighteenth century several waves of people settled there and moved 'to and fro between Chittagong Hills and Arakan (ibid.). In the sixteenth and seventeenth centuries, the kingdom of Arakan had expanded to Chittagong. The situation changed after Burma's occupation of Arakan in 1785.

Burma had invaded parts of India, leading to the first Anglo-Burmese wars, followed by a long period of pacification. Its inclusion as a province of India during the colonial rule till 1937 had dire consequences for many people in the years to come. Following the independence of India and Pakistan in 1947, Burma became independent in 1948 (Steinberg 2010: 5).

After the Anglo-Burmese War, Burma was forced to sign the Treat of Yandabo (1826) which resulted in the confiscation of Arakan by the British, facilitating multiple cross-border movements between Bengal and Arakan.[24] Apparently, the word 'Rohingya' is derived from *Rohang*, the ancient name for Arakan. Historically, the people belong to a community that was developed from many stocks of people including Burmese, Arabs, Moors, Persians, Bengalis and others. They are supposed to be an ethnic blend of indigenous Hindu populations and the Mongols who arrived in the ninth century (Yegar 1972). The relationship between the Muslims residing in the northwestern part of Arakan and the Buddhists in central and southern Arakan was tense, because these refugees were settled by the British for their own economic interests (Basu Raychaudhuri and Samaddar 2018: 6). At present, Buddhists constitute the ethnic majority in the Arakan region and speak a Burmese dialect.

During the ninth century, the Arakan region along with the neighbouring Chittagong region of southeastern Bengal (today's Bangladesh) came into contact with Muslim Arab merchants. Rohingyas claimed to be descendants of those first Muslims and they established themselves as an ethnically distinct group because they were genealogically mixed with Bengalis, Persians, Mughals, Turks and Pathans who came later to settle there. They have many etymological similarities and bear resemblance with the Bengalis in Chittagong district, in terms of customs, traditions and religion (*Human Rights Watch* 1996; Karim 2000).

Burma became a British colony on 1 January 1886. The British ruled Burma as a part of India from 1919 until 1937 when Burma was made a crown colony of Britain. As the British began to establish their control over the territory, there was massive immigration of male workers, mostly as seasonal agricultural workers, from Chittagong to Arakan. Till the Second World War these two communities of the Burmese and the Rohingyas lived in harmony and did not show any sign of enmity and hostility. In 1942 when Japan attacked Burma, the first communal clashes broke out in Arakan between Rakhine Buddhists and Rohingya Muslims (Smith 1991). After independence, under the new constitution of 1974, the name Arakan was changed to 'Rakhine' in a bid to preserve the Buddhist culture, which has been also perceived by many as a step towards erasing the Islamic culture and history of the Muslims like Rohingyas living there.

In 1978, a military operation code named 'Ye The Ha' was launched in the mountains of north Arakan around the Sittwe plains, together with an unusual census operation to check identity papers in the border region for the first time.[25] These operations in 1978 forced some 200,000 Muslims to live elsewhere, especially in the neighbouring country of Bangladesh, formed in 1971 (Lintner 1991). This was the first exodus. Then, in 1982, the Burmese government framed a new citizenship law. Under this act, three categories of citizens—national, associate and naturalized—were created. Full citizenship in Burma was henceforth only for national ethnic groups, such as the Burmans, Mons or Rakhines, or those who could prove that their ancestors had resided in Burma before the first Anglo-Burmese war.[26] This was a daunting task for most Muslim residents like the Rohingyas.

This Act also excluded the Rohingyas from the 13 recognized national ethnic groups in Myanmar. Hence the Rohingya Muslims were stripped off their citizenship rights and as a result they became *stateless*. So, effectively, they became a stateless population in 1982 with the creation of the revised Myanmar Citizenship Law. They could still have continued to live within the geographical territories of Myanmar had they been not persecuted to the extent of leaving their land to seek refuge in neighbouring countries like Bangladesh and India. This has triggered new waves of mass population movement across the borders between Myanmar–Bangladesh–India. Since the Indian subcontinent was partitioned in 1947, the borders have witnessed continuous trans-border and internal migration caused by ethnic violence, economic compulsions and other factors. The borders dividing India, Bangladesh and Myanmar in the postcolonial period are porous, defying their governments to control population flows. Illegal migration has also inevitably increased manifold, due to the long complex processes of formal mobility, resulting in trafficking and smuggling nexuses.

The argument that the Rohingyas are actually Bengali immigrants who had entered Myanmar during British rule has been widely claimed and reinforced through the constitution by Burmese officials in order to exclude them from the history of Myanmar. Partha Ghosh (2016) has traced this historical context of the pre-partition mobility that actually forms the basis of their marginalization when the new state of Myanmar was created in 1948. He also documents the migration of people, who are now citizens of India, to erstwhile Burma before and after the partition, that is, from the period of colonial rule to the post-independent era.[27] Migration from India to Burma was frequent and on a regular basis after 1852. Before 1937, there were about 900,000 Indians working in various fields in Burma and every living resident was by default considered as a member of the country. Things however changed after Myanmar's independence in 1948, when the new citizenship law entailed a proof of ancestry from before 1823 and Burmese was made the official language. This one step took away the right of an entire Rohingya population to claim citizenship from the state, rendering them as non-citizens, devoid of a state, since the Rohingyas are not considered as original settlers of the land and speak the language 'Bengali', derived from the Chittagongian dialect, which is different from the official language of the state. While many Indians living in Myanmar during the pre-independence era came back, particularly Tamil refugees, others continued to live there in a life of extreme precarity, in a kind of a void, devoid of nationality and voice. There are more reasons why the Rohingyas could not continue to live albeit as stateless people within the geographical boundaries of Myanmar and were persecuted to the extent of the history of their existence in Myanmar being eradicated.

Arakan is the westernmost state of Myanmar and is now officially known as the Rakhine state. Its geographical location is extremely strategic. It borders Chin state to the north, Magway, Bago and Ayewardy in the east, Bay of Bengal in the west and Chittagong District (now in Bangladesh) in the northwest. Rakhine has four districts, 17 townships and 3,871 villages, according to a government report published by Myanmar in 2001. It has an area of more than 36,000 sq. km and is located in the tri-junction of Myanmar, India and Bangladesh. There are primarily two major groups, namely, the Rakhine ethnic group and the Rohingya ethnic group inhabiting the region for centuries. The Government Divisional Administration (2011) has estimated that there are about 1,033,212 Rohingya population in Arakan state. The Buddhists constitute the majority and Muslims are the second-largest group in Arakan. The Census Report (2015) of the Government of Myanmar estimates that there were about 2,045,559 people in Arakan State in 1983, which increased to 3,188,807 in 2014. But it excluded the non-enumerated Muslim population and showed only 2,098,807 people in 2014 excluding 1,090,000 people. The data in Table 6.1 show that the density of population increased from 56 persons in 1983 to 57 in 2014; only 1 person has increased in 31 years whereas with enumerated data the density has increased to 87 in the same year.

The district is also covered by a long range of deep mountains in the east that has kept the region isolated from the central region

Table 6.1. Absolute Population of Rakhine State from 1973

Rakhine	Years			
	1973	1983	2014*	2014
Population	1,712,838	2,045,559	2,098,807	3,188,807
Density	47	56	57	87

* signifies that the non-enumerated population was excluded.
Source: Department of Population, Government of Myanmar (2015).

of the Republic of the Union of Myanmar. Its accessibility by sea with Bangladesh is greater than its access to the rest of Myanmar. Even today a communication system is scarce between the centre and Rakhine state, rendering it till now a remote and underdeveloped district compared to other regions in Myanmar. However, this is changing now and that is exactly the reason why of late systematic violence against the Rohingyas has increased. China has taken an active part in developing the infrastructure of Rakhine state. It has started new investments there, for instance, a multibillion project of Kyaukphyu Special Economic Zone (SEZ) that involves building a deep seaport and industrial park. On the one hand, in November 2010, the China Development Bank and Myanmar Foreign Investment Bank have signed a $2.4 billion loan deal to construct a 1,060 km pipeline from Kyaukphyu to Kunming province in China. On the other hand, in April 2008, India has signed a Framework Agreement for facilitating the Kaladan Multi-modal Transport project with Myanmar, as part of its 'Look East Policy'. This project aims to connect Kolkata with Sittwe port in Myanmar through the Bay of Bengal. All these projects have made Rakhine state economically an attractive option to the neighbouring provinces of Myanmar.

The crackdown of the Rohingyas in August 2017 in response to Rohingya militants attack on the army base there, has resulted in a crisis in Bangladesh. Although the government of Bangladesh and people had opened their homes and hearts initially, recently tension is increasing. There are ample reports of violence inside the camps, although not all are tested or proven. A few government officials I could speak to unofficially expressed their discontent on not being able to repatriate the Rohingyas till now. They had believed the influx to be temporary. For instance, a top official of the Refugee Relief and Rehabilitation Commission said,

> This cannot be a long-term solution. When we opened our homes and hearts to the refugees, we had thought they could be repatriated back in a year, however, it's already two years now and the repatriation process too has failed. We do not know what would be the solution, as for a small country like us it is difficult to sustain one million refugees, in addition to our own population. The neighbouring countries in South Asia and Myanmar along with big international powers should come together and either provide the Rohingyas with citizenship status in Myanmar

or think of other alternatives, as Bangladesh cannot go on housing them forever.[28]

The greatest fear that the refugees in Cox's Bazar have is that they might become victims once again to a renewed wave of violence. In the last two years, the Bangladesh government has been determined to repatriate the refugees, but the process has not been fruitful till now. In August 2019, another attempt at repatriation failed. Although the Bangladesh government has acted in a much more humane manner after the August 1917 violence, patience appears to be dwindling. The country had signed a repatriation agreement with Myanmar in November 2017, the vague terms of which have triggered fear among the refugees that they will be pushed again to a life of unsafe precarity.

III AS ILLEGAL MIGRANTS

The vulnerability of the West Bengal–Bangladesh border becomes even clearer with a visit to the Balurghat Correctional Home in South Dinajpur in India, a place very low in development with poor transportation and remote in terms of accessibility. South Dinajpur is basically a part of the West Dinajpur district which has been created out of the erstwhile Dinajpur district during the partition of India in 1947. The rest of the Dinajpur district is now in Bangladesh. Partition suddenly divided the region into two countries but the socio-cultural similarities across the border could hardly be over-emphasized. It is surrounded from three sides by Bangladesh, one side by Malda and one by North Dinajpur. As a result, the nearest border point of South Dinajpur—Hili—is an important point of trade between the two countries. According to a local news report of Balurghat,[29] because Dakshin Dinajpur is surrounded by Bangladesh on three sides it is through here infiltrators enter. It is mainly Rohingya Muslims who enter through this border apart from regular Bangladeshis (Bhaumik 2013). They are a stateless community within Myanmar, as mentioned earlier, because of a citizenship law in 1982. The Rohingyas thus enter India through Bangladesh, via Chittagong and Cox's Bazar.

Although the UNHCR has been issuing refugee cards to the Rohingyas in order to give them refugee status, they are being arrested and put behind bars for illegal infiltration. The major problem regarding the Rohingyas is that there is a general lack of awareness among the authorities concerned regarding the policy to be followed. Often the persons who are caught do not even divulge their true identity and declare themselves as Bangladeshi, thinking that this might go in their favour. According to a news report, a person was arrested recently for being suspected as a terrorist as he could speak seven different languages. However, on being caught he said that he was a Rohingya and after police interrogation declared himself to be a resident of Kolkata.[30] Another report stated of an increasing involvement of school students and youth in illegal business in the border areas, particularly in Dhalpara Pagyul and other villages under Hili Gram panchayat.[31] Cows, Phensedyl, spices and drugs like heroin are smuggled rampantly through the Hili border, and women are often used as carriers, according to the Day Jail superintendant, K. Ghosh.

At the time of this research, Balurghat Correctional Home had officially eight Rohingya women.[32] The women had come together in a group of 20 from Fanshi, Quarbil, Bali Bazar, Bugrishaw and Bohbazar areas of Rakhine District, Myanmar.[33] All of them, Noorjahan, Nurkalima, Belma, Mumtaz Begum, Samjhu Nahar, Manohara, Mabia Khatun and Fatema Khatun, said they were compelled to flee because of mass violence that was unleashed on them for a long time. Fresh ethnic violence erupted from 2001 that devastated them. Their children were not allowed to go to madrassas (educational institutions for Muslim children), they were not allowed to pray, and did not have freedom of movement. Some of these women have lost their husbands to brutal torture. They came through Chittagong in Bangladesh, via a long route to reach India, in order to go to Jammu where some of their relatives have settled in the Rohingya camps. The Dumdum Correctional Home and Behrampur Correctional Home now have a considerable number of Rohingyas and their fate is even graver than the Bangladeshi nationals since they are basically a stateless community who cannot be repatriated or sent back to their country as the Government of Myanmar does not recognize them as citizens and tries pushing them to Bangladesh. So repatriating them is difficult. Most of them claim their nationality as Bangladeshis but the differences in linguistic and cultural traits give them away easily. Therefore, even after a Rohingya becomes a *jaankhalash* (a released prisoner—an unnameable and unclassified being) he/she suffers in prisons till a decision is reached. For instance, Mumtaj Begum (30 years) has already spent a year and nine months in confinement in Balurghat. She has four children, all of whom are staying at two homes. Despite serving a prison term of 19 months she still remains an under-trial person without appearing even once at the court.

The Balurghat Correctional Home has however directly made contacts with the Delhi office of UNHCR in order to rehabilitate the Rohingyas in refugee camps, particularly those women who already have got refugee cards like Noorjahan. The Jail Superintendent is regularly in touch with the officials concerned in UNHCR, Delhi; the process again takes up a lot of time. The interesting thing is that Balurghat jail officials are trying this completely out of their personal initiative. But for the Rohingyas in other prisons, the wait is ceaseless. Some have spent almost two years in prison after release just because a consensus has not been reached regarding where and how they would be resettled.

CONCLUSION

Over the last few years, the Bangladesh government had decided to resettle registered Rohingyas in a different region as Cox's Bazar is primarily a tourist area and the smuggling-trafficking nexus in the region has led to a lot of anti-social activities, including drug smuggling. The place where the registered camps might shift to is a barren island called the Bhashanchar. It is Prime Minister Sheikh Hasina's desire that the Rohingya people be relocated, says the police chief of Hatiya, Mohammad Nazrul Huda.[34] The government, however, is silent about the fate of the unregistered refugees. Hence, despite being recognized as stateless or refugees by the UNHCR, the Rohingyas have been living in extreme adversity, sometimes even denied proper shelter. Some of them have received temporary refugee cards from the UNHCR, but have still been subjected to violation of basic human rights. While the registered Rohingyas in Bangladesh are comparatively better off in terms of receiving food and shelter from the UNHCR, sanctioned by the government, they live in appalling conditions, denied freedom of movement or access to sufficient food, water and sanitation. The government has now taken the initiative to distribute cards to families of registered refugees, with which they can buy the necessary quantity of food. This has been a positive development since previously only a fixed amount of food was distributed by the authorities per family. While the camp refugees we spoke to are happy with this step, it is not enough since there is a limit on the quantity a family can buy with the food cards. According to recent research (Refugees and Migratory Movements 2014), 17 percent of children below five were found to be suffering from malnutrition. Neither the registered Rohingya children nor the unregistered have access to formal education. Children of the registered camps can study till class seven in the official camps, following a Myanmar curriculum.

Article 33[1] of the 1951 Refugee Convention also clearly states that refugees or asylum-seekers cannot be returned to the territory where their lives are under threat. This refers not only to the country of origin from where they are fleeing, but also includes the territory where they might face a threat to security:

> Rescued persons who do not meet the criteria of the 1951 Refugee Convention definition of a 'refugee', but who fear torture or other serious human rights abuses or who are fleeing armed conflict may also be protected from return to a particular place (*refoulement*) by other international or regional human rights or refugee law instruments.

This is applicable even for maritime migrants if they are asylum seekers. Clearly a violation of rules repeatedly has occurred with the Rohingyas even when they have been recognized by international organizations as refugees. Even recently, the decision of the Government of India to deport seven Rohingyas violates international laws.[35] Is going back at all an option, when till now the government of Myanmar has not guaranteed a safe life to them? Will a return without the promise of a citizenship status hold any meaning?

States concerned feign ignorance of the plight of the Rohingyas. Pushing back Rohingyas travelling either over land or sea has been the policy followed by most governments. As a result many Rohingyas have either perished in the seas or have been living in detention camps as bonded labourers along the Thai-Malaysian border. On the other hand, when it comes to employing people in the most labour-intensive industries, it is the Rohingyas who are chosen. Thus, the expansion of a well-knit trafficking network, connecting Myanmar, Thailand, Indonesia, Malaysia and Bangladesh to take innocents on perilous journeys was with the bait of providing work opportunities. The sea is the most accessible route since Rohingya settlements in Bangladesh are mainly in Cox's Bazar, which is a coastal area. While young men are trafficked to Thailand, Philippines and Malaysia and robbed, women and children are increasingly being trafficked for sexual exploitation to these countries and to India. Economic considerations are major pull factors for young boys, since they are not allowed to work in Bangladesh, even if they are registered with the UNHCR.

A media report argues that the Rohingyas are branded by many countries as illegal infiltrators', but unless they are provided with citizenship, this will persist. The problem also is that the concept of statelessness is not recognised by international law.[36] Martin Stiller, a lawyer from Vienna, having written his thesis on statelessness says that 'even if it is frowned upon by many countries and international organizations, statelessness isn't forbidden by international law', adding that every country has the right to determine the requirements a person must fill to acquire nationality.[37] The Indian government categorically states that allowing Rohingya refugees to stay in India would lead to 'social unrest' in the country, to quote, 'the Muslim people who are fleeing Myanmar to escape what the United Nations has branded ethnic cleansing'.[38]

On 12 October 2018, India was elected to the United Nations' top human rights body, getting 188 votes, for a period of three years. It is ironical at this juncture as the same member states have consented to sign the global compact that looks at changing things in the Global South so far as refugee rights and protection are concerned. This would mean that even if India is not a signatory to the refugee conventions, it still has some moral responsibility owing to being a member of the human rights body. However, the current position of India on border issues, especially in the context of the Rohingyas, is quite grim. The electoral campaign of the current rightist government of India, the Bharatiya Janata Party, before coming to power in 2014, had issues concerning 'international borders' as one of the major focal areas. Prime Minister Narendra Modi had mentioned in the run up to the general elections that 'as soon as we come to power at the centre, detention camps housing Hindu migrants from Bangladesh will be done away with. We have responsibility towards Hindus who are harassed and suffer in other countries. Where will they go? India is the only place for them. Our government cannot continue to harass them. We will have to accommodate them here' (*Hindustan Times*, 3 September 2019). The situation, however, has only worsened. With patience wearing thin in both Bangladesh and India, what the future lies for the Rohingya is yet to be seen; however, the only one slim light of hope is the enlightenment of at least a few Rohingya women despite fierce protests of male patriarchy.

NOTES

1   By Bengal Borderland I mean the West Bengal–Bangladesh border.

2   Personal conversation with the author, 2 March 2019.

3   This fieldwork was part of my doctoral studies and was undertaken between January-April 2019.

4   I had visited the Rohingya camps in Bangladesh in 2015 too. But there are significant changes in Bangladesh's policy and overall scenario of refugee settlement after the massive influx of Rohingyas in August 2017. The place has grown to become a spectacle now, drawing researchers, journalists, NGO workers, care givers and so on from across the world. During my brief stay of three months, I had meetings with researchers and faculty members from some reputed institutes in Europe, besides Asia. This is a far cry from 2015 when I had first visited the camps. At that time there was minimal empathy towards the Rohingyas settling in Bangladesh for asylum or limited scope of formal camp access. The entire camp structure has undergone a massive change. Among the thirty plus camps, International Organization of Migration (IOM) is officially in charge of the unregistered camps because Bangladesh does not call the Rohingya living in camps as refugees but 'Unidentified Myanmar Nationals' (UNM).

5   I mention the hours here in order to point out the distances I normally covered in a day and the long hours spent to do justice to my field work in the Rohingya camps.

6   This is what I learnt from some of my fellow PhD female colleagues, on their field work experiences, that in order to avoid too caring or protective men as respondents, they decided to interact more with women. Any fieldwork certainly entails risks for a lone woman and most times as women we prepare ourselves to face that: from understanding the ground situation to changing our dressing pattern, understanding the local culture, and so on, are part of that preparation. However, until one is directly confronted with an unpleasant sexual advance or a similar situation like what I have mentioned above, one realizes no preparation is enough. Something

similar I found in the writing by a fellow researcher at https://medium. com/@documents.meenakshi/navigating-the-field-doing-fieldwork-as-a-woman-d77d3eebbb1f, accessed 3 September 2019.

7   For instance, there were concerned men who often cautioned against going unaided to the camps. While, security concerns are understandable, yet most times they were encroaching in privacy with their vigilance and interrogation regarding my appointments with interviewees. Often they would instruct who is important to meet and otherwise. This was a constant challenge that I had to deal with during my field work.

8   I have taken this from a concept note written by the Research Initiatives Bangladesh in June 2019 that was shared with me.

9   There are several constrictions, but not prevailing fear like in Myanmar, that paves way for freedom. The camps are like open prison, where freedom and obstructions, formal mobility and informal flows are part and parcel of the daily lives of people, including the women.

10   Paula Banerjee shared this information from her 2011 paper with me.

11   Information gathered from the field.

12   Information gathered from the field.

13   Interview with Ali on 10 March 2019, at Camp 9, Balukhali.

14   It was an attack by ARSA on a army base camp in Rakhine state that had triggered the violent exodus in August 2019.

15   Personal Interview on 14 March 2019 in Balukhali, Ukhiya.

16   Personal interview in March 2019. A version of this has been published recently in https://www.thequint.com/voices/opinion/rohingya-crisis-life-in-bangladesh-refugee-camps-as-seen-by-field-researcher, accessed 2 September 2019.

17   Ibid.

18   Ibid.

19   Information from Razia Sultana during one of our conversation on 3 August 2019.

20   I have taken her consent to use her name; interview taken on 10 March 2019.

21   Personal Interview on 10 March 2019.

22   Traditional dresses worn by Rohingya women.

23   In the eighteenth century, a building and a system of control designed by the English philosopher and social theorist Jeremy Bentham; the way it was designed supposedly allowed all prisoners to be watched by a single guard, and as the inmates believed they were being watched, they controlled their behaviour.

24   https://montrealserai.com/article/emergence-of-a-stateless-population-fleeing-rohingyas-of-myanmar/, accessed 2 September 2019.

25   Ibid.

26   Ibid.

27   The names Burma and Myanmar are at times used interchangeably in this paper without any political connotation. The Burmese government

changed the name of the country from Burma to Myanmar in 1989, but the older generation of people living in India or Burma, Bangladesh often refer to the country as Burma and not Myanmar, it is in that spirit that I have used the two words to denote the same place here.

28 Personal interview in March 2019. I have mentioned this in a media piece recently at https://www.thequint.com/voices/opinion/rohingya-crisis-life-in-bangladesh-refugee-camps-as-seen-by-field-researcher.

29 *Dakshin Dinajpur Barta*, 15 September 2014.

30 '*Satti bhasha jana Yusuf Islam ke Balurghat theke greptar*', *Antah Salila Falgu*, 2 November 2014.

31 '*Bidyalayer chhatra o kom boyeshi chhelera chokarbarer sathe jarito*,' *Antah Salila Falgu*, November 2014.

32 The research was conducted on 4 and 5 December 2014, the official entry was given till 4 December. The next day, five more women were brought but that was not updated officially at time of this research.

33 This data was given to us by the Balurghat District Correctional Home authorities.

34 http://www.economist.com/news/asia/21659769-oppressed-myanmar-muslim-rohingyas-are-unwelcome-bangladesh-too-exile-island?frsc=dg%7Cd, accessed on 28 August 2015.

35 'India to deport 7 Rohingyas to Myanmar Thursday', *The Economic Times*, 3 October 2018, https://economictimes.indiatimes.com/news/politics-and-nation/india-to-deport-7-rohingyas-to-myanmar-Thursday/articleshow/66055792.cms?utm_source=facebook.com&utm_medium=Social&utm_campaign=ETFBMain, accessed 2 September 2019.

36 https://www.dw.com/en/rohingya-crisis-demonstrates-consequences-of-statelessness/a-41212883, accessed 2 September 2019.

37 Ibid.

38 https://www.hindustantimes.com/india-news/the-world-s-most-persecuted-community-who-are-the-rohingyas/story-PgNwZ4URpdpMpZXNryw88I.html, accessed 3 September 2019.

REFERENCES

Agamben, Giorgio. 2005. *State of Exception*. Chicago, IL: University of Chicago Press.

Ahsan Ullah, A. K. M. 2011. 'Rohingya Refugees to Bangladesh', *Journal of Immigrant and Refugee Studies* 9: 152.

Banerjee, Paula. Unpublished paper, 2016. 'Rohingyas: The Archetypal Nowhere Community',

Basu, Raychaudhuri, Sabyasachi, and Ranabir Samaddar. 2018. *The Rohingya in South Asia*. New York: Routledge.

Bhaumik, Subir. 2013. 'The East Bengali Muslims in Assam and Rohingyas of Myanmar: Comparative Perspectives of Migration, Exclusion, Statelessness', *Refugee Watch: A South Asian Journal on Forced Migration* (June).

Department of Population, Government of Myanmar. 2015. *Census Report*, vol. 2. Myanmar: Government of Myanmar.

Ghosh, Partha. 2016. *Migrants, Refugees and the Stateless in South Asia*, New Delhi: SAGE. Department of Population, Government of Myanmar, Human Rights Watch. 1996. 'The Rohingya Muslims: Ending a Cycle of Exodus?'(1 September) https://www.hrw.org/report/1996/09/01/rohingya-muslims-ending-cycle-exodus accessed 2 September 2019.

Ibrahim, Azeem. 2016. *The Rohingyas inside Myanmar's Hidden Genocide*. London: Hurst.

Kabeer, Naila. 1988. 'Subordination and Struggle: Women in Bangladesh', *New Left Review* 1, 68.

Karim, A. 2000. *Rohingyas: A Short Account of Their History and Culture*. Chittagong: Arakan Historical Society.

Lintner, Bertil. 1991. 'Diversionary Tactics: Anti-Muslim Campaign Seen as Effort to Rally Burmans', *Far Eastern Economic Review* (Hong Kong), Proquest ABI / INFORM.

Mezzadra, Sandro. 2013. 'The Proliferation of Borders and the Right to Escape', *Refugee Watch: A South Asian Journal on Forced Migration*.

Paasi, Anssi. 1998. 'Boundaries as Social Processes: Territoriality in the World of Flows', *Geopolitics* 3, 1: 69–88.

Refugees and Migratory Movements Research Unit. 'Addressing the Plight of the Rohingyas Summary' in 'Labour Migration from Bangladesh: Achievements and Challenges', Annual Policy Brief (March), Dhaka: 2–3.

Samaddar, Ranabir. 2016. 'Forced Migration Situations as Exceptions in History', *International Journal of Migration and Border Studies* 2, 2.

———. 2015. 'Returning to the Histories', *EPW* (10 January): 49.

———. 1998. 'The Spectre Facing the Nation', in *The Marginal Nation: Transborder Migration from Bangladesh to West Bengal*. New Delhi: SAGE Publications, (p. 44).

Sen, Anandaroop. 2015. 'A Lost Population? East India Company and Arkanese "Refugees" in Chittagong', *Refugee Watch*. Kolkata: Calcutta Research Group.

Smith, Martin. 1999. *Burma: Insurgency and the Politics of Ethnic Conflict*. London: Zed Books.

Steinberg, David I. 2010. *Burma/Myanmar: What Everyone Needs to Know*. New York: Oxford University Press.

UN and UNHCR. 2019. Gender Profile No.2 for Rohingya Refugee Response, Prepared by the Inter Sector Gender in Humanitarian Action Working Group, under the Inter Sector Coordination Group, UN Women and UNHCR (February). Retrieved from https://drive.google.com/file/d/14z ASIR0SnzSuOxXKQSlEn92JSaS2yaj3/view, accessed 2 September 2019.

Yegar, Moshe. 1972. *The Muslims of Burma: A Study of a Minority Group*. Heidelberg: Sudasien-Institut, Heidelberg University.

PART II
MIGRATION AND ASSIMILATION

7

Female Migrants at the Doors of Fortress Europe: The Case of Slovenia

SANJA CUKUT KRILIĆ

MIGRANTS PLAY A crucial role in European labour markets. Demographers have pointed to the growing need for migrants in European societies because of ageing and low-fertility populations. But European governments have continuously attempted to limit migration into their national territories. Although a discourse on open Europe and the free movement of people is increasingly present in political debates and in the wider public, most researchers in migration studies would agree that one of the main characteristics of European Union migration policy is its increasing restrictiveness towards individuals from third countries. Harsh control over external borders, measures to curb immigration and limit the number asylum seekers and recognized refugees figure amongst the key elements of a migration regime that has often been labelled a 'European fortress'. The right to free movement and related social, economic and political rights are limited mainly to European Union nationals, which results in rising insecurity of third-country nationals.[1] Such insecurities are gendered, as female migrants may face particular insecurities, as current immigration and asylum policies are pushing them into situations in which they are at greater risk of experiencing numerous vulnerabilities (Freedman 2016; Zavratnik and Cukut Krilić 2018).

If migrants are defined by policy-makers and in public discourses in opposition to nationals, they are categorized as those that are non-belonging. Such a classification is one of the mechanisms through which migrants are restricted in their right to employment, social security, and political activity (Kofman et al. 2000). Promoting the integration of migrants is thus becoming an increasingly prominent issue in a growing number of European Union countries. Issues such as citizenship, social inclusion and exclusion, and the political and everyday strategies of migrants (Ali 2009) are now more current, whereas the economic aspects of migration had been the principal topic of focus in earlier migration studies.

Currently, at the international level, women represent almost half of all international migrants. It is in this respect that in the last few decades some researchers speak of the feminization of migration (Castles and Miller 2003; Freedman 2003). The reasons behind this trend are complex and varied, as Freedman (2003) points out. Particular effects of globalization, especially the feminization of poverty, manifested in the growing number of women in transnational domestic work and in the sex work industry, figure significantly in conditioning female' migratory trajectories. Additionally, the effects of restrictive migration policies are reinforced by an underlying public/private divide that confines women to the private realm and makes them dependent on the status of a male relative, not only in economic terms, but also in terms of their legal status in the new country (Freedman 2003). However, according to Kofman et al. (2000) the significance of women in migration to Europe lies not only in these increased numbers, but also through their contributions to economic and social life in the receiving countries.

Despite these trends, female migration experiences were often overlooked and/or studied in a stereotypical manner. Such classical studies of migration have adopted the premise that individuals migrating to Western Europe in the years after the Second World War were mainly single men migrating for economic reasons. Consequently, women as potential migrants were viewed almost exclusively as individuals migrating on grounds of family reunification, arriving after male migrants. Males were considered a prototype of a migrant, responsible not only for decisions regarding migration, but also acting as the main breadwinner in the family (Anthias 2000; Lazaridis 2000; Sharpe 2001). Women, if analysed at all, were perceived mostly in the family framework and in relation to their children, which perpetuated the stereotype of women migrants as primarily wives and mothers (Lazaridis 2000).

The main aim of this chapter is to correct such an omission of female migrants by focusing on understandings and experiences of women as actors of migration processes. In the empirical part, I focus on life stories of women from countries that once belonged to the Soviet Union and now reside in Slovenia.[2] In line with the increasing restrictiveness of migration from third countries to the European Union, I hold that female migrants' life courses are fundamentally shaped also by such migration policies. I suppose that migration policies in Slovenia contribute to insecurity and vulnerability of female migrants from third countries. Viewing female migrants as social actors will enable the analysis of strategies that women utilize to challenge such restrictive migration policy measures.

IMMIGRATION TO SLOVENIA: THE FRAMEWORK OF THE STUDY

The most characteristic pattern of immigration to Slovenia in the period from the end of the Second World War until the 1990s, when the dissolution of Yugoslavia occurred, were migrations from the former Yugoslavia republics, mostly from Bosnia and Herzegovina, but also from Croatia, Macedonia, Montenegro and Serbia. At that time, such migration was conceptualized as internal, not international migration. It is not an exaggeration to state that it was only after Slovenia acquired independence in 1991 that migration stakeholders started to frame immigration policies more systematically and explicitly at the national level (Zavratnik Zimic 2004, 2006). After 1991, immigration to Slovenia also became more diversified not only in terms of country of origin but also in terms of statistically recorded reasons for migration. With the process of Slovenia's accession into the European Union and the enforcement of the Schengen legal order, researchers in Slovenia increasingly studied the impact of European Union migration policy not only on migration policy in Slovenia, but also on human rights of individual migrants. They usually concluded that such a migration system enables greater mobility within the European Union, while severely limiting mobility of individuals from third countries and causing their social and economic insecurity (Hrovat et al. 2007; Pajnik and Bajt 2012, 2013; Pajnik and Zavratnik Zimic 2003; Zavratnik Zimic et al. 2003).

By studying the impact of the increasingly restrictive European Union migration policy on female migrants, this contribution is in line with findings of those researchers that have studied female migration in a wider European perspective (Kofman et al. 2000). Specific migration experiences of women have been overlooked not only on a European level, but also in Slovenia. Traditionally, female emigrants from Slovenia were studied much more extensively than women who immigrated to Slovenia. Although there was sporadic mention of female migrants in previous research, the lack of systematic engagement with the issue was apparent.[3] In the last decade, two international projects could be described as pioneering regarding the research on female migrants in Slovenia. These projects were entitled *FEMAGE* (*Needs for Female Immigrants and their Integration in Ageing Societies*) in which the Sociomedical institute of the Research Centre of the Slovenian Academy of Sciences and Arts was the Slovenian project partner, and *FeMiPol* (*Integration of Female Immigrants in Labour Market and Society–Policy Assessment and Policy Recommendations*), where the Peace Institute was the project partner in Slovenia. Both projects were conducted from 2006 to 2007. Among other issues, gender dimensions of migration policy in Slovenia were studied within the FeMiPol project (Pajnik et al. 2006a). Researchers have demonstrated that migration policy in relation to gender is formulated in a generalized manner without taking into account the specificity and vulnerability of women. In Slovenia, there exists a gap in studying the specific position of female migrants in public policy as well as in research. Both the interviews with key actors in migration policy within the framework of the FeMiPol project (Pajnik et al. 2006b) and the focus group with stakeholders in migration policy conducted within the FEMAGE project (Černič Istenič et al. 2007) reveal a strikingly similar picture. The recognition of the unique position of female migrants has not yet been placed on the agenda of migration policy stakeholders. However, in the last years, there has been a proliferation of research interest in female immigrants in Slovenia. Among the issues studied were the positioning of female migrants in informal care chains in providing paid domestic work (Hrženjak 2007, 2012; Šadl 2010, 2014) and there was also considerable interest in female immigrants' life stories (for instance, Antić Gaber 2011; Milharčič Hladnik and Mlekuž 2009).

The main rationale behind the decision to focus on the experiences of women coming from countries that belonged to the Soviet Union was at least twofold. Although statistical data demonstrate that migration to Slovenia is primarily a male phenomenon, most migrants from Russia and Ukraine (the most important countries of origin of migrants, the former Soviet Union states to Slovenia) are females. Furthermore, the prevailing discourse of women from former Soviet Union republics is essentialized and stereotypical and does not take into account the diversity of their experiences. Their circumstances are narrowed in public discourses to exotic dancers, prostitutes, and/or mail order brides. The main representation of women from Eastern Europe, as Passerini et al. (2004) argue is that they are victims or sexually threatening individuals endangering the social community. Such a discourse bears wider ideological connotations: particularly with the establishment of a sovereign nation-state in 1991, Slovenia has been trying to establish itself as a Western Europe country by symbolically excluding elements that could be perceived as Eastern European and/or Balkan (Zorn 2003). With the establishment of the new nation-state, a differentiation between foreigners and 'native population' became increasingly prevalent in public discourses. In this manner, not only non-citizens in legal terms but also those that were, in the words of Kuzmanić (2003), not perceived as 'Slovenians' by blood, land, soil, ancestors, language and culture, were now symbolically increasingly perceived as foreigners.

While acknowledging the fact that male and female migrants are subjected to the same formal (legal) provisions in migration policy regarding entry into Slovenia and the acquisition of residence permits and consequent social, political, cultural, and economic rights, my objective is to shed light on the experiences of female migrants in order to correct the previous neglect of the experiences of women in migration research in Slovenia.[4] Multiple forms of marginalization and exclusion of 'third-country' female migrants (cf. Anthias and Lazaridis 2000) will be analysed. In accordance with more recent research in migration studies, female migrants' innovative strategies of challenging such rigidly and restrictively defined migration regimes, will be emphasized. I therefore examine parts of the life histories of female migrants, which demonstrate mutual linkages between their individual experience and the social (structural) context in which they act (Passerini et al. 2004). The notion of difference and heterogeneity is at the core of contemporary gender/feminist studies, as well as research in ethnic and racism studies (Anthias and Lazaridis 2000).[5] In this manner, I do not view gender and ethnicity as homogeneous categories, but in line with the intersectional approach's aim to demonstrate how categories of gender, ethnic group, age, education, legal status (temporary residence, permanent residence, citizenship of Slovenia) and socio-economic position in Slovenia mutually intersect. In the empirical part of the text I sketch prevailing reasons for female migration, I do not attempt to provide a coherent story of migration. It is precisely through an analysis of the heterogeneity of female migrants' life courses that I attempt to uncover the changing meanings of migration in their life courses. The focus, however, is not only on the process of migration, but also on the processes of immigrants' acquiring legal status and their social and economic inclusion into the new society, as, in the words of Anderson (2010) immigration controls are not simply about conditions of entry across the border, but also about conditions of stay.

WOMEN'S STORIES

Changing Social and Economic Status after Migration

For my collocutors, that is, interviewees, family migration was the prevailing type of entry into Slovenia. Most women in this group migrated to Slovenia after marrying a Slovenian national they had met in their home country. In view of the restrictive tendencies in migration regimes, marriage was not so much a matter of tradition to these women, but rather a precondition on the basis of which they could gain a more permanent legal right to stay in Slovenia. None of them narrated such marriage migration in economic terms. Many women stressed that they had a 'good life' in terms of employment, income, housing and social security in their home countries.

Oksana (44 years old) remembers:

I had a very good job, an apartment, my family was never poor, I had a good life in Russia, and so I came just because of my husband. I decided to come to have a family. In Russia, problems are related to this. Women cannot find a man, especially when you are older it is difficult.

Some narrated in quite some length about love and deep emotions that had brought them to Slovenia:

> I met my now husband at the opera. That story and romance went on for three years in Russia. Afterwards, it was a very difficult decision, as we were not young. I was forty years old, but on the other hand I thought, this was the man of my life, the best that ever happened to me. And when he asked me whether I wanted to go, I said 'yes'. (Lidia, 52 years old)

When the company in which her husband worked experienced economic turmoil, she felt she had no other choice but to move to Slovenia, although she thought they would live in Russia for most of the time. Women generally did not speak of their migration as a carefully thought out rational plan, but described a process of constant negotiation and communication between themselves and their partners/husbands. Some did, mention economic and social turmoil brought by the break-up of the Soviet Union, but did not relate this historical development more specifically to their migration.

Women who came to Slovenia as family migrants described their position on the labour market as the most problematic aspect of their initial stay in Slovenia. Long periods of unemployment and/ or performing (usually temporary) jobs that were not in line with their educational achievements were described as the most pressing issue. They also had to undertake occasional jobs that were not legally regulated. For instance, Olga (25 years old) from Ukraine came to Slovenia to join her husband a few years ago, illegally worked in the kitchen of a restaurant for quite some time despite having completed higher education. In the beginning, she worked for thirteen hours a day, without any social security and protection. As she was legally a foreigner, she says, she could not make the same amount of money citizens of Slovenia would. Her description is quite indicative:

> He [her husband] helped me to get to Slovenia. In the beginning, of course, I had no choice regarding employment, as I do not have acquaintances or relatives here in Slovenia to help me. In the beginning, if you do not know

the language, you have only one option, I began to work in the kitchen, later, when I learned the language, I worked at the bar and it was a little better.... We have been here in Slovenia for quite some time now, we know more people.... This company also invited me as they needed a Ukrainian translator, so I started to work there; they helped me so now I am also learning the Slovenian language to get this job.... In the beginning, it was hard. It is not hard to work physically, but psychologically it is hard. If you are important at home [in Ukraine], you know the language, you studied, completed higher education, and then you come into another country and you are washing dishes. I was very depressed and wanted to go back.

The story of Nadia from Russia (37 years old) is also typical of female family migrants' experiences:

In the beginning, I was a housewife, for quite a while, since in my profession, I am an economist with a university degree, I could not find a job. I searched persistently, wrote applications, with no success. So I dedicated myself to my family, childcare, learning Slovenian, adjusting to local circumstances.

After working in a shop as a sales assistant, Nadia found employment at a bakery. The experience of de-skilling seems to be a perpetual one for some migrant women. For example, Angelika (32 years old) from Russia feels she will never be able to get a job in her profession (translation) in Slovenia. Lidia (52 years old) was a university professor in Russia, and unemployed for a long time before acquiring employment that is still not in line with her educational and professional qualifications. It seems that age was an important factor in her life course as well, as she was told at the Employment Service that she was *no longer young*.

None of my collocutors had actually undergone a divorce during the period when their more secure legal status in Slovenia had not yet been determined. However, many of them mentioned divorce as a pressing issue when referring to other women (they mentioned, for instance, women from Russia they personally knew) who found themselves in such positions of power inequalities between partners.

Some women also reflected on cumbersome and lengthy procedures at the borders and recalled how they were subjected to surveillance while already residing in Slovenia. Nadia (37 years old) from Russia explained how policemen came to check whether she was actually living with her husband at her permanent address. She related this experience to living in a small, rural community. However, Natasha (41 years old), from Ukraine, who is living in the Slovene capital, Ljubljana, shared a similar story.

WOMEN AS AUTONOMOUS MIGRANTS: CHANGES AFTER LABOUR MIGRATION

Another group consisted of women who had come to Slovenia mainly through contacts with other migrants. These contacts included social networks of Russians or Ukrainians, for example, those already living in Slovenia, who had invited them to come to Slovenia to work. These women recalled how they wanted to explore and see the world. Much like the group of marriage migrants, they did not express their motives in economic terms, but more in terms of self-realization autonomy and freedom. The major turning point for them was usually meeting their future husbands (partners) and consequently staying in Slovenia on a more permanent basis. Also, coming to Slovenia to work (sometimes only with a tourist visa) was a way for these women to enter Slovenia legally, although work was in their self-representation not a primary reason for migration. Angelika from Russia (32 years old) maintains it was impossible for her to come to Slovenia as a tourist due to the numerous strict conditions for obtaining a Slovenian visa. Although she reports on being out of Russia on professional grounds on several occasions, she realizes leaving Russia to travel around Europe would be extremely difficult for her:

> I don't know if I had any expectations, I just wanted to see the world around me. It was hard for me to leave Russia, since I had no financial possibility to come alone. And this family brought me to Slovenia, on their own expense. I didn't have any opportunities due to the fact that it is extremely difficult to get a visa. I could buy myself a tourist holiday and live in a hotel, but since I had no financial possibilities, I realised it was extremely hard for me to leave my country.

It is quite indicative that she does not want to report about her experience while working as a domestic worker. After a couple of months, she met her future husband which caused a change in her life orientations as she decided to stay in Slovenia on a more permanent basis.

Natasha's story is somewhat similar as she mentions she merely wanted to travel and gain new experiences. She first arrived in Slovenia to work:

> They had invited me to come here to teach, so I accepted the offer and came. My friend was already here so they asked him to find another woman, so I accepted the offer. (Natasha, Ukraine, 41 years old)

Those collocutors who came to Slovenia to perform skilled work (e.g., at an international university or at a branch of an international corporation) also described such 'self-realization' motives in their decision to migrate. Since their employers were very instrumental in helping them, they seem to have experienced fewer difficulties in arranging residence and work permits. Nevertheless, their initial plans to stay in Slovenia only on a temporary basis were usually altered when meeting their partners/husbands.

Some interviewees in this group also utilized self-employment to acquire a more secure legal status in Slovenia. For Natasha from Ukraine (41 years old), self-employment was a strategy she resorted to after being unsuccessful in finding a suitable job. Her story points to upward social mobility. In her self-representation, this is more a result of her own initiative and inventiveness than a result of systematic active employment policies. For Lilia, an artist from Russia (48 years old), securing her work status as a freelance artist was a prerequisite on the basis of which she could stay in Slovenia with her family. Although she did not experience a reduction in professional status or de-skilling in Slovenia, she perceives herself as essentially unemployed.

MIGRATION FOR REASONS OF STUDY

Collocutors who came to Slovenia to study were usually under-age at the time of their migration. They typically described their migration as to some extent involuntary, as it was more a result of their parents' will than their own wishes. Their parents already had established professional contacts in Slovenia. Typically, Katerina (28 years) remembers:

> My parents had worked abroad before and as they were returning a group of construction workers, actually a project leader, invited them

to Slovenia.... Coming to Slovenia was a catastrophe for me. I was a very successful student in Russia and started to prepare myself for my profession beforehand.... I came for the holidays and thought, ok, three months, and then I go back. Actually, I was bothered for some time that coming to Slovenia was not my choice and thought, what if I came back?

From Katerina's story, it is quite clear she was aware that her abilities to make an autonomous decision regarding her migration at the age of fifteen were limited. She seems to have resolved this conflict by her professional success in a profession that requires mastery of the Slovenian language. Masha (26 years) from Ukraine gives a similar account of her migration:

I first came with my parents ten years ago.... At the time, the Soviet Union was just falling apart and there was chaos in Ukraine, we didn't know what will happen. So basically I came to Slovenia due to greater social security at fifteen years of age. They enrolled me in school and I stayed because I liked it. Actually, the first time I came I thought I was coming for holidays, I didn't know I was being moved. I liked life in Ukraine back then.... Then they told me they rented me an apartment and I did not like it. I said I would be here for a year and then return. Well, then I decided to stay.

Quite possibly also due to the fact that this group of collocutors studied at schools/universities in Slovenia and were thus quite proficient in the Slovenian language, they usually held jobs that were more in line with their educational levels than the group of women that came to Slovenia for reasons of marriage. This could be attributed also to their young age when searching for employment. Nevertheless, they also described typical cases of discrimination on ethnic grounds. Despite finishing university in Slovenia, Katerina (28 years old) describes how many employers were not willing to give her a chance due to her supposed 'foreignness'.

PAPER NARRATIVES

Lengthy bureaucratic procedures to acquire necessary papers in order to secure individual social and economic rights in Slovenia were described almost universally by my collocutors, regardless of their reason for coming to Slovenia. They narrated how they were sent back and forth for documents, described the difficulties in obtaining original papers from their home countries, and complained about the lack of information and the unfriendly and unhelpful attitude of employees at the office for foreigners.

For instance, getting married was sometimes marked by problems that resulted from complicated bureaucratic procedures. Nadia (37 years old) from Russia recalls how she had to get married at the Russian embassy in Ljubljana:

> We had some problems, because my husband wanted a Slovenian wedding, but things went wrong in acquiring my identity documents, so we solved this by getting married at the Russian embassy in Ljubljana. My husband was primarily disappointed with his country, since he did not imagine such complications would arise.... At the registry office, they could not understand why in my passport my name was different because in translation, my name was written with one letter less. But the translator also noted it had to be written in this way, since we have passports that are issued in French, due to the international agreement.

Travelling to other countries was also perceived as problematic. Lilia (48 years old), an artist from Russia, recalls how she experienced severe problems in acquiring a visa for Germany, where she had established professional connections, during the time Slovenia was not yet a part of the Schengen area. Similarly, Masha (26 years old) from Ukraine expressed frustration that obtaining a visa for Ukrainian citizens is so difficult. Her international mobility is hampered; she reports, for example, how her visa application to travel to Croatia on tourist grounds was rejected.

My interviewees also expressed great concern over the issue of dual citizenship, which most of them are not allowed to possess, except in exceptional cases, when having special merits for Slovenia. A further problem arose if a woman already acquired Slovene citizenship and had had to give up her Russian/Ukrainian citizenship. This was especially problematic if she chose to return to her home country, which could result in an inferior status in terms of social, economic, and political rights in the home country. Giving up their original citizenship has led to many negative practical consequences for these women: by doing so, they now are required to obtain visas in order to visit their families and/ or travel to their countries of origin on business. Difficulties in matters of real estate (for example, maintaining property) also arise. Oksana (44 years old) comments on this:

> I knew a couple of cases, my acquaintances, they acquired Slovenian citizenship, their husbands literally kicked them out, so they returned to Russia, they had no place to go, there is the issue of children, how to protect not only yourself, but also children. Many open questions remain.

With respect to exercising retirement rights in Slovenia, the women referred to their working years in Russia and Ukraine as a pressing issue, since bilateral agreements between Slovenia and Russia/Ukraine have not yet been ratified. Procedures for the recognition of vocational qualifications and diplomas were long and cumbersome. An extreme case is that of a professor of Russian, who had to write her diploma anew in Slovenia. The interviewees also described the 'vicious circle' of not being able to get a job without citizenship and the necessity of having sufficient economic means in order to obtain citizenship.

Many women were not in an economic position to afford a Slovenian language course. This further contributed to their exclusion from the labour market, as knowledge of the language is generally a prerequisite for applying for jobs requiring higher education and professional skills. Economic and other contacts with Russian-speaking countries or, for example, jobs in translation and Russian language teaching represented a solid starting point for integration in the labour market in Slovenia. Many of these women were thus creatively using their knowledge of Russian as an asset and found jobs mainly through social networks, that is, through friends and colleagues, often of shared ethnic background.

Public stereotypical views of Russian/Ukrainian females as mainly dancers were also exposed in the interviews, as well as prejudice connected to Russia as a former communist state. In this manner, Olga (27 years old) remembers how state officials were suspicious of her when she first came to Slovenia on a three-month visa:

> At the border, they inspect you quite thoroughly, they ask you where you are going as you are a young female, ask you where you will be working, a hundred questions.

Most women reported on such an attitude particularly when not accompanied by a Slovenian citizen and/or when travelling alone.

Some discussants were quite critical of such practices. Natasha (41 years old), for example, firmly maintained that she *does not have to prove herself to anyone.*

COMPLEXITIES OF MIGRATION

It seems that a conservative, restrictive approach to migration management has contributed to an increasing insecurity and vulnerability of third-country nationals residing in the European Union. The verbal accounts of female migrants from the former Soviet Union point to some weaknesses of such a migration regime. First, marriage is one of the few available options through which migrants can gain the right to reside in Slovenia on a long-term basis. Such a model favours a classical model of family life (marriage as an institution) over other forms of extra-marital community and thus fails to take into account the diversification of contemporary family life. Furthermore, the rights of a spouse are linked to her partner, which can be potentially threatening in cases of divorce before a woman has obtained permanent residence and/or citizenship, which can create opportunities for subordination of particular women (Guličová-Grethe and Schlenzka 2006; Kofman et al. 2000).[6]

Going to Slovenia for purposes of work is another option for migrants from third countries hoping to gain legal residency in Slovenia. However, the meanings attributed to such a migration were usually not framed in economic terms by the discussants. Rather, the women spoke of the possibility for self-realisation, individual fulfilment, and the opportunity to gain new experiences and insights. The way they spoke could conceal other individual motives and also reveal strategic decisions in a woman's life. These strategies could present a response to the inability to engage in other forms of international mobility.

Consequently, it seems that an empirical distinction between different types of migration is impossible to sustain. The term 'migrant' can even be considered a strong form of categorization particularly for those who do not consider such a label as relevant and appropriate to their everyday lives (Gárdos and Gödri 2014), as qualitative research across different migration contexts has pervasively demonstrated. Constable (2003) rightly states that female migrants are often labelled too narrowly as either labour or marriage migrants. Clearly, such narrow statistical typologies do not encapsulate the diversified nature of contemporary migration processes. Typologies, as Brettell argues (2000), present us with a static and homogenized picture of a process that is dynamic throughout the course of an individual's life. Additionally, this process differs widely among individuals and changes throughout time with changes in the social context. Crosby (2006) holds that because of the way we label, define, and categorise people who move, we obscure and make invisible their actual lived experience. It thus becomes clear why migration policies can also be referred to as 'containment policies' that define and hold people within particular definitional boundaries and objectify them.

Policies of Categorization

This bears important consequences for the implementation of migration policies that generally do not take into account the diversity and complexities of migrants' lived experiences, but are devised according to statistically defined typologies of migration (for instance, labour migrant, marriage and family migrant, and asylum seeker/refugee). As Kofman (2004) aptly states, although female labour migrations and family-related migrations are treated as analytically separate in migration studies, family migrants are a major source of female migrant labour. In this regard, she continues: 'women may seek to combine work, career and marriage but these multiple rationalities are difficult to grasp using a classification of migratory moves based on a single reason, such as labour, family or asylum'. As Kofman (2012) argues in another text, skilled female migrants who enter through family routes (for instance, marriage, family reunification) are also a significant, although an under-studied group of migrants. Their specific problems both on the labour market as well as in family life were also documented in the presented study. In this manner, Erel (2009) points to the social construction of skill: The categories of skilled or unskilled migrants are not simply descriptive. Instead, gendered constructions, migration regimes as well as racist stereotypes contribute to the social construction of these categories themselves.

Thus at different times in their migration history, the same individual may be classified as an undocumented, unskilled or skilled migrant. The categorization of a migrant often does not take account of their factual skills or professional experiences. Therefore, categories used to control migration and migrants' access to the labour market should not be taken for granted, but deconstructed.

Residence Permits

The procedures to obtain residence permits are complicated and lengthy, the recognition of pensions between the countries has not yet been arranged, and women's skills and qualifications are often not formally recognized. The inability to gain dual citizenship can further hamper the transnational movements of migrants across national borders due to complicated visa procedures if a woman is forced to give up the citizenship of her country of origin. The category of citizenship remains linked to a specific nation-state, as European citizenship as a formal legal category does not exist. More inclusive citizenship, according to Hansen (1998) can thus be achieved accepting the notion and practice of dual citizenship. Within such citizenship models, it is assumed that citizenship is based on a singular and exclusive membership in a given nation-state (uncritically defined as clearly demarcated communities of shared identity and culture), thus excluding possibilities of belonging to multiple national territories.

Informal Sector Jobs

Restricted job opportunities for third-country nationals mean that working in the informal sector becomes an important source of income, which creates further possibilities for exploitation. This is corroborated by the fact that a couple of female migrants coming to Slovenia to work in the domestic sector did not generally wish to report about their experiences. The interviewees frequently mentioned de-skilling, downward social mobility, long and irregular working hours, and on and off part-time and contract jobs. Limited job opportunities because of the non-citizenship (foreigner) status of third-country nationals, coupled with ethnic discrimination in the labour market, produce instances of exclusion and delayed entry into the labour market. Some researchers hold that the experiences of female migrants from Eastern Europe are different from those from the Third World due to their higher education levels and almost universal participation in the labour market in former socialist states. Contrary to this, our research corroborates the finding that female migrants, regardless of their country of origin, face similar problems due to downward professional and social mobility and experience a discord between their professional potential and structural chances on the labour market (Remennick 1999).

Despite instances of ethnic discrimination and their third-country nationals/non-citizen status that places restrictions on their possibilities to perform paid work, many of the women interviewed have been able to use their ethnic background (especially Russian language skills) to gain access to the labour market (for example, in translation, administration, and in tourist agencies that cater to Russian tourists). They successfully mobilized various personal resources (such as social networks of friends and acquaintances) to acquire a more stable position in the labour market and to obtain information about their rights in Slovenia. Self-employment was also reported as a strategy to overcome blocked upward mobility in the labour market. Rather than viewing migrant women as victims or passive agents, their active decision-making and strategies to overcome restrictive and discriminatory practices were revealed in the interviews.

Diverse experiences of the interviewees demonstrate that politics of inclusion should account for various factors such as gender, age, educational level, socio-economic position, social networks and legal status to a greater extent. It is clear that such factors intersect to fundamentally shape experiences of migration. Although early feminist research on female migrants aimed at highlighting the importance and specificities of female migration, it is imperative to study also other axes of difference (Silvey 2004). To study individual differences in their life-stories, qualitative research methods are of vital importance as they enable us to analyse socio-political processes as experienced by individual social actors. As Passerini et al. (2004) write: the women's accounts are much more than personal stories.

NOTES

1   Rozenhek (2000: 52) argues that host country migration regimes generate structures of constraints and opportunities within which political actors define their goals and strategies of action. On the basis of such institutional configurations, policies of regulation and control of migrants' entry to the national territory, as well as policies related to the economic, social, and political status of migrants, are designed and implemented.

2   In this chapter, I utilize data gathered in the framework of the project *FEMAGE: Needs for Female Immigrants and Their Integration in Ageing Societies* of the European Commission, 6th Framework Programme (contract number—SSP4-CT-2005-022355, duration 2006–2007, web page: www.bib-demographie.de/femage/). Besides interviews conducted within this project, some interviews were conducted within my PhD project entitled *Gender and Migration: Experiences of Female Migrants in Slovenia*, which I defended in 2008 at the Faculty of Social Sciences at the University of Ljubljana, Slovenia. In a slightly revised form, it was published in a monograph *Spol in Migracija: Izkušnje Žensk kot Akterk Migracij* (in Slovenian language, English translation: Gender and Migration: Experiences of Women as Actors of Migration) in 2009. Previous versions of this paper were presented at the post-graduate course *Feminisms in a Transnational Perspective: Voicing Feminist Concerns*: Dubrovnik, Croatia, May 26–30, 2008 and at the conference *Inclusion and Exclusion in and on the Borders of Europe:* Portorož, Slovenia, 6–7 June 2008. The revised conference paper is published online at: www.mirovni-institut.si/data/... Lev/cukut%20author%20reviewed.doc. Parts of the text were previously published in the scientific article entitled: *Examining the Dynamics of Migrant Categorisations throughout the Life Course*. Temperanter, 2010, vol. 1, 2/3, pp. 35–44. The analysis in this contribution builds on my previous research on this issue, and upgrades it by adding selected theoretical and methodological sources and giving more extensive reference to the interview material.

3   An exception was the issue of human trafficking that was researched quite systematically (e.g., Zavratnik Zimic et al. 2003).

4   In 2006, I talked to a total of nineteen women using a biographic approach. I also participated in some of their social activities (for example meetings and gatherings) and recorded my observations in an ethnographic diary. The aim of the interviews was not to gain accurate statistical representation of female migrants, but to acquire a more thorough understanding of their migration and inclusion into the 'new society' through a detailed analysis of case studies (cf. Riaño and Baghdadi 2007). Nevertheless, the sample was chosen to represent a variety of life situations including age, education, socio-economic background, reason for entry, time of residence and residence status in Slovenia, and marital status. The contacts with

potential collocutors were established through personal contacts, the 'snowball technique', and through contact with associations that bring together Russian-speaking people. The vast majority of women I talked to migrated to Slovenia from Russia and Ukraine; two came from Belarus and one from Latvia. The main themes of the interviews were the following: life in the society of origin, family background, division of labour and relationships within the family (both in the society of origin and in Slovenia), decision for migration, arrival in Slovenia, formal and informal social networks, economic, social and political integration into the new society, paid work, expectations regarding retirement and understanding of integration.

5   Addressing ethnic discrimination and acknowledging the connection of migration processes with nationalism (for an analysis of the Slovenian case see, for example, Bajt 2009), by analysing social representations of national identities (Černič Istenič and Knežević Hočevar 2006), can further explain prevalent anti-immigrant attitudes and instances of discrimination on ethnic grounds.

6   Although this is not a gender-specific provision, such restrictions would apply to male migrants as well.

REFERENCES

Al-Ali, N. 2009. 'Women, Gender and Migration in Europe'. Retrieved from http://www.comune.forli.fo.it/Documenti/39/gender.pdf, accessed on 24 January, 2015.

Anderson, B. 2010. 'Migration, Immigration Controls and the Fashioning of Precarious Workers'. *Work, Employment and Society* 24, 2: 300–17.

Anthias, F. 2000.' Metaphors of Home: Gendering New Migrations to Southern Europe', in F. Anthias and G. Lazaridis, eds. *Gender and Migration in Southern Europe.* Oxford: Berg, 15–47.

Anthias, F. and G. Lazaridis. 2000. 'Introduction: Women on the Move in Southern Europe', in F. Anthias and G. Lazaridis, eds. *Gender and Migration in Southern Europe.* Oxford: Berg, 1–14.

Antić, M. G., ed. 2011. *Na Poti do Lastne Sobe* (Towards One's Own Room). Ljubljana: i 2.

Brettell, C. B. 2000. 'Theorizing Migration in Anthropology: The Social Construction of Networks, Identities, Communities, and Globalscapes', in C. B. Brettell and J. F. Hollifield, eds. *'Migration Theory: Talking Across Disciplines'.* London: Routledge, 85–135.

Castles, S., and J. M. Miller. 2003. *'The Age of Migration: International Population Movements in the Modern World'.* Houndmills: Macmillan.

Constable, N. 2003. 'A Transnational Perspective on Divorce and Marriage: Filipina Wives and Workers. Identities', *Global Studies in Culture and Power* 10, 2: 163–80.

164   Sanja Cukut Krilić

Crosby, A. 2006. 'The Boundaries of Belonging: Reflections on Migration Policies into the 21st Century'. Retrieved from http://interpares.ca/sites/default/files/resources/2006–06 BoundariesofBelonging.pdf, accessed on 24 January, 2015.

Černič Istenič, M., D. and Knežević Hočevar. 2006. '*Ali so stališča prebivalcev evropskih držav do priseljencev povezana s stališči, ki se nanašajo na odnose med spoloma, rodnostno vedenje in vrednotenje otrok?*' (Are the Attitudes of Europeans towards Immigrants Related to their Attitudes towards Gender Roles, Fertility Behaviour and the Meaning of Children?). *Dve domovini/ Two Homeland*, 24, 21–46.

Černič Istenič, M., D. Knežević Hočevar, and S. Cukut. 2007. 'Needs for Female Immigrants and Their Integration in Ageing Societies, Work package 4: Focus Groups with Stakeholders', National Report Slovenia. Wiesbaden: Bundesinstitut für Bevölkerungsforschung: (Federal Institute for Population Research), unpublished report.

Erel, U. 2009. '*Migrant Women Transforming Citizenship: Life-Stories from Britain and Germany*'. Farnham: Ashgate.

Eggebø, H. 2013. 'A Real Marriage? Applying for Marriage Migration to Norway'. *Journal of Ethnic and Migration Studies* 39, 5: 773–89.

Freedman, J., 2003. 'Introduction: A Gendered Analysis of Migration in Europe', in J. Freedman, ed., '*Gender and Insecurity: Migrant Women in Europe*'. Farnham: Ashgate, 1–15.

——. 2016. 'Engendering Security at the Borders of Europe: Women Migrants and the Mediterranean Crisis', *Journal of Refugee Studies* 29, 4: 568–82.

Gárdos, Éva, and Gödri Irén. 2014. 'Analysis of Existing Migratory Data Production Systems and Major Data Sources in Eight South-East European Countries', Hungarian Demographic Research Institute, Budapest.

Guličova-Grethe, M., and N. Schlenzka. 2006. 'Female Marriage Migration: Definition, Problems and Related Phenomena', in N. Schlenzka, ed. '*Female Marriage Migrants: Awareness Raising and Violence Prevention*'. Berlin: Edition Parabolis, 9–11.

Hansen, R. 1998. 'A European Citizenship or a Europe of Citizens? Third Country Nationals in the EU', *Journal of Ethnic and Migration Studies* 24, 4: 751–68.

Hrovat, L., M. Gregorčič, and V. Bajt. 2007. 'Integration of New Female Migrants in Slovenian Labour Market and Society and Policies Affecting Integration: State of the Art', Working Paper No. 8 – WP4. Retrieved from http://www.femipol.uni-frankfurt.de/docs/working_papers/wp1/Slovenia. pdf, accessed on 30 January, 2015.

Hrženjak, M. 2007. '*Nevidno Delo*' (Invisible Work). Ljubljana: Mirovni Inštitut (Peace Institute).

——. 2012. 'Hierarchization and Segmentation of Informal Care Markets in Slovenia', *Social Politics* 19, 1, 38–57.

Kofman, E., A. Phizacklea, P. Raghuram, and R. Sales. 2000. *Gender and International Migration in Europe: Employment, Welfare and Politics*. London: Routledge.

Kofman, E. 2004. 'Gendered Global Migrations', *International Feminist Journal of Politics* 6, 4: 643–65.

———. 2012. 'Gender and Skilled Migration in Europe', *Cuadernos de Relaciones Laborales* 30, 1: 63–89.

Kuzmanić, T. 2003. '*Ksenofobija vs Nekdanji SFR Jugoslaviji in v Postsocialistični Sloveniji* (Xenophobia in the former Yugoslavia and in Postsocialist Slovenia), *Poročilo Skupine za Spremljanje Nestrpnosti* (Intolerance Monitor Report), 2, 2: 14–33.

Lazaridis, G. 2000. 'Filipino and Albanian Women Migrant Workers in Greece: Multiple Layers of Oppression', in F. Anthias and G. Lazaridis, eds. *Gender and Migration in Southern Europe*. Oxford: Berg, 49–79.

Milharčič Hladnik, M. and J. Mlekuž, eds. 2009. *Krila Migracij. Po Meri Življenjskih Zgodb* (The Wings of Migration: Life Stories). Ljubljana: Založba ZRC (ZRC SAZU Publishing House), ZRC SAZU.

Pajnik, M. and S. Zavratnik Zimic. 2003. '*Med Globalnim in Lokalnim vs Sodobnih Migracijah: Predgovor*' (Between Global and Local in Contemporary Migration: Introduction), in S. Zavratnik Zimic and M. Pajnik, eds. *Migracije, Globalizacija, Evropska Unija* (Migration, Globalisation, European Union). Ljubljana: Mirovni Inštitut (Peace Institute), 5–14.

Pajnik, M., N. Kogovšek and S. Zupanc. 2006a. 'Mapping of Policies Affecting Female Migrants and Policy Analysis: The Slovenian Case, Working Paper No. 8, WP 1. Retrieved from http://www.femipol.uni-frankfurt.de/docs/working_papers/wp1/Slovenia.pdf, accessed on 10 January 2015.

Pajnik, M., V. Bajt, and S. Zupanc. 2006b. 'Policies Affecting Female Migrants', Report on Key Informant Interviews in Slovenia, Working Paper No. 8, WP2. Retrieved from http://www.femipol.uni-frankfurt.de/docs/working_papers/wp2/Slovenia.pdf, accessed on 10 January 2015.

Pajnik, M., and V. Bajt. 2012. 'Migrant Women's Transnationalism: Family Patterns and Policies', *International Migration* 50, 5: 153–68.

———. 2013. 'Migrant Women's Work: Intermeshing Structure and Agency', *Arts and Humanities* 7, 2: 163–76.

Passerini, L., R. Braidotti, J. Gazsi, I.-M. Conradsen, and N. Alexsandrova. 2004. 'Gender Relationships in Europe at the Turn of the Millenium: Women as Subjects in Migration and Marriage' (GRINE, final report). Retrieved from ftp://ftp.cordis.europa.eu/pub/citizens/docs/kina21249ens1_grine.pdf, accessed on 17 January 2015.

Pellander, S. 2015. 'An Acceptable Marriage: Marriage Migration and Moral Gatekeeping in Finland', *Journal of Family Issues* 36, 11: 1472–489.

Remennick L. 1999. 'Women with a Russian Accent in Israel: On the Gender Aspects of Immigration', *The European Journal of Women's Studies*, 6, 4: 441–61.

Riaño, Y., and N. Baghdadi. 2007. 'Understanding the Labour Market Participation of Skilled Immigrant Women in Switzerland: The Interplay of Class, Ethnicity, and Gender', *Journal of International Migration and Integration* 8, 2: 163–83.

Rozenhek, Z. 2000. 'Migration Regimes, Intra-State Conflicts, and the Politics of Exclusion and Inclusion: Migrant Workers in the Israeli Welfare State', *Social Problems*, 47, 1: 49–67.

Sharpe, Pamela. 2001. 'Introduction: Gender and the Experience of Migration', in P. Sharpe, ed. *Women, Gender and Labour Migration: Historical and Global Perspectives*. New York: Routledge.

Šadl, Z. 2010. 'Globalizacija Družbene Reprodukcije: Skrbstveni Deficit in Globalne Verige Skrbi' (Globalisation of Social Reproduction: Care Deficit and Global Care Chains). *Teorija in Praksa* 47, 1: 139–55.

——. 2014. 'Perceptions of Stigma: The Case of Paid Domestic Workers in Slovenia'. *Teorija in Praksa* 51, 5: 904–27.

Silvey, R. 2004. 'Power, Difference and Mobility: Feminist Advances in Migration Studies', *Progress in Human Geography* 28, 4: 490–506.

Zavratnik Zimic, S., U. Kavčič, M. Pajnik, and P. Lesjak-Tušek. 2003. 'Where in the Puzzle: Trafficking from, to and through Slovenia', Assessment study. Ljubljana: International Organisation for Migration.

Zavratnik Zimic, S., and M. Pajnik, eds. 2003. 'M Mirovni Inštitut (Peace Institute), igracije, Globalizacija, Evropska Unija' (Migration, Globalisation, European Union).

Zavratnik Zimic, S. 2004. *Migration Trends in Selected EU Applicant Countries*, vol. 6, *Slovenia: The Perspective of a Country on the Schengen Periphery*, Vienna: International Organization for Migration.

——. 2006. 'Contemporary Immigration and Asylum Policies in Slovenia: Rethinking Questions of Entrance and Integration', *Annales* 16, 2: 343–54.

Zavratnik, Zimic S. and S. Krilić Cukut. 2018. 'Addressing Intersectional Vulnerabilities in Contemporary Refugee Movements in Europe, *Družboslovne Razprave* 34, 87: 85–106.

Zorn, J. 2003. 'Etnografija Vsakdanjega Življenja Ljudi Brez Slovenskega Državljanstva janstva' (Doktorska Disertacija) (Ethnography of Everyday Life of People without Slovenian Citizenship), PhD thesis, Fakulteta za Družbene Vede (Faculty of Social Sciences), Ljubljana.

8

Care Relations of Resettled Refugees: Case Study, Finland

KATI TURTIAINEN

THE SITUATION OF forced migrants is unbearable in many parts of the world. More than 68 million individuals have been forced to leave their home country or region of origin as a result of persecution, conflicts, generalized violence, or human rights violations. The situation of forced migrants gives a huge challenge to the international community. I focus on refugees, which is one group of forced migrants. The other forced migrants are Internally Displaced People (IDPs), asylum seekers, victims of trafficking and smuggled and stateless persons. By the end of 2017, some 25 million persons were refugees under the UNHCR (United Nations High Commissioner for Refugees) or UNRWA (United Nations Relief and Works Agency for Palestine Refugees in the Near East) (UNHCR 2017).

Refugees are a group of forced migrants who have been given the status of refugee according to International Refugee Law, the Convention 1951 and its 1967 Protocol (UNHCR 2011). The essential criteria of refugee status are: first the person's flight must be motivated by the persecution, which means of serious harm against which the state of origin is unwilling or unable to offer protection. Second, the risk faced by the person must have a connection to his or her race, religion, nationality, membership in a particular social group, or political opinion. Third, there must be a genuine need for and legitimate claim for protection[1] (Hathaway 1991). The definition reflects the fact that the bond of trust, as a form of protection and assistance between the citizen and the state, constitute the normal basis of society. It asserts the moral claim by positing the existence of the minimal relation of rights and duties between the citizen and the state. It asserts that the actual consequences of the severed bond between the person and the state are always persecution and alienage, that is, the state of becoming an alien (Shacknove 1985).

The refugee definition is rooted in the European context. Even if refugee definition has been widely regarded as universal and generally accepted, at the same time it has been described as a product of the Cold War and as eurocentric (Chimni 2000). Refugees may live in a provisional situation without any state protection for decades. UNHCR gives temporary protection and tries to find durable solutions for them. One possibility is to resettle refugees from the refugee camps and other temporary places to the developed countries (UNHCR 2006). The context of this article is the resettlement of the refugees to Europe and especially to Finland. Finland is one of the oldest European refugee resettlement countries. The yearly quota of resettled refugees is 750 individuals. In the year 2017, around 65,000 new migrants, including asylum seekers, applied for residence permit in Finland (The Finnish Immigration Service 2018).

Resettlement doesn't automatically solve the problems of refugees. After resettlement to the new country, refugees become dependent on the stakeholders of the new society. Therefore, successful settlement takes place when the integration process is built. Also, integration needs relevant actions by the host community, society and the state in order to meet the needs of refugees and other forced migrants. In Finland, public authorities are in the frontline of settlement and integration of refugees, but as my previous studies (Turtiainen 2011) show, the relationship between refugees and public authorities could sometimes be based on negative dependency, where the former become dependent on support received. Therefore, the needs of the resettled refugees were not necessarily met by the stakeholders of Finnish society. My interest here is the refugees' care relations, which are one essential element of settlement process (Turtiainen 2012). Raghuram (2012) also states that analysis of the local specific dynamics of care in different geographical contexts is needed.[2]

CARE RELATIONS

First of all, refugees as vulnerable human beings require social and emotional support. I approach the concept of care as a vital human need and, therefore, care relations must form a basis of well-being in the new society they find themselves in. Refugees may have a background of serious denial of care, which could deteriorate into a form of abuse and even torture. According to Honneth's theory of recognition (1995; 2007)[3] this kind of violence threatens the integrity of a person by destroying self-confidence. Honneth, as well as the theorists of ethics of care (Baier 1995; Sevenhujsen 1998; Tronto 1993) highlight the relational nature of the care, and also the need for care as a part of the human condition. My starting point here is that building care relations are vital to the resettled refugees in the early stages of integration in order to maintain positive self-relations as bases of a good life and integration process in the new society.

In Finnish society, taking care of people's needs is an essential part of social welfare, which also covers resettled refugees. Thus, I study how refugees form their prior care relations with whom in the early stages after arrival in Finland. I question whether there are gender differences in the formation of care relations. The data are based on the interviews with the refugees. I start by looking at the European context of forced migration and refugee resettlement as one durable solution used by UNHCR. Second, I discuss how the concept of care is understood in this study. Lastly, the research frame and the results of this study are presented.

EUROPEAN CONTEXT OF CURRENT FORCED MIGRATION

The number of forced migrants entering European territory has increased during the last few years. However, the distinctions within the category of forced migrants are an artefact of policy concerns rather than of empirical observation and scientific enquiry (Turton 2003).

UNHCR (2010) speaks about the migration-asylum nexus, which means that many migratory movements involve both economic migrants and forced migrants. According to Betts (2013) there is a lack of terminology to clearly identify people who should have the entitlement not to be returned to their country of origin on human rights grounds. He proposes that these individuals may be referred to as 'survival migrants'. Also the perspective could be changed from the particular cause of movement to identifying a threshold of fundamental rights. The number of refugees and other forced migrants without any state protection are increasing due to unrest in the different parts of the world. In 2017, around 705,000 asylum seekers applied for international protection in the Member States of the European Union. This was just a half of applications recorded in 2015 and 2016, when nearly 1.3 million asylum applicants were registered. In 2017, EU Member States granted protection to more than 538, 000 asylum seekers (Eurostat 2018). Western European states have developed a battery of measures designed to reduce asylum claims. These measures are, for example, carrier sanctions, pre-inspection regimes in foreign countries and interdictions to prevent asylum seekers from accessing national territory (Gibney and Hansen 2003). Despite this, individuals are still trying to reach Europe across the Mediterranean. In 2015, more than 1 million people arrived in Europe across the Mediterranean Sea, compared to the 200,000 in 2014, and around 172,000 during 2017. The main countries of origin of the people claiming asylum in Europe are Syria, Iraq and Afghanistan. The main destination countries are Germany, Italy and France (IOM 2018).

In 2017 in Finland, the number of asylum seekers was around 5000, but in 2015 the number of new claims were about 32,000. (The Finnish Immigration Service 2018). In 2016, there was a hardening of policy in the Finnish Aliens Act concerning the possibilities of getting protection. Finland has been traditionally an emigration country since the Second World War. Until now the number of foreign citizens was only about 4 percent of the population. Whom NHCR has identified to be the most vulnerable persons, such as women at risk, survivors of torture or other kinds of violence, chronically ill and elderly persons.

While the EU is blocking the mobility to the north, the so called migration industry is expanding since people have to rely on informal networks or 'people smugglers'. The migration industry embraces a broad spectrum of people who earn their livelihood by organising migratory movements (Castles and Miller 2009). As a consequence, after 2014 until December 2018, around 15,000 human lives have been lost in the in the Mediterranean, which is considered to be the deadliest migration route in the world (Missing migrants 2018). Brian and Laczko (2014) report that there is no exact information available on the gender of the deceased or missing migrants globally or in Europe. It is only reported that there is no information on 96 percent of these lost human lives. It is known that 3 percent are females and 1 percent are males. Gerard and Sharon Pickering (2013) state that the 'EU policy is blind to the lived realities of those who seek refugee protection in the EU and urgently need to address the structural contradictions exacerbating violence experienced by refugee women in transit'.

There is an urgent need to solve the enormous human catastrophe by the international community. Yet there are no simple answers to the mixture of problems, such as war, ethnic hatred, political instability, economic failure which force people to flee their homelands, nor any simple way to elicit the international political will needed to ameliorate them (Gibney 2006). The status of asylum seekers at the moment of entry into a new country without appropriate papers is not very different from that of a criminal. To be without papers in the state-centric world is a form of civil death (Benhabib 2001). Pirjola (2009) highlights that the virtues of liberal democracies are not to be found in their capabilities to close their borders or to build frontiers, but to hear from those who are excluded. According to Finnish resettlement policy the persons selected for resettlement in Finland are mainly among those whom UNHCR has identified to be the most vulnerable persons, as mentioned above.

THEORETICAL PERSPECTIVES TO CARE AS REFUGEE RECEIVING WORK

In general, trust is an essential element in creating a cohesive society (Simmel 1978) and relations of care are an element of trust formation between people. Therefore, building care relations is an important part of the integration of refugees in the new society where everyday life has to be built again. According to my previous studies (Turtiainen 2012), safety can be built through emotional, social and practical support and by fostering feelings of acceptance. Trust and care are closely connected to each other. Individuals respond to signs of the people's good will in order to trust them (Koehn 1998: 97). Therefore, experiences of care or a caring attitude can be a sign enabling mutual trust formation. If refugees can identify, for example, civil servants, as persons who care for the service users' well-being, refugees could trust them (Turtiainen 2012). Thus, I approach the concept of care as a vital human need of all individuals; to be taken care of in a reciprocal relationship is fundamental to being a human (Honneth 1995; Sevenhuijsen 1998). Besides, I discuss care as a public sphere.

I approach the concept of care as a part of German philosopher Honneth's theory (1995) of recognition. In the recognition theory, care, or love, as Honneth calls it, is derived from the object-relation theory by Winnicott (1971) and Mead (1934). In this sense, care is a base for self-confidence and it is developed in early relationships between needy children and their carer. Good care relations also help to develop all further attitudes of self-respect (Honneth 1995).[4] Also another social philosopher, Selma Sevenhuijsen (1998) states, based on the feminist ethics of care,[5] that subjects come to understand themselves through their relationships with others. She states that human subjects develop their moral and rational capacities in connection and interaction with others, in the first instance with those who care for them and on whom they are dependent'. Also for Honneth (1995) the person as a moral subject (self-respect) is developed in the reciprocal relationship. For him, this morality, the respect, is seen in the legal relations and especially through the legislation.

In the Nordic societies care relations are connected to the political responsibility that all citizens' and residents' needs must be recognized. Thus, it is important here to consider the dynamics of care in public space. The human condition as needy and vulnerable beings gives a basis for dealing with political morality to care about all people living in the society. For this reason, as Tronto (1993) states, we have to develop our capacity to care beyond the sphere where we give care on a daily basis. She states that in the democratic society in which all people are responsible for seeing that the care for all is the premise of justice, 'we would expect that collective power will be used not to exclude or degrade any groups' (ibid.). Therefore, taking care of the needs of refugees is also a concern of the public authorities. Ikäheimo (2003; also Honneth 1995) states that care concerns human beings as such, not as a result of their particular features or skills but for their own sakes. However, authorities take care of a person's needs because they care about the person's well-being, regardless of what kind of person he or she is.

The political debate about caring for the needs of all residents, refugees and especially irregular migrants, is topical in the European Union and also in Finland. Thus, their recognition is conditional. The conditionality is connected directly to their contribution by their professional skills. Therefore, migrants are considered more as labour but not in need of protection. It means that values have changed so that individuals must take care of themselves (Dahl and Eriksen 2005). This is because people are seen as instrumental for some other goals, usually economic; not just persons deserving care and a good life. At the end, people are considered as workers and consumers in the different fields. Warness (2005) states that the most privileged groups can ignore much of the strain care entails because they never have really faced it. Tronto (1993) calls this a 'privileged irresponsibility'. Therefore, in the political discourse, care ethics is often considered to belong to the private sphere. Thus, the most vulnerable refugees, such as single mothers or elderly people, may be seen just as a burden for the society. According to Finnish legislation, not all forced migrants are taken care by Finnish society. For example, undocumented migrants cannot get public health care services before they are recognized as residents of the country.[6] Jönsson (2014) states that undocumented immigrants are excluded from many services and social practices in Sweden too.

METHODOLOGY

The data of this study are based on the interviews of experiences of resettled refugees in Finland. First I am primarily interested in knowing that as the interviewees arrive in a new society, with whom do they form the primary care relations? Second, I look to see if there are gender differences in the data. The concept of care is a basis of the analyses; I understand care as a social and emotional mutual relationship. The premise is that care is a fundamental need which concerns all people, not only those who are considered to be the most vulnerable ones. In Nordic countries taking care of the residents has been the policy choice since the Nordic welfare state has been built mainly after the Second World War.

My data consists of interviews with 13 resettled refugees living in Finland. The interviewees represent a heterogeneous group in terms of ethnicity, education, age, and gender. Half of them are women and half men of whom six are either single or are single mothers and seven married with children. Some of them are illiterate without any basic education, some are students and the others have vocational or a university education. Some of them are unemployed and the others are working or studying. They come from different countries in Africa and Asia, and their ages range from 20 to 60. At the time of the interviews, they had been living in Finland between 4 and 13 years. Half of the interviewees are so-called strong cases (Patton 2002) who are somehow working for their own ethnic community. This can also be called as an elite sampling, which means that these informants can offer the best possible information about the migrants (Tuomi and Sarajärvi 2002). In this case, they can provide information also about their own ethnic community. I will not provide more detailed background information of the interviewees in order to avoid identification of the interviewees. Ethically, it is important that, at the time of the interviews, they were no longer users of the services to which the interviews pertained, and thus could speak freely about the services without being dependent on them.

All the interviews were multi-voiced, which meant that interviewees were not speaking only about themselves, but also about other refugees and factors that could help them in their relations with the authorities. Potter (1996) calls this the principle of footing, where a particular piece of speech may be necessary to distinguish whose position the talk is meant to represent, the author, who does the scripting or the animator who says the words. I also include these narratives in my analyses.

The interviews conducted were based on contact information for refugees from the immigrant services in one town. I explained what this research was about over the phone and none of the refugees contacted refused. Before starting the interview I explained again, both orally and in writing, the purpose of the interview and asked for their consent. Some of the interviews took place at the interviewees' homes or work places and the rest of them in my office, lasting for one to two hours. At that time I worked as a director of immigrant services and interviewees told me that they are pleased to tell me their experiences with authorities and settlement services. I knew all interviewees somehow beforehand due to my work. None of the interviewees were personally my clients. I was surprised how openly interviewees spoke about their lives and problems with authorities in Finland. We were looking back to many events which were common to both of us. They also mentioned that I knew how their lives were in the refugee camps because I had visited there, and then they continued their narration. Jocobsen and Landau (2003) write about the willingness to satisfy the researcher and tell such things that they expect the researcher would like to hear. This kind of willingness to satisfy the researcher is known as 'reactivity' in field work. I did not have an impression of this kind of reactivity during the interviewees; they were critical of the services and described how these could be improved in order to better meet the needs the refugees. I collected the data by trying to make the time of the interview into a joint process. By this, I mean that the interviewees and the researcher together actively shaped the form of the interviews. Hydén (2008: 123) calls this a circular process, where both parties are trying to make continuing sense of what they are talking about.

MAIN FINDINGS

I found six different kinds of experiences of positive care relations in the early stages of arrival in Finland. These relationships are formed between the interviewees' own ethnic community or association, Finnish civil servants, religious communities and Finnish people, such as neighbours. One group of extracts are about those refugees, who did not find any people outside their family on whom to rely in the early stages of arrival to Finland. There are also experiences where the prior dependency relations are between those who are still living in their countries of origin. The resettled refugees are still responsible for the well-being of their dependents in the countries of origin and therefore their own settlement and integration seem to be in the secondary place in their lives. Next, I'll introduce the analyses of these relationships.

Own Community or Ethnic Association

The main source of care is the relationship with a refugees's own ethnic community and associations formed by the immigrants who have arrived to Finland earlier. The experiences of care relations are expressed next:

> W: They are lucky because we came here before and we are helping them, for them everything is possible because I just say, call me whenever you need help ... They [immigrant services] are not coming here ... It is really very different culture. They are afraid here.
> M: Our association can help, because we know what people need. You [civil servants] know also but when a person says that I come from the village we know what that village means and due to that we need cooperation.

The role of own communities and association was the first place while asking help and building care relations in these extracts. This role is diverse in the data. First, the data show that refugees ask help from their own community for learning to know how the everyday life practices function. They may not have very strong future goals to integrate to the new society, but they would like to keep their past cultural habits as strongly as it is possible. These people may benefit from the activities of the ethno-cultural associations already in the early stages of arrival. They do not ask help from civil servants and also they may not find help beyond their own community due to lack of language and other skills. This type of associations exits in the many areas of Finland, which aim at strengthening the identity of immigrants mainly by organizing social and ethno-cultural activities (Pyykkönen 2007; Saksela-Bergholm 2009).

According to my previous studies some refugees may need a long time to build safety and trust to the stakeholders of the new society. The signs of care and moral behaviour of the civil servants were the guarantee that they are worth trusting and it is possible to ask help from them (Turtiainen 2009b). Another type of relationship with associations during the settlement period concern those who would like to integrate immediately with the inhabitants and activities in the new society. Their aim is to build relations beyond the associations not only to the members of their own ethnic group. There are such societal associations in Finland, which provide services for immigrants, such as counselling (Pyykkönen 2007; Saksela-Bergholm 2009: 273). Besides, there are societal associations, which focus on their activities in helping immigrants into the labour market and educational system (ibid.).These activities can help the informants, who have a school background and study skills. Many refugees did not have a possibility to go to school or study due to the unrest in their countries or they did not have an access to school or to study in the refugee camps. Saksela-Bergholm (2009) has mapped the Finnish immigrant associations and she found out that most of them belong to the integrative category.

Immigrant associations have an important role in meeting and responding to the immediate needs of the newly arrived refugees in Finland. According to my data there were no gender differences in these extracts. Both female and male are able to be positively dependent on the associations and their own community. Associations can strengthen the self-confidence by providing care in a mutual relationship (Honneth 1995).

Civil Servants

My previous studies show that it often took time before refugees identify civil servants as care givers.[7] But there were also trust stories and positive dependency to civil servants. Refugees would like be cared for as women, as single mothers and their background recognized, including sorrows, traumas and fears. Often it took a long time before the trust formation towards civil servants took place (Turtiainen 2009a; 2012). The following extract explains the basis of the relations between refugees and civil servants:

M: It helps when it is said a word 'help' that already helps me and gives me peace.

According to my data, in many extracts, civil servants are identified as care givers. It is seen in the next extracts:

> W: As a single mother, it is so hard. It went so well because they took care of the practical things... My child is handicapped and I am a single mother, I have the most difficult situation ... A social worker came to me because here the state is behind the people, thus it is not only a person from next door whom to be dependent on.
>
> M: It was so important when you [civil servants] listen to our stories ... by listening, you know how to help us ... We had so terrible experiences and here we had an opportunity to release our feelings.
>
> M: I felt so good when I realised that somebody cares about how I feel ... we had that group with the psychologist and it has helped me until these days.

In these extracts, the Finnish welfare state was understood as a source of help and care. Before coming to Finland the only source of help may be the neighbours whose good will she had to rely on and be dependent on them. Refugees often come from weak states where there is no infrastructure to fulfil the immediate needs of the people. For the refugees, the reason to escape from their own countries is the lack of state protection. Public authorities, such as police, could be a perpetrator of persecution of the refugees. Moreover, the state supports groups who persecute refugees. Therefore, it is obvious to have doubts about the good will and morality of the public authorities. In Finland, the idea is that the provision of care and safety is taken over by the receiving workers and new networks because the family or other close relations may not be available. Also practical help is needed since the beginning due the life situation, such as being a single parent or having health problems.

Sometimes there is a confusion of the role of civil servants because, for example, the expertise of the social workers is not something familiar. This was expressed in one extract:

> W: Tell them directly who you are that you are not policemen ... and you are like a friend, ok, not like a friend but you want to help.

Social and also emotional care relations with refugees and civil servants are possible just after arrival to Finland. Even if Honneth (1995: 129) situates this kind of care in the family context, but because care is understood as an attitude, and as the opposite of a lack of concern, and indifference towards the well-being of other people, care must be expected to take place in the public sphere. The gender differences are not seen essential in the experiences of care relations between refugees and civil servants. The only difference is that men speak more about the experiences of healing from the traumatic experiences and women needed more practical support in order to build an everyday life. This could be also a consequence of the life situation of the women who are single mothers and they have to take care of the daily needs of their dependents. There were also experiences of the young boys who took care of the family and relatives before coming to Finland. After arrival they benefit from the help of the civil servants because they could have relief and more autonomy for their own future goals, such as studies.

Religious Organizations and Churches

A special type of positive care relations are formed with the religious communities, churches and mosques.

> W: The church, they pray for me and I can tell them my situation and I can trust them as I can trust my friends ... they help a lot.

This experience shows how important the church could be after resettlement. My data show that refugees often rely on the churches or faith-based organizations and communities during the escape from persecution in their own countries and in the country to which they escaped. Therefore, it is easy to contact the organization which was already known in their own country, besides, they also know that one aim of the religious community is to provide help for those in need. Also, Martikainen (2004) states that in general, people with a Christian background 'join already established congregations, which is significantly easier than organizing new religious activities'. In addition, the universal feature of Christian organization is understood by the immigrants. Therefore, according to Martikainen, Christians attend more often the communities than the members of other religious communities. This kind of continuity, inside the community in concern, is known as a 'chain of trust' (Coleman 1990: 180–188), which enables asking for support from the members of the already familiar community. Gallo (2014: 4), for example, states that among the South Asian migrants in Europe, religion supports framing of collective diasporic identities. Also in Finland the substructures, for example, based on a shared language inside the religious communities, may benefit formation of such collective diasporic identities.[8] In my data the religious communities have an important role in the early stages of arrival in Finland and no gender differences exist.

Finnish People

A relationship to local Finnish people after arrival in Finland is emphasized in the data as it is expressed here:

> W: It will be very good, if there would have been a Finnish friend, such a support person for us. I have a feeling that in the beginning you need such a teacher … so that a person can show by her or his behaviour how it is here.
>
> M: In the beginning [after resettlement] it feels that here we were born again.

There are extracts where the contact to Finnish people is desired as early as possible after arrival. The urgent need to get integrated into the new society is also mentioned, which could also reduce the embarrassment of trying to belong without enough knowledge on how to 'behave' in the new society. This is an experience of how people became dependent on the people living in the same area. There are no problems in getting support from the Finnish people but refugees could not find such people very easily.

> W: It is hard for me if a migrant [from my own community] comes to my home. If a Finn comes, then it is normal, for example, if I am sick I can ask help from Finnish people such as, please, water my flowers, can you clean a little bit, and at the same time, please help yourself and make coffee … But if an immigrant comes, you know. One person [mention the ethnicity] said, I never can be a friend to Finn, but I say the Finnish people are the same kind of persons as I am, they are like me.

In my data, not all the informants are willing to have contacts with their own community. It is also mentioned that they did not feel good to be with their own community because of the pressure to use cultural signs such as scarf. As expressed in the extract, there is a pressure and also a demand to behave according to the cultural role expectations as a woman. So, for the women it can be relieving to depend on the people without role expectations. This is expressed by the single mothers, who also sometimes experience harassment by the men from their own ethnic group. If they don't find Finnish people and if there is no trust for authorities, these women could be isolated inside their homes.

Myself

My data (next extracts) show that there are experiences of the refugees who are very alone in their new situation:

> W: Because we did not find our own community, therefore we [family] had to rely on our own help.
> W: I say to myself that I have to study a lot ... In the beginning I did not trust Finnish people, they help only each other. But I am black. I try to cope by myself.
> W: I have told that we have to help each other because we don't have anybody (relatives) here for us.

These experiences of refugees describe the survival without any remarkable networks outside their own family. The main reason for being alone is the lack of their community in that area. Civil servants are there but they are not identified as care givers. This can hardly be named as positive dependency. However, the self-confidence as a survivor still exists and a possibility to take care of their own well-being in a new situation. In my previous studies, I name this kind of relationships with authorities as negative dependency (Turtiainen 2011). By this, I mean that even if people really need help, they did not ask for it from anybody. It appeared in the data, for example, that refugees used a lot of time and energy to do practical things alone without help. These refugees systemically denied help, which could be available. On the other side, Finnish social services can appear distant, inflexible and not gender- and ethnic-sensitive in their response (Vuori et al. 2012). Also Tiilikainen's study (2007) on Somalian women and families shows that women prefer to build transnational networks in order to help each other while encountering problems, such as difficulties in bringing up their children, divorce or family violence.

As a Source of Care

My data that some prior dependency relations are linked to the countries of origin.

> M: It was very difficult in the beginning but through our co-operation [civil servants and service users] many problems are solved … but we are so-called hard cases because many problems are even worse and in the beginning [help needed in their home country] they are still there.
> W: Our situation is the same, nobody helps us, and our son is still there.

Refugee families shape a special form of global care chain (Piper 2006: 145–146) in a transnational context, with a strong emotional, social and economic dependency. The family members are often in the state of limbo in their countries of origin. There could be an expectation that family members will help and even rescue those who still live in the countries of origin. Their own settlement and integration is in the secondary place while the prior concern is a moral responsibility to help family members in the homeland through different organizations. In Finland, there are still quite few transnational associations, which aim at transnational activities such as improving the living conditions of their countrymen, mainly women and children, in their homeland. Transnational activities were organized mainly by people living in the diaspora, such as the Kurds and Somalis (Saksela-Bergholm 2009; Wahlbeck 1999). Often females are preferred to carry the responsibility for the relatives in the transnational networks (Piper 2006). In my data, both male and female informants express a strong obligation to take care of their relatives in their countries of origin.

CONCLUSION

In my data, I found six types of different kinds of primary care relations, which refugees rely on after arrival in Finland. The role of their own communities or associations is essential after resettlement. These associations have been established by persons who have come to Finland earlier from the same areas. Relations are built based on information sharing, assisting in building everyday life and being available when needed. These associations also build a bridge between the public authorities and societal activities, enabling the agency of the newcomers in a new society. Also the role of the host community is an important stakeholder in the integration of the new refugees in the new country. Besides, the transnational networks have an impact on the well-being of the resettled refugees because refugees may have their prior care relations in the countries of origin.

The major gender differences are not seen in the data. The only difference that is seen is that single mothers benefit from a strong presence of social services and they were happy to get more autonomy for their future plans which was never possible before resettlement. Another difference is seen that victims of torture and violence were male and they benefit from the services as well. Due to the qualitative research being limited, any further conclusions are not possible.

In the current economic recession and discriminatory public opinion towards forced migrants, there is a political debate concerning the size of the quota of resettled refugees, as well as the level of social welfare and social security in general. However, the current situation where there are constantly increasing numbers of asylum seekers and refugees waiting for resettlement, the pressure should be in the opposite direction, that is, the refugee quota should be increased. This study shows that resettlement is a human way of finding the sustainable solutions for the refugees living without any state protection. Finland, even if it has a small immigrant population, has developed a quite functional programme to resettle refugees.

This programme is in the process of promoting and empowering the stakeholders within the public sphere and has a tendency to co-operate with migrant communities. It looks humane and also very rational to continue already established practice of receiving quota refugees in co-operation with UNHCR. Besides, Finland as a member of UN and European Union has a responsibility to share the responsibility of the asylum seekers coming to European territory. The problems in the integration process seems to be minor ones compared to the desperate journey to seeking asylum and waiting decisions in Europe, or as is happening, drowning in the Mediterranean Sea.

NOTES

1   Article 1 A (2) of the 1951 Convention Relating to the Status of Refugees (UN General Assembly 1951) defines a refugee: as someone who has left his or her country or is unable or unwilling to return to it 'owing to a well-founded fear of being persecuted for reasons of race, religion, nationality, membership of a particular social group or political opinion' (UNCHR 2011).

2   There is a comprehensive literature on global care and care chains concerning paid and unpaid care work (e.g., Lutz 2008); e.g., Lisa Widding Isaksen's (2010) significant article collection on gender and migration in Nordic countries explains the migrant women's situation in labour market.

3   The other components are social esteem, which concerns person's capacities such as knowhow and skills, which contribute to the common good of the society and respecting rights of the people. Also Canadian philosopher Charles Taylors's theory of recognition (1992) is an important aspect. For him recognition is also a vital human need. The American feminist philosopher, Nancy Fraser (1997) with her broader theory of justice, is a third significant academic who has contributed to this theory.

4   Respect concerns our rights and therefore us as legal individuals (Honneth 1995).

5   Feminist ethics of care highlight the relational nature of ethics instead of applying hierarchical rules in a hierarchical order. The pioneer of the feminist ethics of care is Carol Gilligan (1982). Later, the care ethics have been developed for example with many other authors, by Nel Noddings (2003), Annette Bair (1994), Joan Tronto (1993), Selma Sevenhuijsen (1998) and Daryl Koehn (1998).

6   In Spring 2015, there were an initiative for new law for the irregular migrants' right to get health care for serious chronic diseases and also health care for migrant children and pregnant women. This initiative was not accepted. The supporters of the law say that health care is a human right and opponents claim that paperless people are just 'health tourists', who do not deserve health care.

7   I have earlier studied the trust formation, recognition and negative dependency between refugees and Finnish civil servants (Turtiainen 2009a, 2009b, 2011, 2012). I have looked closer to regocnitive attitudes of respect and social esteem. Care is the third recognitive attitude and I look at it here from the point of view of positive dependency.

8   Globalization with regard to religions in Finland is a rather new phenomenon, starting from the latter part of the nineteenth century (Martikainen 2004).

REFERENCES

Anis, Merja. 2012. Isäkuvat Monikulttuurissa Lastensuojelun Kohtaamisissa (Images about Fathers in Multicultural Child Welfare Service Encounters), in Suvi Keskinen, Jaana Vuori and Anu Hirsiaho, eds, '*Monikulttuurisuuden Sukupuoli. Kansalaisuus ja Erot Hyvinvointiyhteiskunnassa*' (*Multicultural Gender: Citizenship and Differences in a Welfare Society*). Tampere: Tampere University Press, 321–48.

Baier, Annette. 1995. 'Trust and Antitrust', *Ethics* 96: 231–60.

———. 1994. *Moral Prejudices: Essays on Ethics*. Cambridge, MA: Harvard University Press.

Benhabib, Seyla. 2001. *Transformation of Citizenship: Dilemmas of the Nation State of the Era of Globalization: Two Lectures*. Amsterdam: The Department of the University of Amsterdam, Koninklijke Van Gorcum.

Betts, Alexander. 2013. *Survival Migration: Failed Governance and the Crisis of Displacement*. Ithaca: NY: Cornell University Press.

Brian, Tara, and Frank Laczko. 2014.' Fatal Journeys, Tracking Lives Lost during Migration', (IOM) International Organization for Migration. Retrieved from http://www.iom.int/files/live/sites/iom/files/pbn/docs/Fatal-Journeys-Tracking-Lives-Lost-during-Migration-2014.pdf, accessed on 10 June 2015.

Castles, Stephen, and Mark J. Miller. 2009. *The Age of Migration, International Population Movements in the Modern World,* 4th ed. New York: Palgrave Macmillan.

Chimni, B. S. 2000. Who Is a Refugee?, in B. S. Chimni, ed., *International Refugee Law. A Reader*. Thousand Oaks, CA: SAGE Publications, 1–8.

Coleman, James S. 1990. *Foundations of Social Theory*. Cambridge, MA: Harvard University Press.

Dahl, Hanne Marlene, and Tina Rask Eriksen. 2005. 'Introduction', in Hanne Marlene Dahl and Tina Rask Eriksen eds. *Dilemmas of Care in the Nordic Welfare State, Continuity and Change*. Farnjam: Ashgate, 1–14.

Eurostat 2018. Retrieved from https://ec.europa.eu/eurostat/statistics-explained/index.php/Asylum_statistics#Number_of_asylum_applicants:_drop_in_2017, accessed on 8 December 2018.

Fraser, Nancy. 1997. 'From Redistribution to Recognition? Dilemmas of Justice in a "Post-Socialist" Age', in Nancy Fraser, ed. *Justice Interrupts: Critical Reflections on the "Post-Socialist Condition"*. London: Routledge, 11–39.

Gallo, Ester. 2014. 'Introduction. South Asian Migration and Religious Pluralism in Europe', in Ester Gallo, ed., *Urban Anthropology: Migration and Religion in Europe: Comparative Perspectives on South Asian Experiences*. Farnham: Ashgate, 1–27.

Gerard, Allison, and Sharon Pickering. 2013. 'Gender, Securitization and Transit: Refugee Women and the Journey to the EU', *Journal of Refugee Studies* 27, 3: 338–59.

Gibney, Matthew. 2006. *The Ethics and Politics of Asylum*. Cambridge: Cambridge University Press.

Gibney, Matthew, and Randall Hansen. 2003. 'Asylum Policy in the West: Past Trends, Future Possibilities', Reseach Discussion Paper No. 2003/68. World Institute for Development Economics (3 **September**): 424–29.

Gilligan, Carol. 1982. *In a Different Voice: Psychological Theory and Women's Development*. Cambridge, MA: Harvard University Press.

Hathaway, James C. 1991. 'The Development of Refugee Definition in International Law', in James C. Hathaway, *The Law of Refugee Status*. Toronto: Butterworths, 1–24.

Honneth, Axel. 1995. *The Struggle for Recognition—The Moral Grammar of Social Conflicts*. Cambridge: Polity Press.

———. 2007. *Disrespect. The Normative Foundations of Critical Theory*. Cambridge: Polity Press.

Hydén, Margareta. 2008. 'Narrating Sensitive Topics', in Molly Andrews, Corinne Squire and Maria Tamboukou, eds. *Doing Narrative Research*. Los Angeles, CA: SAGE Publications,122–36.

IOM 2018. Retrieved from https://www.iom.int/, accessed on 8 December 2018.

Ikäheimo, Heikki. 2003. 'On the Genus and Species of Recognition', in Heikki Ikäheimo, ed. *Tunnustus, Subjektiviteetti ja Inhimillinen Elämänmuoto. Tutkimuksia Hegelistä ja Persoonien Välisistä Tunnustussuhteista* (Subjectivity and the Human Life Form: Studies on Hegel and Interpersonal Recognition). Jyväskylä Studies in Education, Psychology and Social Research 220. Jyväskylä: University of Jyväskylä.

Jacobsen, Karen, and Loren B. Landau. 2003. *The Dual Imperative in Refugee Research: Some Methodological and Ethical Considerations in Social Science Research on Forced Migration', Disasters, Issues in Refugee Research*, Working Paper No. 90, UNHCR, Geneva. Retrieved from http//www.unhcr.ch/, accessed on 20 May 2010.

Jönsson Jessica H. 2014. 'Local Reactions to Global Problems: Undocumented Immigrants and Social Work', *British Journal of Social Work* 44 (Supplement 1), 35–52.

Keskinen, Suvi, Vuori, Jaana, and Anu Hirsiaho, eds, 2012. *Monikulttuurisuuden Sukupuoli. Kansalaisuus ja Erot Hyvinvointiyhteiskunnassa* (Multicultural Gender: Citizenship and Differences in a Welfare Society). Tampere: Tampere University Press.

Lutz, Helma. 2008. *Migration and Domestic Work. A European Perspective on a Global Theme*. Farnham: Ashgate.

Koehn, Daryl. 1998. *Rethinking Feminist Ethics: Care, Trust and Empathy*. London: Routledge.

Martikainen, Tuomas. 2004. *Immigrant Religions in Local Society: Historical and Contemporary Perspectives in the City of Turku*. Åbo: Åbo Akademi University Press.

Mead, George Herbert. 1934. *Mind, Self and Society from the Standpoint of a Social Behaviourist*, edited with Introduction by Charles W. Morris. Chicago, IL: University of Chicago Press.

Missing Migrants 2018. Retrieved fromt http://migration.iom.int/europe?type= arrivals, accessed on 8 December 2018.

Noddings, Nel. 2003. *Caring: A Feminine Approach to Ethics and Moral Education*, 2nd. ed. Berkeley: University of California Press.

Patton, Michael Q. 2002. *Qualitative Research and Evaluation Methods*. Thousand Oaks, CA: SAGE Publications.

Piper, Nicola. 2006. 'Gendering the Politics of Migration'. *IMR* 40, 1: 133–64.

Pirjola, Jari. 2009. 'European Asylum Policy—Inclusions and Exclusions under the Surface of Human Rights Language', *European Journal of Migration and Law* 11: 347–66.

Potter, Jonathan. 1996. *Representing Reality. Discourse, Rhetoric and Social Construction*. London: SAGE Publications.

Pyykkönen, Miikka. 2007. *Järjestäytyvät Diasporat. Etnisyys, Kansalaisuus, Integraatio ja Hallinta Maahanmuuttajien Yhdistystoiminnassa* (Organizing Diasporas. Ethnicity, Citizenship, Integration, and Government in Immigrant Associations). Jyväskylä: University of Jyväskylä.

Raghuram, Parvati. 2012. 'Global Care, Local Configurations—Challenges to Conceptualizations of Care', *Global Networks* 12, 2: 155–74.

Saksela-Bergholm, Sanna. 2009. 'Immigrant Associations in the Metropolitan Area of Finland: Forms of Mobilisation, Participation and Representation', Faculty of Social Sciences, Department of Sociology, Nr 27. Swedish School of Social Science, University of Helsinki.

Sevenhuijsen, Selma. 1998. *Citizenship and the Ethics of Care. Feminist Considerations on Justice, Morality and Politics*, translated from Dutch to English by Liz Savage. London: Routledge.

Shacknove, Andrew E. 1985. 'Who Is a Refugee?', *Ethics* 95, 2: 274–84.

Simmel, Georg. 1978. *The Philosophy of Money*. London: Routledge.

Taylor, Charles. 1992. *Ethics of Authenticity*, Cambridge, MA: Harvard University Press.

The Finnish Immigration Service. 2018. Retrieved from http://tilastot.migri. fi/#applications/21205?l=en&start=564&end=575, accessed on 8 December 2018.

Tiilikainen, Marja. 2007. *Somaliäidit ja Transnationaali Perhe* (Somalian Mothers and Transnational Family), in Tuomas Martikainen and Marja Tiilikainen, eds. *Migrant Woman: Integration, Family and Work*, Väestöntutkimuslaitoksen Julkaisusarja D 46/2007. Helsinki: Väestöliitto, 266–84.

Tuomi and Sarajärvi. 2002. *Laadullinen Tutkimus ja Sisällönanalyysi* (Qualitative Research and Content Analysis). Helsinki: Tammi.

Tronto, Joan. 1993. *Moral Boundaries. A Political Argument for an Ethic of Care*. London: Routledge,

Turtiainen, Kati. 2012. 'Possibilities of Trust and Recognition between Refugees and Authorities: Resettlement as part of Durable Solutions to Forced Migration', Jyväskylä Studies in Education, *Psychology and Social Research* 451, Jyväskylä: University of Jyväskylä.

——. 2011. *Riippuvuus Pakolaisia Vastaanottavassa Sosiaalityössä* (Dependency in the Refugee Resettlement Social Work), in Aini Pehkonen and Marja

Väänänen-Fomin, eds., *Sosiaalityön Arvot ja Etiikka* (*The Ethics and Values in Social*). Sosiaalityön tutkimuksen Seuran Vuosikirja. PS-Kustannus, Jyväskylä, 139–64.

——. 2009a. 'Recognition and Recognitive Attitudes between Refugees and Authorities. A Finnish Example' in Vesna Leskosek, *Theories and Methods of Social Work. Exploring Different Perspectives*, Faculty of Social Work. University of Ljubljana, 149–61.

——. 2009b. Kertomuksia Uuden Kynnyksellä—Luottamuksen Rakentuminen Kiintiöpakolaisten ja Viranomaisten Välillä (Stories on the New Step after Arriving to Finland. Trust Building between Quota Refugees and Public Authorities). *Janus* 4, 17: 329–45.

Turton, David. 2003. 'Conceptualizing Forced Migration'. RSC Working paper 12. Retrieved from https://www.rsc.ox.ac.uk, accessed on 20 May 2015; http://www.unhcr.org/refworld/docid/45339d922.html, accessed on 10 June 2015.

UNHCR. 2006. 'Conclusion', on 'Women and Girls at Risk', 6 October 2006, No. 105 (LVII) 2006, accessed on 15 November 2017.

——. 2010. *Statistical Yearbook 2009*. 'Trends in Displacement, Protection and Solutions'. Retrieved from http://www.unhcr.org/, accessed on 14 August 2017.

——. 2011. *The Convention 1951 and Its 1967 Protocol Relating to Status of Refugees*. Retrieved from http://www.unhcr.org/1951-refugee-convention. html, accessed on 15 November 2017.

——. 2017. *Global Trends, Forced Displacement in 2017*. Retrieved from https://www.unhcr.org/statistics/unhcrstats/5b27be547/unhcr-global-trends-2017.html, accessed on 8 December 2018.

Vuori, Jaana. 2012. *Arjen Kansalaisuus, Sukupuoli ja Kotouttamistyö* (Everyday Citizenship, Gender and Integration Work), in Suvi Keskinen, Jaana Vuori and Anu Hirsiaho, eds. *Monikulttuurisuuden sukupuoli: Kansalaisuus ja Erot Hyvinvointiyhteiskunnassa* (Multicultural Gender: Citizenship and Differences in a Welfare Society). Tampere: Tampere University Press, 235–62.

Wahlbeck, Östen. 1999. *Kurdish Diasporas: A Comparative Study of Kurdish Refugee Communities*. London: Macmillan.

Warness, Kari. 2005. 'Social Research, Political Theory and the Ethics of Care in a Global Perspective', in Hanne Marlene Dahl and Tina Rask Eriksen, eds. *Dilemmas of Care in the Nordic Welfare State. Continuity and Change*. Farnham: Ashgate, 15–32.

Widding Isaksen, Lisa. 2010. '*Global Care Work. Gender and Migration in Nordic Societies'*. Lund: Nordic Academia Press.

Winnicott, Donald, W. 1971. *Child, the Family and the Outside World*. Harmondsworth: Penguin.

9

Requestioning Identity: Female Descendants of Immigrants from Former Yugoslavia in Slovenia

MATEJA SEDMAK

THE HIGHLY CURRENT topic of migrations and migration experiences has been receiving considerable research attention within the social sciences. As a result of the universal presence of migrations, which are in the globalized world actually becoming a total phenomenon, and expectations that this trend will continue to increase throughout the world as a result of economic, political, as well as ecological and other reasons, do not seem to be losing steam. From the macro-social perspective, migrations represent an important economic and political issue.

In the last few decades there is an increasing interest on the gender perspective of migration and some authors are even speaking about the feminization of migration. However, it could well be that there is essentially no change in migration patterns but a rising interest of researchers on questions of the relationship between the gender and migration phenomena (Vezzoli et al. 2014). The general invisibility of women in migration studies starts to change in the 1980s and 1990s with the development of the feminist approach in the study of migration and emergence of interest in issues of migration patterns associated with gender, such as the correlation between gender, class, ethnicity and migration, the violence against migrant women, influence of women's migration on family, women labour migration on the axis of brain drain—care drain, and so on.

What is also important to emphasize while discussing the gender perspective is the trap of stereotypes and normative expectations which too often present women migrants as one dimensional personages (victims, passively accompanying husbands, domestic workers) and denies the diversity of migration experiences and the participatory and decision-making approach.

An approach to research on the women migrants could be from the macro- and micro-perspective, exploring, for example, the social and economic consequences of their migration or subjective individual trajectories and everyday perspectives.

This chapter will focus on *subjective experiences* and narratives of migrants. More specifically, these will be women, the descendants of immigrants.

Why *female descendants of immigrants?*[1] The international professional and academic community share a relatively common stance concerning expectations from the first generation of migrants: their decision to move has been either voluntary or made forcedly under the threat of political persecution or war, among other reasons. Upon arrival in their host country they are *foreigners* who fail to understand the seemingly obvious routines of everyday life and culture codes of the new environment (Schutz 1987). They need to confront numerous problems related to cultural adaptation, segregation and discrimination. Some opt to return to their homelands, others may create families in their new environment. Countries have adopted different approaches to solving the problems encountered by immigrants and providing assistance programmes for facilitating faster, and more efficient adaptation/assimilation which are in line with their actual social policy orientations. However, when the focus is placed on female and male descendants of immigrants, social expectations change.

Descendants of immigrants, children who have been born and socialized in the formal system of their parents' host country, are expected to be well integrated or, more than that, assimilated into the new social milieu of their parents. In addition, descendants of immigrants have not *made the decision* to move to another cultural environment but were born in their parents' host country. The consequences of denying the complex issue of integration of the descendants of immigrants into society (of the host country and usually the only country that they perceive to be their homeland) have become a subject of increased academic interest only after the empirical reality of European countries has pointed out their unbearable situation (here we recall street riots in the suburbs of London and Paris at the turn of the millennium). These revolts personify the powerlessness of a young generation which has been rejected by the country and the society in which they were born. These are acts of rebellion on the part of a group that is experiencing social and spatial segregation, lower educational opportunities, unemployment, and social hopelessness instead of social equality, whereas on the other hand, the society is nourishing unreal expectations that their adaptation to or assimilation into their parents' host country would be unproblematic. As mentioned earlier, despite being the only home that they actually know and thus have nowhere else to 'go back to', society at large continuously reminds them that they are not its equal members.

Why *women*? From the feminist perspective the experiences of women (migrants) differ from those of men. Men are traditionally entitled to more freedom to make personal choices, more opportunities, and activities. Female migrants are thus exposed to double discrimination: as migrants and as women. The narratives of female respondents presented further on in this chapter bear witness to a higher degree of 'restraint' or lower degree of freedom to make entirely independent choices, and a higher degree of adaptation to the customs and expectations of the nuclear family, relatives and cultural environment. These may intensify if their culture of origin is strongly committed to traditional and patriarchal norms.

I take a narrow focus on an aspect of the migration experience that critically marks the whole person: this will be *identity* or a subjective answer to the question '*Who am I?*' in relation to requisitioning one's ethnic, cultural, and state affiliation. Based on the case of female descendants of immigrants who had left the territories of the former Socialist Federal Yugoslavia and moved to Slovenia, an attempt will be made to reject assumptions of the existence of singular and exclusive identities, and to present the complex, plural, hybrid, and transcultural nature of ethnic and state affiliations. Within this context, three closely linked, intertwining and yet separate issues will be examined: *(i)* the problematic nature of monoethnic definitions; *(ii)* the fact that ethnic boundaries do not necessarily overlap with state and cultural borders; and *(iii)* the complexity of self-perception processes and identity bricolage. The reflection on the complexity of identity definitions will reject the erroneous assumption concerning the unproblematic ethnic assimilation of female descendants of immigrants into the dominant culture of the environment into which they were born and in which they underwent formal and institutional socialization through educational and other systems. In addition, their in-between status of being caught between two cultural worlds will be presented.

SOCIO-HISTORICAL AND POLITICAL BACKGROUND OF IMMIGRATION FLOWS

Let us consider the identity of female members of the nations of former Yugoslavia whose parents emigrated to Slovenia. Therefore, some facts and circumstances regarding the socio-historical and political background of these migrations will be presented. Slovenia was at one time a part of the former Yugoslavia between the Second World War and 1991 when it gained independence.[2] Within the common political, economic as well as monetary system, Slovenia was economically the most developed and richest republic. As a result, it was an attractive destination for economic migrants from other parts of the former common state (in particular Bosnia and Herzegovina and Kosovo but also Serbia, Croatia, Montenegro and Vojvodina). Geographically speaking, having borders with Italy in the west and Austria in the north, Slovenia represented Yugoslavia's point of contact with the West. The other two political neighbours are Hungary, and Croatia after 1991 and its secession from Yugoslavia.

Immigration from territories of the former Yugoslavia can be divided into two waves. The first wave which took place after the Second World War reached its peak in the 1970s (Klopcic et al. 2003) when the developing industry required and invited manual workers, in particular, men with low levels of formal education. These were internal (intrastate) economic migrations. The second wave of immigration happened in the 1990s, following Slovenian independence and the disintegration of the once common state, when political immigrants were forced to leave their homes during the war in the Balkans. During this period, refugees from war-stricken Bosnia and economic migrants sought refuge in Slovenia. These had become interstate migrations, which further complicated the procedures for the acquisition of residential and work permits. In order to better understand the status of immigrants from the territories of former Yugoslavia, we should bear in mind that despite the relatively high numbers of their members, these groups have not managed to acquire minority status with special protection rights similar to those granted to the Italian and Hungarian autochthonous minorities.[3] This status grants special rights, for instance, formal bilingualism in the areas where autochthonous or traditional minorities live, the right to education in their mother tongue, political representation at the local and national (parliamentary) levels, and other special measures aiming at the preservation and protection of formally acknowledged national minorities.

In the common state of Yugoslavia, the question of ethnicity and ethnic identity were not a priority or, in other words, it was 'under-communicated' (Eriksen 1993). Moreover, in the 1970s the phenomenon of affiliation to a 'Yugoslav identity' started to spread and numerous citizens of Yugoslavia declared their nationality to be 'Yugoslav'. Therefore, the definition of their ethnic identity was supra-ethnic or adjusted to state affiliation. The irrelevance of ethnic identity was being consolidated further by 'brotherhood and unity', one of the key ideological principles of the former common state. Unfortunately, the developments following the disintegration of Yugoslavia and in particular the war in the Balkans with a significant underlying ethnic conflict highlight the fact that the ethnic issue in former Yugoslavia was not at all as unproblematic as presented. The non-unproblematic nature of the ethnic issue is corroborated by the ever-present Slovenian pejorative stance toward all immigrants from territories 'to the south of Slovenia' (i.e., from territories of former Yugoslavia) and the concomitant high degree of acceptance and even admiration of immigrants from developed western states of Europe and the world. Discriminatory treatment, ethnic prejudice, and stereotypes in relation to the immigrants from territories of former Yugoslavia have been subject to extensive research (see also Klopcic et al. 2003; Komac and Medvescek 2005).

As far as the number of immigrants from the former Yugoslavia is concerned, there seems to be a consensus that despite the recorded (hence formal) high degree of immigration, their number is actually even higher.[4] Until 1991 these migrations had been intrastate migrations. This could indicate that a significant share of migrants did not have their arrivals registered and the actual statistics should be viewed as a resource for observing trends rather than providing actual migration data.

IDENTITY BRICOLAGE OF FEMALE DESCENDANTS OF IMMIGRANTS

Numerous economic migrants created their new homes and families in Slovenia and stayed there despite the possibility that this may not have been their original intention. The next section discusses the narratives of female descendants of immigrants whose parents had come to Slovenia from other republics of the former Yugoslavia.[5] As mentioned in the Introduction, the three key questions which expose the in-between status and complexity of ethnic identities of second generation female migrants will be covered. My final comments are on the denial of the erroneous predisposition regarding the predominant and unproblematic ethnic assimilation of the female descendants of immigrants into the dominant culture, language, and religion of the environment into which they were born and in which they underwent formal and institutional socialization through educational and other systems.

Question One: The Problematic Nature of Monoethnic Definitions

The life stories of women—descendants of immigrants from the territories of former Yugoslavia who had moved to Slovenia and stayed there primarily for economic reasons—expose the problem of simple and singular or monoethnic definitions. The problem of a monoethnic definition, either following the ethnicity of their parents or that of the majority ethnic group (i.e., being 'Slovenian'), emerges in several different ways.

For instance, in an attempt at self-definition and in the quest for an answer to the question '*Who am I?*' in terms of ethnic affiliation, the narratives of female descendants of immigrants reveal a phenomenon that can be referred to as 'fluidity of ethnic identity'. The term 'fluidity' is used here to denote the shifting of a person from one identity to another and back, which can occur several times, take multiple directions, and adopt varying levels of intensity during different periods of one's life. The fluidity of ethnic identity can be presented through the example of M., aged 38, descendant of Bosnian parents, who says:

> I can't be Slovenian. I'm actually Muslim. This means—Bosnian.... I always spoke Slovenian to mother because mother wanted us to stick to 'this system' because we are here in Slovenia].... But when I was little, I wanted to be Slovenian. I have a house here, my home's here, I was born here.

Among other things, M.'s words reveal her own and her mother's wish to be 'Slovenian'. However, the environment constantly reminded her of her different ethnic origin and the fact that her parents are Bosnian, which inhibited her from simply adopting the definition of being 'Slovenian'. Her narrative expresses the continual process of bargaining between two identities: Bosniac and Slovenian. During one period of her life M. felt more Slovenian than Bosnian (e.g., in her early childhood) but later the ethnic prejudice and stereotypes present in her living environment (teasing her for the non-Slovenian names of her parents, insinuation of bad body odour for being Bosnian, and so on.) 'reminded' her of not being Slovenian. M. largely adopted a Bosnian identity after getting married to a first generation Bosnian migrant who does not speak Slovenian and is a practising Muslim. However, she does emphasize that she is a 'tourist' when visiting Bosnia.

A second example that exposes the problematic nature of singular, monoethnic definitions among female descendants of immigrants is the answer 'I don't know', when asked to give an explicit answer to the question 'Who are you? Are you Slovenian, Croatian? Are you Bosnian or Slovenian?'

This is clearly shown by the narrative of A., aged 32, daughter of Bosnian parents who had moved to Slovenia in the late 1970s for economic reasons. A.'s reply to the question 'Who are you?', referring to national affiliation and identity, was 'I don't know. I truly don't know.' On a different occasion she said: 'I'm mixed', and 'My mother tongues are Slovenian and Bosnian.' An interesting aspect that should be reflected upon is her self-definition as a bilingual person given her exclusive use of the Bosnian language in her communication with her mother and father since birth. Nevertheless, she perceives herself as bilingual and a bearer of two mother tongues. She feels both languages to be hers and could not choose one over the other. The 'language aspect' that also M. mentioned in her narrative is another important element. The majority of linguistic and ethnic studies automatically define the mother tongue as the language that a child has learnt and used in their earliest years with their mother, father, or caretaker. The phenomenological and subjective, self-defining approach is what should be followed instead. Despite being ethnically mixed and incapable of singular ethnic definition, A. displays a revitalization of her Muslim ethnic identity after her marriage to a Bosnian, a Muslim from Bosnia, whom she met in Bosnia and who moved to Slovenia to be with her. Together they have two sons.

The narratives of the respondents reveal the general problem of articulating one's 'mixedness'. Despite their clear feelings and awareness of belonging to different cultures, they find it difficult to put these into words which would adequately describe their situation. How can the inability to offer a singular definition and the concomitant inability to define oneself as being mixed be explained? A possible answer lies in the process of the establishment of modern nation-states, which required a clear equation between the nation and the state or political territorial entity covered by one language, one culture, and one nation. As a result of specific socio-historical and political processes (the emergence of nation-states), Europe has internalized the discourse of nationalist ideology that has prevailed in science and politics as well as in everyday life. Hence, today we are used to 'thinking in terms of singular and exclusive definitions' within the boundaries of our (home) lands, cultures, and languages. The same can be applied to the field of identity, both ethnic and state identities. In Europe we bear witness to the ideological dictatorship of singular ethnic identities (I am a Slovenian, a German, or an Italian, for instance) and the conviction concerning the congruity of identities. In other words, each cultural identity should encompass a specific linguistic, religious, and state identity. In the lay, political, and academic discourse, the general stance is that, for instance, Slovenia is the home of primarily ethnic Slovenians who speak the Slovenian language, are Catholic, and who largely identify with the Slovenian state and its national symbols. What is more, ethnic identity as such generally represents the essential and central element of self-identification and identification from others. The reason for this, as mentioned above, lies in the very foundations of the emergence of modern nation states (in the eighteenth century) when newly established states had to be imbued with 'content', which were individuals who would be loyal members of these political entities. The establishment and prevalence of singular ethnic identities held key value for the founders of modern states. It would be exceptionally difficult to keep registers of the population, citizens, and taxpayers if, according to Vedery (1996), 'they are one thing at one point, another thing at another'. In addition, 'not only the forging of various 'identities' has been important in effecting control but also the idea that to have 'identities' are normal, and that any given person can 'have' only one identity of a certain basic kind (ethnic, national, gender)' (ibid.)

Therefore, the logic of (singular and exclusive) ethnic definitions gained ground through official censuses, statistical records, demographics, and school registers at local and national levels. Finally it slowly slipped into the general imaginary of the European continent. The self-definitions of Europeans are thus mostly mononational, monoethnic, linguistically exclusive and so forth (in relation to what we are not). Given that most population censuses and other statistics do not allow for the possibility of being dual or multiple, or have not done so until recently, exclusiveness is perceived as the norm (Sedmak and Zadel 2015).

These perceptions of (singular and exclusive) ethnic identities, so self-obvious to Western Europeans, make it difficult to 'think beyond' and yet these perceptions are certainly not the only ones possible. Empirical cases of ethnic identities from other cultural environments (e.g., Southeast Asia or the Middle East), where the flexibility, variability, and situation-dependency of ethnic definitions are much greater, show that different perceptions are possible. These have been discussed within theoretical reflections of postcolonial studies

(Jeffs 2007), and by advocates of transcultural (e.g., Welsch 1995) and hybrid (e.g., Homi Bhabha 1990) identities. In fact, similar to other social phenomena, ethnic identity is a social construct. This is why singular and exclusive ethnic definitions prevalent in modern day Europe primarily have to be seen as such.

Question Two: Incongruence between Ethnic, State and Cultural Boundaries

Let us explore ethnic, cultural, and state identities of female descendants of immigrants, whether these overlap or what is the relationship among them. *State identity* is understood as deriving from citizenship, the most tangible and objectively measurable identity. Nevertheless, one might not feel proud of or as though they actively belong to a state despite being a formal member of that state. *Ethnic identity* is understood as *national identity* (the term 'nationality' (Slovenian *narodnost*) would be generally used in the territory of the former Yugoslavia and is used instead/as a synonym of the term 'ethnicity'). On the other hand, *cultural identity* is understood as the identity that entails key cultural elements, such as language, religion, values, dietary habits, dress codes, folk music or, in other words, material and immaterial culture in its broadest sense. In this chapter the main criterion that defines cultural identity will be the mother tongue or 'first' language.[6]

The answers to the presented research questions theoretically lean onto the central idea of anthropologist Barth (1970, 1996) as presented in his *Ethnic Groups and Boundaries*. His work represents the turning point from the static approach to the research of ethnicity to an interactionist approach, emphasizing the importance of boundaries and preservation of group boundaries. Summarizing Barth, inter-group cultural differences do not have a key importance for the definition of ethnic identity given that ethnic boundaries and cultural boundaries do not necessarily overlap. In addition, equating ethnic groups with cultural groups allows a simplified and erroneous assumption of the unproblematic preservation of boundaries, and indicates the possibility of the existence of ethnic groups in isolation. According to Barth, a common (homogeneous) culture is a result of a long-term process and not a primordial characteristic of groups per se. Inter-group cultural variations are in fact a consequence of and not a cause for group boundaries. It is the production and reproduction of differences in relation to the external others that is at the very essence of the creation of internal similarities among us. Thus, an ethnic group is primarily a form of social organization in which the crucial role is played by the subjective self-perception of group members as members of a specific ethnic identity. An ethnic group has to be recognized as such from the *inside*—by the members of this group, and from the *outside*—by others.

The key element in this respect are boundaries that are, however, variable and changing. Therefore, we can experience changes of group culture without changing ethnic boundaries. Ethnic groups can become culturally closer while ethnic boundaries become stronger. This means that cultural variety is not essential until it is recognized as such by the ethnic groups in contact. It is the intensity of contact among groups that defines an ethnic community; in fact, isolated ethnic communities are least ethnically self-aware.

The narratives provided by female descendants of immigrants corroborate the fact that cultural and ethnic (and state) identities do not necessarily overlap as they do not display any congruence between ethnic and cultural (and state) identities. All respondents defined their state identity to be Slovenian (they have been citizens of Slovenia since birth) but the relationship between cultural and ethnic affiliation seems to be more complex.

N., aged 28, daughter of Orthodox Serbs, self-defines as being Slovenian in terms of state identity but 'Orthodox' (i.e., of Orthodox Christian religion) by culture, and says that her mother tongue is Serbo-Croatian but she is Slovenian by ethnicity. She emphasized that among all identities (state, ethnic/national, and cultural) the one that defines her most is cultural identity, more specifically religious identity. She perceives herself primarily as being 'Orthodox'.

The incongruence between ethnic and cultural (and state) identities adopts a different pattern with M., aged 38, and A., aged 32, who define their ethnic identity as Muslim. The state identity of both respondents is Slovenian (self-definition). M.'s ethnic identity is Muslim with a strong religious component while she says that her mother tongue is Slovenian (element of cultural affiliation). This is yet another case of incongruence between cultural and ethnic boundaries. A.'s words confirm that she is incapable of self-definition of ethnic identity. The answer she gives to the question '*Who are you in terms of ethnic/national identity?*' is '*I don't know, I really don't know. I should be Muslim because my parents are Muslim but …*' When asked about her mother tongue she defines herself as being bilingual while in terms of religion she is Muslim.

Likewise, the respondents whose parents had come from Croatia —a state that is culturally closest to Slovenia (similarity of languages, same religion, and so on)—do not exhibit congruence among ethnic, cultural and state identities.

L., aged 29, who has been using the Slovenian language to communicate with her mother since her birth, came to Slovenia as a child and is linguistically assimilated. She is Slovenian by nationality and in terms of culture she is not different from her Slovenian peers in any way (her mother tongue is Slovenian, values, dietary habits, dress codes, and so forth, are 'Slovenian'). Nevertheless, her self-definition of her ethnicity is Croatian, emphasizing this to be an entirely intimate decision that she is unable to explain rationally.

> Yes, ok, the language is one of the indicators of identity but it's not the only one. My father and my mother always said we're Croatian, when there was some political tension, but also in general, when we spoke of cultural things. I feel I'm Croatian, yes. I was probably brought up a little this way, it's self-obvious, I can't say that I'm Slovenian, not at all!

The narrative of B., the 21-year-old daughter of immigrants from Croatia, highlighted another problem regarding any objective 'measurement' of linguistic (and cultural) identity. In her case, we can observe a split between the declared 'mother tongue' and the language that she actually uses in all speech situations, including conversations in the personal domain (within the family circle, with her siblings and parents). In B.'s words: 'Blood is not water. I'm Croatian. My mother tongue is Croatian.' B. is a practising Catholic and her other cultural elements do not significantly differ from 'Slovenian' ones. Therefore, we can assume that both her ethnic and cultural identities are Croatian. A doubt in her Croatian cultural identity is nevertheless instilled by her use of the Slovenian language in communication with her siblings as well as parents, therefore, in her personal domain. As a result, when can the mother tongue or first language be defined as such? Is this the language that one has learnt to speak first, is this in fact the language of the mother, is this the language that one perceives as their mother tongue (by self-definition) despite not using it with their parents, not even in their private domain, when they could?

These questions provide the grounds for a discussion of differences between passive and active (ethnic and cultural) identity, and the differences in relation to one's own ethnic (cultural) community: from a passive to an active, and from a cognitive to an emotional and activity-based attitude (Mikolič 2004). Thus, ethnic identity is a synthesis of affiliation and awareness, where *affiliation* 'merely' denotes one's personal characteristic while *awareness* refers to a conscious and free definition to belong (or the activity-based component). In the words of Mikolič: 'Similarly to what national awareness is to an upgrade of ethnic or national identity, an upgrade of citizenship is loyalty to a state that entails an active attitude of an individual.' (2004) One's active attitude or awareness can then further be divided into the cognitive, emotional, and activity-based aspects of operation.

If these theoretical premises are applied to the narratives of the respondents, B.'s case might indicate a differentiation between a passive and an active stance or the difference between affiliation and awareness: B. *belongs* to the Croatian ethnicity and her mother tongue is (*passively*) Croatian. She nourishes an awareness of identity in relation to her Croatian ethnic identity, which is the activity-based component. However, this cannot be observed in relation to the Croatian language where another language is in active use instead (Slovenian), which is an example of the split between the principle and the actual 'first' language.

Question Three: Complexity of Self-Perception and the Identity Bricolage

Based on what has been presented so far in this chapter, we can now turn to our next issue: in the case of female descendants of immigrants whose parents had moved to Slovenia from other territories of former

Yugoslavia, the existence of *mixed identities* can be observed. Mixed, compound, hybrid, or transcultural identities have been subject to extensive research. Mixed identities have been examined within postcolonial studies, whose representative Bhabha speaks of 'hybrid identities' (1990; 1996). The authors of mixed race policies talk about 'mixed races' (Suki 2011; Sundstorm 2001), Welsh (1995) speaks of transculturality and 'transcultural identities' (see also Eigeartaigh and Berg 2010) while Milharčič-Hladnik (2011) uses the term 'compound identities' to describe identity mixing and so forth.

What these approaches have in common is an advocacy for the right to be mixed, dual or multiple, to be bilingual or plurilingual, to be bicultural or pluricultural, to be 'biracial' or 'multiracial', and to be complex. In addition, they share a common rebellion against the dictatorship of singular cultural, 'racial', and linguistic definition.

Although the discussion regarding mixed identities usually refers to children born of mixed marriages (Breger and Hill 1998; Sedmak 2001; Sedmak and Zadel 2015), mixed identities can also be observed among other population categories, for instance, migrants (Eigeartaigh and Berg 2010) or traditional minorities, in which cultural elements of the homeland culture and the culture of the living environment intertwine (Sedmak 2009, 2011a, 2011b; Sedmak and Medarić 2014; Sedmak and Zadel 2015). The Anglo-Saxon world is traditionally more dedicated to 'racial' mixedness whereas recently research has also turned to ethnic and cultural mixedness (Edwards et al. 2012), which prevails in eastern and central European countries and hence in the territories of former Yugoslavia as well.

The narratives of female descendants of immigrants clearly reveal the mixedness of their identities or, in Homi Bhabha's words (1990), the 'third space' or 'intermediate space' that hybrid identities personify. Bhabha views the third space as a metaphor for the space of cultural contact in which new (hybrid) identities are born through the processes of cultural hybridization and transculturation. Cultural identity is understood as an unstable space or unresolved question between several intersecting discourses. Identity is not static or unchangeable but can be processing and evolving (Bhabha 1990). Hybridization does not only mean simple mixing (a person is partly a member of one culture, and partly a member of another) but is rather an expression of the selective appropriation of meanings whereby different parts of the identity combine with others in relation to different social power relations. Hybridity is a process in which identities do not separately change on their own. Instead, elements of different cultures compound to create a different culture. The identity of the subject is or can be similar to the previous one but is not entirely the same. In this process we must, as Bhabha stresses, take into account the importance of relations of social power.

The collected narratives of female descendants of immigrants corroborate the importance of relations of power between the dominant Slovenian culture and the culture of migrants in (each occurrence of) identity formation. In addition to being in an a priori position of lesser social power, the culture of immigrants has less symbolic power. M., aged 38, as mentioned earlier, the daughter of Muslim parents, consciously wanted to be Slovenian in her childhood, but her conscious decision must be placed into the context of the social domination of Slovenehood. In addition, this same person, after becoming an adult, 'recognizes' that she is not and cannot be Slovenian. A thorough examination of her narrative reveals that it was the (Slovenian) environment that did not allow her to be Slovenian and thus 'forced' her into the ethnic identity of origin of her parents.

> I 'found out' at school that I'm not Slovenian when, fighting, the girls from my class would say 'get lost to Bosnia'. But I didn't understand why … and 'Bosnian louse' and 'your mother dresses like a Gypsy'. (G, aged 32)

> I saw that I was different in the fifth grade. The teacher asked us to say the names of our parents aloud. My parents are E. and D. (typical Muslim names). Everybody laughed and since then they started calling me D. [her father's name] and not M. [her actual name] … Mother and father did not know how to protect me. (M., aged 38)

> I actually made the decision that I'd learn to speak Slovenian so nobody could notice that I'm not Slovenian. (U. speaks standard Slovenian). But they said they could see (physically) that I'm not Slovenian. (U., aged 26)

In addition to social power relations, all narratives indicate the mixed or hybrid identities of the respondents. Their mixed identities may be more or less explicitly expressed and reflected:

> I speak Slovenian and Bosnian, both are my mother tongues. With my parents in Bosnian, with my children in Bosnian and Slovenian because

my husband is from Bosnia and couldn't speak Slovenian when he came to Slovenia.... I became Muslim after getting married, I like my religion but I drink alcohol and eat pork.... I know that at home, in our flat, I didn't have the same culture as Slovenians, which you could also tell from the outside. I couldn't go with my friends to the seaside, we don't do this, my mother said.... I make pita and burek [typical Bosnian dishes] at home and prepare Slovenian food, too, mixed. (A. aged 32)

I'm mixed, a Croat who speaks Slovenian and is like a Slovenian [laughter]. (L. aged 30)

I feel one and the other, I speak Slovenian at home, so I'm neither this nor that, I take care that my children pray to God [respondent is Muslim], a lot about it is food, it's different, but I cook both, I make sure my children attend folklore [Muslim folk dance group], I don't force them to go to religion class if they don't want to. What is important is who your friends are, the society that's around you. If you're in more religious, Muslim, society, you're more there .... Most of this is about feelings, I feel good here in Slovenia, I feel good when I'm making pita. (M. aged 38)

The preservation of the ethnic identity of parents frequently is the explicit wish of the latter:

If you want to or not, you sometimes have to [practice the parents' culture of origin through religion], because the parents are like that, what others say. (M. aged 38)

Yes, my mother wanted me to marry someone from our religion, a Muslim. She thought it'd be easier for me that way ... when I was younger and I wanted to go to the seaside with my female friends, I couldn't. Mother said we don't do this. It was different with my brother. He could. (G. aged 32)

CAUGHT IN-BETWEEN

In conclusion, I would like to emphasize some other findings resulting from the case study of female descendants of immigrants from the former Yugoslavia that are equally important for the understanding of the dynamics of identity definitions and a broader understanding of the phenomenon of women's migrations. The narratives of female descendants of immigrants in Slovenia reject the thesis concerning an unproblematic assimilation into a new cultural environment. It actually seems that women born in Slovenia but who are descendants of immigrants from other cultural environments remain caught somewhere in-between, between two cultures, between two symbolic worlds or, in accordance with Berger and Luckmann (1988) 'between two fundamental realities of everyday life'. A crucial role in these processes is played by the response of the broader society. The environment (kindergarten, school, peer group, colleagues and so forth) is the element that these women, born in Slovenia but having a different culture of origin of their parents, are told that 'they are not and cannot be Slovenians'. They are not Slovenian either for their 'wrong surname', a different pronunciation of Slovenian words,[7] or their parents' wrong names. However, a tolerant environment can make a difference. If the respondents have lived and have been socialized in a multicultural and tolerant environment, there are fewer comments related to the culture of origin of their parents and questions of ethnic identity are not as exposed.

The narratives of women from the second generation of migrants indicate an ambivalent attitude of their primary families to cultural assimilation: on the one hand their daughters are encouraged to learn the Slovenian language (also by discontinuing the use of their language themselves and attempting to use Slovenian in communication with their daughters) and assimilate into Slovene society. This, however, is accompanied by the explicit wish of the parents that their daughters should get married to one of 'their own' because they would have 'fewer problems' or, in other words, conscious reminders of the family's cultural origins. This is particularly explicit in Muslim families. Their narratives demonstrate that it is exclusively women (and not their brothers, for instance) who are encouraged to 'marry a Muslim' and live in accordance with Muslim norms whereas men have significantly more freedom to live in line with the expectations of the Slovenian environment as far as, for instance, dating is concerned. Moreover, the narratives reveal that the respondents are willing to follow their parents' and families' wishes that are retrospectively evaluated as well meant and the 'right' decisions. One of the respondents who declined to subject to the will of her (Muslim) father regarding (in)appropriate behaviour left home very early, at the age of 18, and broke off all contact with her family for two years.

The 'in-between' status can be perceived in the following typical statement: '*I was born here, my home is here, I wouldn't go anywhere else, but my children have to know where they come from.*'

Another significant finding is that the in-between status of female descendants of immigrants in this case study demonstrates feelings of uprootedness and incomplete affiliation to one or the other cultural environment, which results in quests for one's identity and feelings of insecurity and unacceptance. In my opinion, a key element that contributes to these feelings is the status of inferiority frequently attributed to immigrants from territories of the former Yugoslavia by Slovenians. In fact, other studies have shown that cultural duality or mixedness between 'Slovenianhood' and another culture that Slovenians perceive as being superior (e.g., Italian) may be reflected in pride and, more than that, feelings of superiority (Medarić, 2014; Sedmak 2005, 2009, 2011a, 2011b).

NOTES

1   The literature, in particular that of the Anglo-Saxon world, prefers the term *second* generation of female migrants. However, this term can be perceived as discriminatory, misleading, and inaccurate. By emphasizing the migrant status of the 'second generation of migrants', we do not clearly express the fact that descendants of immigrants were actually born in the host country of their parents and are therefore not migrants.

2   Slovenia is a small country in the northwest part of the Balkans with a population of slightly less than 2 million.

3   These are traditional or indigenous minorities that the Constitution of the Republic of Slovenia defines as being 'autochthonous'.

4   In accordance with the 1961 population census, the share of citizens of Slovenia who declared their nationality to be Slovenian was approximately 96%. This decreased to approximately 94% in 1971, approximately 90% in 1981, and approximately 88% in 1991. In the entire post-war period, migrations to Slovenia originated from territories of the former Yugoslavia. As a result, the presented data can be interpreted as indicating shares of immigrants from these territories. However, they can only be interpreted as indicators of immigration trends rather than actual numbers of immigrants.

5   This chapter presents excerpts from life stories of 11 women—female descendants of immigrants, aged between 21 and 38, whose parents had moved to Slovenia from Croatia, Bosnia and Herzegovina, Serbia, and Vojvodina. All of them were born in Slovenia and have lived there all their lives. Some are married and have children, others are single or cohabit with their partner but have no children. The collection of narratives for the needs of the present study took place in May 2014. (The article is partly based on previous comprehensive research studies made by the author, for instance: Sedmak, 2001, 2005, 2009, 2011; Sedmak and Žadel, 2015.)

6 In the professional and academic linguistics community the term 'first language' seems to be prevailing over the term 'mother tongue'. The 'first language' refers to the language that speakers use in their everyday communication or accept as the 'first language' of their communication in the personal or public domain irrespective of their actual 'mother tongue' – the first language that they have acquired. Moreover, the use of the term 'mother tongue' is being discontinued because the mother, despite most often being the one, may not be the transmitter of the 'first' language to a child.

7 For instance, the use of a broad 'l' is a typical sign of recognition of a non-Slovenian speaker, or interference of Croatian, Serbian or Bosnian words.

REFERENCES

Barth, F. 1970. *Ethnic Groups and Boundaries: The Social Organization of Culture Difference*. Bergen: George Allen & Unwin.

——. 1996. 'Ethnic Groups and Boundaries', in J. Hutchinson and A. Smith, eds. *Ethnicity*. Oxford: Oxford University Press, 75–82.

Berger, P. L., and T. Luckmann. 1988. *Družbena Konstrukcija Realnosti* (Social Construction of Reality). Ljubljana: Cankarjeva Založba,

Bhabha, H. K. 1990. 'The Third Space. Interview with Homi Bhabha', in J. Rutherford. ed., *Identity: Community, Culture, Difference*. London: Lawrence and Wishart, 207–21.

——. 1996. 'Culture's In-Between', in V. S. Hall and P. Du Gay, eds. *Questions of Cultural Identity*. Thousand Oaks, CA: SAGE Publications, 53–60.

Breger, R., and R. Hill., eds. 1998. *Cross-Cultural Marriage*. Oxford: Berg.

Edwards, R., S. Ali, C. Caballero, and M. Song, eds. 2012. *International Perspectives on Racial and Ethnic Mixedness and Mixing*. London: Routledge.

Eigeartaigh, A. N. 2010. 'Editors' Introduction: Exploring Transculturalism', in Wolfgang Berg ed., *Exploring Transculturalism: A Biographical Approach*. Germany: Deutsche Nationalbibliothek.

Eriksen, T. H. 1993. *Ethnicity and Nationalism: Anthropological Perspectives*. London: Pluto Press.

Jeffs, N. ed. 2007. 'Zbornik Postkolonialnih Študijev' (*Proceedings of Postcolonial Studies*). Ljubljana: Krtina.

Klopčič, V., M. Komac, and V. Kržišnik-Bulić. 2003. *Albanci, Bošnjaki, Črnogorci, Hrvati, Makedonci in Srbi v Republiki Sloveniji (ABČHMS v RS); Položaj in Status Pripadnikov Narodov Nekdanje Jugoslavije v Republiki Sloveniji* (Albanians, Bosnians, Montenegrins, Croats, Macedonians and Serbs in the Republic of Slovenia (ABMCMS in the RS); Position and Status of Members of the Nations of the Former Yugoslavia in the Republic of Slovenia). Ljubljana: Inštitut za Narodnostna Vprašanja.

Komac, M., et al. 2005. *Percepcije Slovenske Integracijske Politike* (Perceptions of the Slovenian Integration Policy). Ljubljana: *Inštitut za Narodnostna Vprašanja*.

Mikolič, V. 2004. *'Jezik v Zrcalu Kultur'* (Language in the Mirror of Cultures). *Založba Annale* Koper.

Milharčič-Hladnik, M. ed. 2011. *Življenjske Zgodbe o Sestavljenih Identitetah* (And Life Stories About Composite Identities). Ljubljana: Založba ZRC, ZRC AZU.

Schutz, A. 1987. *'Tujec: Socialnopsihološki Esej'* (Foreigner: Socio-Psychological Essay). *Nova Revija* 6, 65–66: 1620–1628.

Sedmak, M. 2001. *Kri in Kultura. Etnično Mešane Zakonske Zveze* (Blood and Culture. Ethnically Mixed Marriage). Koper: Založba Annales.

——. 2005. 'Social Inclusion/Exclusion of Immigrant Groups in Urban Slovenia: The Case Study of Istria', *Ethnologia Balcanica* 9, 241–59.

——. ed. 2009. *Podobe Obmejnosti* (Images of Life along the Border). Koper: Založba Annales.

——. 2011a. 'Displacement of Citizenship: The Multicultural Reality of Slovene Istria', in I. Pardo and G. B. Prato, eds. *Citizenship and the Legitimacy of Governance.* Farnham: Ashgate, 59–73.

——. 2011b. 'Culture of Mixedneess: Social and Political Recognition of Social Category of Mixed People', *Annales, Series Historia et Sociologia*, 21, 2: 261–74.

Sedmak, M., and Z. Meddaric. 2014. 'The Management of Interthnic Relations in the European Context', in M. Sedmak, Z. Medaric S. Walker, eds. *Children's Voices: Studies of Interethinic Conflict and Violence in European Schools* (Routledge Research in International and Comparative Education). London: Routledge: 33–48.

Sedmak, M., and M. Zadel. 2015. '(Mixed) Cultural Identities: Construction and Deconstruction'. *Annales, Series Historia et Sociologia*, 25, 1:155–170.

Suki, A. 2011. 'Mixed Race Politics', *Annales Series Historia et Sociologia* 21, 2: 237–48.

Sundstrom, R. R. 2001. 'Being and Being Mixed Race', *Social Theory and Practice* 27, 2: 285–307.

Verdery, K. 1996. 'Ethnicity, Nationalism, and State-Making: Ethnic Groups and Boundaries: Past and Future', in H. Vermeulen and C. Govers, eds. *The Anthropology of Ethnicity: Beyond Ethnic Groups and Boundaries.* Amsterdam: Het Spinhuis, 33–58.

Vezzoli, S., M. Villares-Varela, and H. De Hass. 2014. 'Uncovering International Migration Flow Data: Insights from the DEMIG Databases', IMI Working paper 88; DEMIG Working Paper 17. University of Oxford, International Migration Institute, Oxford.

Welsch, W. 1995. 'Transculturality—The Puzzling Form of Cultures Today', *California Sociologist* 17–39.

10

Precariousness of Migrant Women: Between Structural Constraints and Coping Strategies

MOJCA PAJNIK AND VERONIKA BAJT

WE ADDRESS THE question of migrant women's experiences in accessing the labour market in Slovenia and examine how welfare policies, or the lack thereof, affect migrant workers' lives. We thus problematize these women's perpetual de-skilling and socio-economic exclusion. Drawing on migrant women's narratives we also point to their activity in counteracting experiences of discrimination and downward social mobility.

Demographic trends show that the European population will continue to age and that a smaller portion of citizens will be available for care of the elderly, both financially and in terms of actual care (Lisiankova and Wright 2005). In recent decades, European states have increasingly relegated various forms of care and domestic work to migrant women, which has been the case also historically. Migration theorists tend to use economic paradigms to explain these trends, referring to a push-pull model and the demand and supply dichotomy. Gender sensitive analysis (Anthias and Lazaridis 2000; Lutz 2008, 2011) has proven that such explanations are gender-blind in their arguing that domestic and care work is 'just another kind of work'. Rather, this work is deeply embedded in 'gender regimes', in social constructions that deem this type of work to be women's work, characterized by a high degree of dependency of the female worker on the employer and by highly personalised and emotional work relationships (Lutz 2008).

It seems that theorizing care and domestic work, service and sales work, as well as sex work, all of which are increasingly performed by migrant women, can avoid generalizations of rationalized economic theory only after the interrelationships of gender, class, ethnicity, and other social divisions are taken into consideration. We here draw on the concept of intersectionality (Yuval Davis 2006) that helps us understand how the marginalized positions of migrant women are intermeshed in social divisions functioning around gender, nationality, class, as well as migrant status and labour market segmentation (McDowell 2008). By acknowledging the interrelations of various forms of subordination, intersectionality as a concept reminds us that inequalities emerge at the crossings of positions related to gender, ethnicity, age, class, and so on. The narrations of migrant women presented in this chapter reveal the empirical disempowerment strategies that the intersectional approach has theoretically tried to capture.

Social divisions are manifested in various forms[1] and our analytical focus here is twofold: we analyse divisions that are expressed in the form-specific institutions and organizations such as laws and state agencies, and we are also interested in how migrant women subjectively, exerting their own agency, experience and counteract social divisions in their everyday lives. We acknowledge the need for contextual analysis that does not separate the institutionally reproduced differentiations from the actual experiences with oppression and inequalities (cf. Anthias and Yuval Davis 1983; Milharcic Hladnik 2016).

We also draw on the concept of 'positionality' (Anthias 2002), for it relates to the space at the intersection of structure as position in the system, and agency as individual positioning, meaning, and practice. It is a space between social constructionism and the agency approach, the interrelations of which are even better explained by 'translocations' or 'translocational positionality', which more explicitly captures the various belongings of migrating subjects (ibid.). Such an approach enables us to challenge the hegemonic analysis that reifies institutions and their laws and to avoid the essentialization of specific identities.

Data for several European states show that in the current global financial and economic crisis, the migrant workers are the first to face layoffs (e.g. Pajnik and Campani 2011), yet the trend in hiring migrants for the most precarious jobs remains unabated. Statistics show that, even though the labour market increasingly rejects workers with low levels of education and skills, the overwhelming majority of jobs accessible to migrants in Slovenia are classified as unskilled. The demand has long been the highest for 'unskilled work in construction'—a typically male profession—and 'cleaner'—a paradigmatically female migrant's job.[2] Migrants have traditionally found work in sectors that are socially considered 'dirty' or underpaid. This persists and in Slovenia is connected to the perceived 'female migrant profession' of cleaning. It might appear that the current 'native' workforce, particularly the rising number of long-term unemployed women, could meet such a demand (Hrzenjak 2007). Nevertheless, it is often the case that the work in question is physically demanding, underpaid and garners low levels of social respect. In addition, it is also unregulated and mostly part of the grey economy with known breaching of workers' rights. Not all unemployed women are prepared to or even capable of performing such work.[3] As a result, migrant women are bridging this gap, meeting the demand for services, particularly in the form of undocumented household work, childcare, and care of the elderly. Similar to other developed countries, Slovenia has seen a steady rise in the tertiary sector, reflected in the labour market's demand for services. It remains unclear how many migrant women find work in industrial cleaning, hotels, and restaurants, let alone in informal domestic work, though their shares point to the feminization of these sectors of migrant work.[4]

Overlooked in Policies, Denied of Agency and Equal Labour Market Access

The majority of the foreign-born population in Slovenia comes from the former Yugoslavia; almost half is from Bosnia-Herzegovina. The construction of the European Union's external borders classifies former co-nationals into 'third country nationals', a category inherent in migration and integration policies to the detriment of their full inclusion. Women migrants are also predominantly citizens of Yugoslavia's successor states, especially of Bosnia-Herzegovina. In recent years, more women than men have come to Slovenia from Ukraine and the Russian Federation; and migrant populations from Thailand, Romania, the Czech Republic, Moldova, the Dominican Republic, the Philippines, and Colombia are also largely female. Only a fragment of third-country nationals in Slovenia come from Asia, the Americas, or Africa.

Our data are drawn from 26 biographical interviews with migrant women between 22 and 48 years of age, who have migrated to Slovenia from different countries in the last 15 years, most quite recently.[5] In this perspective, they can be seen as part of 'new' migrants who face even greater difficulties compared to migrants who have lived in Slovenia for a longer time. The women have diverse socio-economic and educational backgrounds, come from different geopolitical contexts, and live and work in various social situations. The diversity of the sample, which at the same time reflects the official statistical trends, enables us to infer from the data that the same structural problems permeate the lives of migrant women, regardless of their education or professional qualifications and their sector of work.

In order to reside and work legally in Slovenia, migrants, particularly 'non-EU nationals' need both work and residence permits. State policies expect employers to arrange the necessary documents for the employment of 'foreigners'. On the one hand, it is helpful for migrants that officially they do not need to arrange all the necessary documentation themselves, especially if they are migrating for the first time and are unfamiliar with the new environment, language, laws, and procedures. Yet at the same time this can also be discouraging for those migrants whose qualifications may not be in great demand or whose potential employers are not familiar with the official procedure of lodging an application for work permits. As a teacher from Croatia explains, she managed to find an employer who upon enquiring about the procedure to employ a 'foreigner', decided it was 'too much hassle'. Melanija was thus told that she would not get the promised job because it was easier to hire a Slovene worker.[6] At the same time, Marija, a university graduate from Moldova, speaks of having to pay high sums of money for her work permit, suggesting that her employer circumvented legal regulations which stipulate the employer's responsibility to cover these costs.

Migrant women in our sample offer various accounts of how a complete reliance on their employers often made them feel they had no choice but to endure discrimination and harsh working conditions for low pay or sometimes no pay at all. The narratives illuminate that being employed on a contract for a fixed-term period of time is disadvantageous compared to regularly employed workers because contract work puts employees at a greater risk with respect to job security and prevents them from being entitled to the same social security or other benefits, such as paid vacation.[7] Migrant workers were dependent on their employers because of their temporary residence permits and employment regulations, which up until 2011 tied work permits to specific employers, rather than allowing free movement of migrants between positions and employers. A particular sub-pattern connected to work could be recognized, where women adopted roles that followed the established patterns of work migration. This led them from their countries of birth, through an apparently smooth transition, to a pre-arranged work setting and accommodation that was tied to fixed-term work contracts. Yet, at least initially, they remained tied to the same employer because the work permit they possessed precluded free choice of employment. In addition to the fact that migrant women are limited in accessing the labour market and often face discrimination, precarious work conditions and limited social security, they have also been reliant on their employer in order to keep their residence permit.

The narratives show that even migrants with personal work permits who were formally equal to Slovene citizens in competing for jobs noted several obstacles in their attempts to find work, as well as problems accessing social welfare. The migrant life stories illustrate that they experienced numerous obstacles in accessing the labour market on a footing equal to that of the 'native' workers; the narratives also reveal, however, that they faced additional hindrance due to language barriers, lack of educational recognition, lack of informal networks, as well as overt discrimination because of their presumed otherness. For instance, even though the Employment Service is supposed to provide administrative help, state institutions in general are slow in fulfilling their obligations towards foreign nationals, leaving several of the migrant women in our sample disappointed at being prevented from participating in the so-called Active Employment Policy programme. The narratives illustrate the need to facilitate better access to the labour market in a manner which would be helpful for all migrants regardless of their status or the type of work permit.

EXPERIENCES OF PRECARIOUS JOBS AND DE-SKILLING

Even though the sample was purposefully designed to examine the practice of migrant de-skilling and low-skill sectors of work, a major finding is the notable de-skilling of migrant women regardless of their status, mode of entry, educational level, or prior work experience. Even in cases where migrants manage to arrange formal recognition of education, their abilities and qualifications remain devalued (Bajt and Pajnik 2015; Zavratnik and Cukut Krilić 2018). Many women speak of being unable to find work suitable to their qualifications, like Melanija, a teacher who works as a cleaner because her Slovene, or Slovenian, is not fluent enough to allow her to teach. Despite valuable work experience and possession of skills that are advertised as greatly needed in Slovenia, Sandra, a medical nurse, works as an undocumented kitchen aide. Ada, a lawyer from Bosnia-Herzegovina, has been unable to find a job suitable to her qualifications, despite trying for several years; her attempts at finding employment in her field included trying to get afoot in the door by volunteering at a courthouse. Though her education is recognized in Slovenia, her lack of work experience prevented her from passing the obligatory bar exam, which further limits her chances of ever finding work suitable to her expertise.

Migrant women are significantly hindered in their attempts to access the labour market, and it is not uncommon for university educated women to work as waitresses or shop assistants. Working in low-skill sector jobs, some report poor working conditions and exploitation by employers. Our sample revealed cases of migrant women discovering that employers never registered their employment or that they registered them for a significantly shorter period than the length of their actual employment. Such violations, though also applied to numerous Slovene citizens, but affect migrants even more because they result in a lack of social insurance for migrants, no paid vacation or right to sick leave, and, above all, problems in accessing healthcare and pension schemes.

Forced 'inactivity' in the formal labour market is a significant problem for migrant women, who experience long periods of time in which accessing the labour market is difficult. This has negative consequences on their self-esteem and can contribute to a precarious existence and the need to seek undocumented work. After a certain period of unemployment, the fact that they cannot find employment aligned with their expertise and education often becomes 'accepted' as an unavoidable predicament. As a result, many migrant women resolve to accept any kind of employment, either because they need the money, or because they wish to avoid seclusion and inactivity. This means that some migrant women resort to undocumented low-skill and low-paid positions, whereas others manage to find jobs at lower levels within their sector. This is a problem that stems from labour policies, which systematically favour the employment of the 'native' workers and restrict the number of work permits issued to 'foreigners'.

The 'third country' status profoundly affects the labour market access of the women categorized as such, because all third-country nationals need to secure work permits in order to work legally and reside in Slovenia. Therefore, their stories describe undocumented work experiences. Some are engaged in 'illicit' work in order to supplement their regular earnings, and all their narratives show that their decision to accept work in the black market was the consequence of inability to find regular employment.

> With higher education ... I was ready to mop the floor only to get that job ... I was aware that I'm going to a foreign country, that it'll be tough and that people are foreign and that it'll be hard to get a place among people. But I said to myself I'll get used to it ... Why are foreign people not appreciated? Why?... Your Slovenia will go on because of that ... Give me normal salary, respect me, and I'll do what you need. Is it so or not? And also Slovenia will in the end prosperous ... And you (a migrant) don't have the right to say anything to anyone! Don't have the right! Can't. Hard.

Really hard. I can see that some don't do anything and they have three times bigger salary than me. And you go and toil away like a horse, and you have lower pay. (Marija, 30, Moldova)[8]

UNDOCUMENTED DOMESTIC WORK: AN ARRANGEMENT TO SUSTAIN THE GENDER DIVIDE

As is the case for women in general, for migrant women who work, employment and family obligations also result in a double burden that constrains what kind of job they can perform and what career opportunities they are able to take on—if they are able to find work at all. Lilia, a qualified seamstress, for instance, supplements her earnings by working as a baby-sitter. She cares for a young boy whose parents need additional assistance because they work at night. This arrangement of childcare is illustrative in two ways. On the one hand, it shows how undocumented domestic work is used as a way to earn money, which Lilia notes, makes her feel more independent, stating: 'A woman needs to have her own money'. On the other hand, the night work performed by the boy's parent shows the need for extra childcare that is not being met by regular state-organized kindergarten facilities. There is an obvious demand for childcare, and this demand provides migrant women with paid but undocumented work. Unless young parents have the support of grandparents or other family members or friends, they resort to employing help for childcare. Illustrating the double burden of female migrants, Marija's case is particularly telling:

Everybody wonders how I manage. Because at my home it is so clean.... I live like robot. From Monday to Friday, work from 7 to 3, or from 8 to 4, I make 8 hours. I go straight to school, take my daughter home–she has that additional at school—come home and I take vacuum cleaner straight away, clean, make the beds, iron, cook dinner. Then my daughter in bed, must go to sleep by 9 because must get up in the morning … And on Saturday I clean up everything, on Sunday I cook. I don't have time ever. (Marija, 30, Moldova)

I like to work, it's not hard for me and not a problem. I'm tired from time to time, especially now when we moved. When I have to be at 6 o'clock (at work), I get up 20 past 4 … And I have to deal with the kid all day, I mean, all day, have to work, and come back, and collect kid from kindergarten, and deal with kid from 4 till 9 in the evening, and at 9, I don't know, clean house a little, do a little this, a little that, and it's 12, 1, and then at 4 I have to get up, and it's really sometimes a problem. But ok. You get used to it. (laughs). (Sandra, late 20s, Kosovo)

Moreover, Melanija, a Croatian with a degree in pedagogy, who is employed as a cleaner in a school and is in charge of domestic work at home, also performs domestic work outside of working hours in her 'free time' in order to earn extra money. Her undocumented additional job, therefore, results in Melanija performing domestic work in three different places: in the school that is her workplace, at home, and in a household where she cleans for cash as an additional undocumented job.

These examples reveal the double burden placed on migrant women who perform domestic work in their homes for their own families as well as in somebody else's household. Outsourcing domestic household and care work to migrant women has become an accepted habit that actually supports the 'institutionalized genderisms' (Lutz 2008), allocating household work to migrant women does not question the traditional gender divide; rather, it sustains it. By calling on the migrant woman to act as a nanny or a nurse, the image of a caring mother is maintained at the crossings of gender and migration regimes that reactivate traditional gender roles.

Performing domestic work in other people's homes represents an additional or sometimes the sole financial resource for migrant women. Since domestic work is performed in the private sphere and in most cases as an undocumented 'arrangement' between the migrant woman and her employer, she is exposed to the usual dangers of illicit employment. Even though in our sample one migrant woman performing such work notes that she is content with cash payments, such arrangements present potential dangers. Most obviously, a migrant may not be paid after performing her job, and since her employment relationship is based on an oral agreement alone, she has no possibilities to demand money that is owed to her through formal official channels. This precarious situation, involving a lack of social security, job security, healthcare, and other benefits, is particularly relevant in the case of undocumented domestic work. In addition, this type of work is profoundly characterized as low status, even if paid or acknowledged as a profession. Furthermore, personalized and emotional work relationships that accompany care work add additional pressure to the already precarious migrant situations (Lutz 2008; Sadl 2007).

MIGRANT WOMEN'S AGENCY THROUGH SELF-EMPLOYMENT AND RE-SKILLING

Contrary to the rhetoric of victimization of migrants (cf. Agustín 2003), the participants in our sample confirm their active agency. This was particularly the case for migrant women working in the area classified as 'dance', a sector that is habitually associated with dubious nightclub 'exotic dancing' related to sex work and trafficking. Most of the narratives show how migrants continuously try to improve their situation. For example, a Czech migrant Nika found a way out of working in nightclubs by working as a cleaner. Similarly, migrants who arrived on work visas as dancers expressed unhappiness with their initial job and had hence put their efforts into changing their line of work. Three migrant women in our sample who began working in Slovenia as nightclub dancers have since become waitresses. Though being a waitress is a low-paid position that may also expose them to unwanted male advances and a precarious socio-economic existence, in their eyes it represents a step up, an improvement. Moreover, night work prevents the women from having a 'normal life'. While they note the pay is good, working at night is physically tiring and prevents migrant women from establishing contacts with local people, forging friendships, or finding a partner. In contrast, being a waitress is presented as a good opportunity to establish new contacts and to practice speaking the local language:

> What I tell you before about that nightclub where I was ... Now I work in ordinary bar. No problem getting that work because I have a friend and he did for me ... I only knew that I don't want dance, I return to Czech Republic. And my friend called (and) said his friend is looking for waitress ... And I said that I don't know. He said that I try one month, two, and I will see, right. Actually I come back (smiles). I called that boss, very kind she was, everything. (Natalija, 24, Czech Republic)

> No, I don't work no more in a bar, I am now in waitress job in a day bar, right in that carwash (smile). Yes, like that. I don't work no more as dancer ... It's better for me here, day work, because night work is hard. Even if

you work two hours, your free time for sleep no good, eh. You cannot only dance all your life, you must change life. That's it. (Irina, 27, Ukraine)

I tell you, when I was dancer—for some time I was dancer, then went home, then come back here—no problem then. That changed now—no dance as such, as before. Before were shows, professional ballet dancers, but no more now ... And when you work like that for so long time you don't enjoy any more ... And cannot find other sort of job straightaway. Cannot find. Simple. So you must look, make effort, find somebody to help you, help you as foreigner, find job. Long-term job also difficult. Well, I got it, I was lucky, eh. And how I was lucky? To change job. To go from that bar to normal company, to work as cleaner. I worked for 6 years. Said YES straight away. I didn't mind, cleaning or whatever, only to go away from that ... I cleaned offices in bank, I was employed, it was quite good. For me it was, for that time, I was very satisfied then because I got normal job, day job, to live normally, like normal people, new environment and all new. (Nika, 35, Ukraine)

Self-employment is another strategy for coping with limited access to the labour market, as well as a way of earning money in a migrant woman's preferred field of expertise. In our sample, self-employment as a coping mechanism is featured in two narratives. Mariana is a hairdresser who saw a market niche in offering her services outside of established hair salons, which she believes are not offering sufficient cutting edge skills; so she decided to give it a go on her own. Even though Mariana encountered problems having her education recognized (she was overqualified) and also struggled to understand Slovenia's regulations, procedures, and tax system when trying to set up her own hair salon, she succeeded. Another example of a self-employed migrant is Xan, a woman who, after working alongside her husband in a Chinese restaurant, eventually decided to leave him and open a shop together with her sister as a business partner.

> Then I decided to make a hair salon, to work for myself ... But then, when I started making my firm, it was so many, so many problems. And you have to have it, up, down, various documents, permits, different things. I don't know, that was really, really hard ... Mhm, because I'm not used to it, right. In Peru we don't have it that hard. If you want to have hairdressing, you have. You don't need permission, paper for ... electricity, for how it looks inside, nothing. There you do it very easy. You have one place, buy ... Here such permissions that you can't, right. Hard, if you don't have money, right. (Mariana, 32, Peru)

> In the beginning I worked in restaurant, every day I get up at 10 in morning and at 11 in evening I finish with work ... Such life I lived for 10 months and then I start thinking about me open little shop and start working alone, then I searched (a Slovene acquaintance) to help me rent a flat.... We don't have this shop with husband, we with my younger sister joined and we have it together, he still works in restaurant ... I couldn't do it myself, there's many things in these (administrative) offices that need to be arranged and they (Slovene acquaintances) help me to arrange all this. (Xan, 33, China)

The two self-employed migrant women in our sample, Xan and Mariana, both spoke of highly complex bureaucratic procedures. Mariana did not fully understand the lease contract, nor did she know whether its provisions were in accordance with the law. Similarly, Xan did not understand the proper formal procedure for opening a store. They managed to overcome the administrative obstacles with the help of the social network of their Slovene friends. These examples speak of a wider problem, namely, that migrants are excluded from all institutional schemes and left reliant entirely on their own social capital. The fact that Slovenia does not stimulate self-employment of migrants is of particular relevance, especially as both interviewees complained about not fully understanding the administrative procedures required for self-employment, the leasing of premises, and so on.[9] Given the total lack of policy measures, which could promote migrant employment, migrant workers are in a disadvantaged position.

CONCLUSION

In examining migrant women's experiences with accessing the labour market in Slovenia it is evident that the existing labour laws and welfare policies result in the exclusion of migrants. They experience de-skilling, lack equal options, and are limited in realizing their full potential. The socio-economic exclusion is particularly apparent with third-country migrant women, whose status renders their positions highly dependent. Reliant either on family reunification policies or the existence of labour market demands in order to secure work permits and thus legal residence, the migrants also experience prejudice and discrimination based on gender, age, ethnicity, religion, and so on.

The narratives in our sample describe how migrant women's access to the labour market is systematically shaped by the intersection of social divisions pertaining to gender, ethnicity, and class, but particularly by their migrant status. Revealing these intersecting influences, the migrant women's stories illustrate the impact state policies have in terms of labour market access and social benefits, particularly since migrants are frequently exempt from state assistance.

We conclude by listing a few policy recommendations, considering the fact that the demand for migrant work, particularly the need for women's labour in terms of personal services and domestic work, not only remains unabated even in the current economic recession, but is expected to increase as the demographic trends of population aging already show. This strongly suggests the need to assist migrant workers in accessing the labour market even if their professions are not in high demand, which at present seems to provide the (only) incentive for employers to put the required extra effort into acquiring the needed migrant workers.

Moreover, correct, fast, simple, and inexpensive procedures for issuing work permits are crucial for ensuring that migrant women can access the labour market, as well as for enticing employers to hire migrants. Also, policies need to seriously consider abandoning the mechanism of work permits that frequently represents the source of migrants' precariousness, address the lack of opportunities for migrant women to find jobs that are not confined to domestic and care work, and thus endeavour to recognize the persistence of a gender divide created with the double burden of domestic work. 'Engendering' of migration regimes seems an appropriate response. In addition, policies should recognize that informal work performed in the care sector is only accessible to those who can afford it. Class divisions are noted here, where migrant women are directed to performing low paid domestic and care work, without having their needs recognized.

NOTES

1   Organisational, inter-subjective, experiential, and representational forms (Yuval Davis 2006, 198).

2   Most jobs available to migrant workers based on quota permits were for low or semi-skilled and low paid positions, mainly found in construction and

heavy industrial sector. Prior to recession, the number of foreign workers in Slovenia was continuously on the rise (it tripled in the last decade) and in 2008 about 90,000 held valid work permits. Comparatively, only 31,000 migrants hold valid work permits in 2013.

3   Most of the long-term unemployed women in Slovenia are above the age of 50, while it is also significant that some are unemployed because of disabilities.

4   Data for 2008, when seasonal permits were still issued for work in 'hotel, catering and tourism industry', show that 55 percent were held by women.

5   Biographical narrative interviews were conducted in Slovenia between 2006 and 2007 as part of the 6FP project 'FeMiPol'—Integration of Female Immigrants in Labour Market and Society: Policy Assessment and Policy Recommendations. For more, see http://www.femipol.uni-frankfurt.de, accessed 28 October 2019.

6   All names are pseudonyms.

7   Eurostat data for 2012 shows that Slovenia exibits above the EU average shares of fixed-term employment.

8   All the quotations have been translated to English without language editing, thus purposefully retaining the language proficiency varieties as these appeared in the interviews with migrant women.

9   The Employment and Work of Aliens Act even stipulates that the government may adopt special measures to restrict the number of self-employed 'foreigners'—as indeed any migrant workers—if 'justified' by, among other reasons, 'the general economic interest or the situation and foreseen shifts in the labour market', which is especially relevant in the current economic crisis.

REFERENCES

Agustín, L. M. 2003. 'Forget Victimization: Granting Agency to Migrants', *Development* 46, 3: 30–36.
Anthias, F. 2002. 'Where do I Belong? Narrating Collective Identity and Translocational Positionality', *Ethnicities* 2, 4: 491–514.
Anthias, F., and G. Lazaridis, eds. 2000. *Gender and Migration in Southern Europe: Women on the Move*. Oxford: Bloomsbury Academic.
Anthias, F., and N. Yuval Davis. 1983. 'Contextualizing Feminism: Gender, Ethnic and Class Divisions' *Feminist Review* 15: 62–75.
Bajt, V., and M. Pajnik. 2015. 'Migrant Education and Employment Equity in Slovenia: Officially Coveted, Factually Negated', in E. L. Brown, P. C. Gorski, G. Lazaridis, eds., *Poverty, Class, and Schooling: Global Perspectives on Economic Justice and Educational Equity*. Charlotte, Va: Information Age Publishing.

Hladnik Milharčič, M. 2016. *'Nadzor nad Nadzorom: Strategije Upiranja in Avtonomnost Delovanja Migrantk v Sodobni in Zgodovinski Perspektivi'* [Contr Peace Institute of Control: Strategies of Resistance and Autonomy of Agency of Women Migrants in the Contemporary and Historical Perspective], Dve domovini/ *Two Homelands*, 43: 35–46.

Hrzenjak, M. 2007. *Invisible Work*. Ljubljana: Peace Institute.

Lisiankova, K., and R. E. Wright. 2005. 'Demographic Change and the European Union Labour Market', *National Institute Economic Review*: 74–31.

Lutz, H., ed. 2008. *Migration and Domestic Work: A European Perspective on a Global Theme*. London: Routledge.

——. 2011. *The New Maids: Transnational Women and the Care Economy*. London: Zed Books.

McDowell, L. 2008. 'Thinking through Work: Complex Inequalities, Constructions of Difference and Trans-National Migrants', *Progress in Human Geography* 32, 4: 491–507.

Pajnik, M., and G. Campani, eds. 2011 *Precarious Migrant Labour Across Europe*. Ljubljana: Peace Institute.

Sadl, Z. 2007. *Delo na ujem omu. Specifične anljivosti aposlovanja v asebnih ospodinjstvih* (Working in a Stranger's Home: Specific Vulnerabilities of Employment in Private Households), in M. Sedmak, Z. Medarič, eds., *Med avnim in asebnim. Ženske na rgu ela* (Between Public and Private: Women on the Labour Market). Koper: Založba Annales.

Yuval Davis, N. 2006. 'Intersectionality and Feminist Politics', *European Journal of Women's Studies* 13, 3: 193–209.

Zavratnik, S., and S. Cukut Krilić. 2018. 'Addressing Intersectional Vulnerabilities in Contemporary Refugee Movements in Europe', *Družboslovne Razprave* (Social Discussions) 34, 87: 85–106.

About the Editor and Contributors

EDITOR

Roli Misra is Associate Professor in the Department of Economics, University of Lucknow. Her areas of interests are gender studies, migration and agricultural economics. She has previously published three books: *Agricultural Growth and Terms of Trade in India Since 1951* (Kunal 2018), *Rethinking Gender* (Rawat 2014) and *Community Participation and Water Resource Management in Uttarakhand* (New Royal 2012). She has made the following documentary films: *Waste-Full Lives: Hardships in Waste-Pickers Life*, *Childhood Lost in Waste: Film on Child Labour* and *Magical Hands: Fading Crafts of Assam; Wounded Identities*, which is based on the problem of identity and migration in Assam, has been screened in leading universities of India and at the University of Colombo and the University of Ljubljana, Slovenia.

CONTRIBUTORS

Veronika Bajt holds a PhD in sociology from the University of Bristol, UK, and works as a researcher and project coordinator at the Peace Institute in Ljubljana, Slovenia. She has published internationally on topics of migration, gender and labour market, nationalism, discrimination, national identity construction and practices of Othering, as well as analyses of collective memory construction and nationalist appropriations of history.

Sanela Bašić is Associate Professor, Faculty of Political Sciences, University of Sarajevo. Her current research interests include social policy, gender, family and labour markets; poverty and social exclusion; domestic and gender-based violence; social justice, peace, and post-conflict peace building. She was a recipient of the Konrad Adenauer Foundation Fellowship (2002–2004) and Academic Fellowship Program of the Open Society Foundation (2010–2014).

Gomati Bodra Hembrom is Associate Professor at the Department of Sociology, Jamia Millia Islamia. She received her PhD in Sociology from the Centre for the Study of Social Systems, Jawaharlal Nehru University, New Delhi. Her research interests include gender studies, tribal studies, social stratification, research methodology and media studies.

Sanja Cukut Krilić is Research Fellow, Socio-Medical Institute ZRC SAZU, Ljubljana, Slovenia, and holds a PhD in Sociology. Her research interests include gender and migration, experiences of female migrants, transnational families and migrants' care work.

Sandhya R. Mahapatro is Assistant Professor, Economics, at A. N. Sinha Institute of Social Studies, Patna. She has completed her PhD from the Institute for Social and Economic Change, Bengaluru. She was a postdoctoral research fellow in a collaborative project on migration with the University of Groningen, and Institute for Social and Economic Change, Bengaluru. She has published research papers on migration, health and employment issues.

Mojca Pajnik is Associate Professor, Faculty of Social Sciences, University of Ljubljana and senior research advisor at the Peace Institute in Ljubljana, Slovenia. Her research focuses on gender inequality, populism, racism, migration and citizenship. Currently she coordinates the research project POP-MED, 'Political and Media Populism: "Refugee crisis" in Slovenia and Austria' (2018–2021).

Mateja Sedmak received her PhD in sociology and is a research councillor and the head of the Institute for Social Studies at the Science and Research Centre, Koper, Slovenia. She was a lecturer at the University of Primorska, Slovenia. At the moment she is the Coordinator of MiCreate 'Migrant Children and Communities in a transforming Europe' Horizon 2020 project. Her research interests are ethnic studies, intercultural studies, migrant children, transculturality, sociology of family and everyday life.

Sucharita Sengupta is completing her PhD at the Graduate Institute of International and Development Studies, Geneva. Earlier she was research assistant at the Calcutta Research Group (CRG). Her research interests pertain to border studies and forced migration, gender, and minority rights.

Nazimuddin Siddique is an independent researcher with many contributions to scholarly journals. He received his PhD in Sociology from Gauhati University. He is a keen observer on the socio-political development in Northeast India. His research interests include society and politics of Northeast India, ethnicity, ethnic conflict, forced migration, human rights and military sociology.

Ena Tripura is undertaking a PhD at the College of Humanities and Social Science, Flinders University, South Australia. She has worked with national and internationals organizations and the United Nations in the Chittagong Hill Tracts (CHT), doing research and actively engaging in policy development and implementation in multiple projects for gender equality. Her research interests are migration, marginalization, social inclusion and ethnicity.

Kati Turtiainen is Senior Lecturer in Social Work. She received her PhD from the University of Jyväskylä in 2012. She also worked as the director of immigration services for the city of Jyväskylä. She has participated in various national and international development projects on multicultural work with forced and voluntary migrants.